HOLY
CONFESSIONS

Bill & Kim,

Great knowing you &
enjoying many new moments
to come.

Seek Truth!

Thadd

HOLY CONFESSIONS

A *365* DAY
DEVOTIONAL TO DEEPEN AND
STRENGTHEN YOUR FAITH

THADD KUEHNL

TATE PUBLISHING
AND ENTERPRISES, LLC

Published by Tate Publishing & Enterprises, LLC
127 E. Trade Center Terrace | Mustang, Oklahoma 73064 USA
1.888.361.9473 | www.tatepublishing.com

Tate Publishing is committed to excellence in the publishing industry. The company reflects the philosophy established by the founders, based on Psalm 68:11,
"The Lord gave the word and great was the company of those who published it."

Published in the United States of America

ISBN: 978-1-62854-098-7
1. Religion / Christian Life / Devotional
2. Religion / Christian Life / General
13.11.13

FOREWORD

I am pleased to commend to you Thadd Kuehnl's *Holy Confessions–Daily Devotions for God's People*. Thadd draws from the venerable Westminster Standards which come to us from 17th century England. Though the Westminster Standards have been available for some time, they are not time bound. In fact, they are an excellent exposition of the very teaching of God's Word.

Not only does Thadd begin with a time-honored and beloved treasure trove of Biblical teaching and wisdom, he also has the rare gift of breaking the material down into easily digestible portions. What's more, Thadd writes clearly and he gets straight to the point!

It would be my desire that Thadd Kuehnl's book would lead you into a greater understanding of the Scriptures and the teaching which it conveys. Most importantly I pray that this volume will lead you into more intimate fellowship with the Triune God of Scripture: Father, Son, and Holy Spirit.

Taste and see that the Lord (and his teaching) is good.

—Rev. Jeffrey C. Waddington, PhD
Communications Director
Alliance of Confessing Evangelicals

INTRODUCTION

In my endeavor to deepen my understanding of the doctrines of God, his word, and my responsibility to the Creator, I began my study into the general tenants of the Christian faith. I had three documents in front of me that first January morning; the *Holy Bible*, the *Westminster Confession of Faith (WCF)*, and the *Westminster Larger Catechism (WLC)*. I also had my trusty notepad and pen, which are paramount at every study.

Nothing was new at first. I scribble notes during all of my studies. I read in a fairly deliberate manner and often put the pen to the paper for an important point, rephrasing it to reinforce my understanding and retention. In fact, when I study through a full biblical book, I typically paraphrase every verse. I also explore the meaning important words, making reference to their use in other passages. So, it was unexpected, as I was already several days into my *WCF* study, to look back and think to myself, "This could be something to share with my family."

That the book would pattern into a "daily devotional" was self evident. Beginning with the *WLC*, the question/answer format had already lent itself to several short, two or three-paragraph reviews. Sticking with this format, the concept becoming a reality proved to be a much more difficult matter. I no longer could allow myself liberty to ramble on, but now had be concise and clear for third party eyes. Add a fourth tool to my mix...a *thesaurus*.

My favorite biblical teachers are those who clearly teach and explain passages, then get out of the way to let Holy Spirit do the transforming. There are many dynamic speakers who know how to work up an audience into an emotional frenzy, playing on the psychology of the individual. However, they often dethrone the Master, the only true author and finisher of our faith. My goal in this is to avoid my opinions and keep our focus on God's Word.

This devotional has over a thousand footnotes[1]. These footnotes are critical for the reader to see the biblical proof texts which support every devotional topic. My only valuable opinions are those which whole-

---

[1] Footnote: this is the location you will find valuable future references. Use them.

heartedly agree with the Holy Scripture. To this end, I have strived to provide helpful thoughts, true only to the biblical perspective.

Finally, although this book is written per a calendar year, do not feel like you need to wait until January 1st to begin. Because the book is topical, feel free to begin on any date. Some dates are continuations, but you shouldn't have to go back more than a day to two to catch up. Now, please let me to step into the shadows of the Almighty and allow you to begin your journey into the review of these Westminster Standards.

Grab your Bible and let's go. To God be the Glory!

January 1

To God Be the Glory

The Westminster Confession begins its catechism with the question, *What is the chief and highest end of man?* To which the faithful answer is *to Glorify God[2] and enjoy Him forever.[3]*

What have we accomplished on our own? Society gives the answer of *everything*. Our pride wants to agree with this. *I work all day. I build things. I am a doctor and save many lives.* Name the talent. However, every answer we could come up with is impossible without God.

The truth is that, not only are our talents God-given, but every facet of the universe is created and sustained[4] by him. From the first cell division to the last breath that will enter our lungs, these are all from God. The diversity of talents and our ability to use them are not ours to boast, but should humbly be recognized as *gifts*.

When we give proper thanks to God and use our talents to his glory alone, we will not only enjoy his creation, but will be fully satisfied and able to enjoy him in this life and in eternity. Put your trust in him, draw near, and declare his works. How many blessings will you count today?

---

[2]   Rom 11:36, 1Cor 10:31
[3]   Ps 73:24-28; Jn 17:21-23–WLC Q1
[4]   Col 1:16-17

JANUARY 2

DESIGN EQUALS DESIGNER

Have you ever looked at a car and exclaimed, "What an amazing machine!" If we found a car in the desert, would we ever say, "This thing must have taken millions of years of evolution to get to this stage." Of course not, because we know that from the windshield wipers to the headlights, from the air in tires to the fuel that feeds the engine, this car was designed and made with purpose. It must have a designer and a creator.

The very light of nature in man, and the works of God, declare plainly that there is a God;[5] but his Word and Spirit only, do sufficiently and effectually reveal him unto men for their salvation.[6]

The Scriptures tell us that every accountable human being recognizes that there is a God, whether or not they have ever been told. Just as we understand that the car has a designer and a painting has a painter, we recognize God through his creation. But although we might understand that God exists, it is not enough to know him personally.

Our purpose on earth is not only to know of the One True God, but also to entrust him with our lives and declare him to the world. Pray for boldness that you will point others to the Bible that they too may intimately know their Creator.

---

[5]   Ro 1:19,20; Ps 19:13; Ac 17:28
[6]   1 Co 2:9,10; 2Ti 3:1517; Isa 59:21–WLC Q2

JANUARY 3

THE WORD OF GOD

God could have chosen any way he wanted to convey the truth of his existence and our purpose here. He could proclaim it audibly from heaven. He could take his finger and write it in the sky. But he has provided us his Word through men who were instruments of his very breath to both proclaim and record every truth he would have us to know.[7]

The holy Scriptures of the Old and New Testaments are the Word of God. Therefore, the only rule of faith and obedience.[8]

God's people are not like the world, making up a religion that best suits them. We cannot pick and choose what is truth. But that does not mean we cannot know truth. God's Word is the only source of truth, and it is only through the proclamation of his Word that we can know about God, his salvation, and his purpose for our lives.[9]

How much time do you spend in God's word? Are you taking time to even look up the supporting verses provided? We cannot claim to know God without knowing his proclaimed truths. Christianity is not a godly life on autopilot; we must dig into his word and meditate on his counsel.

---

[7] 2 Ti 3:16; 2Pe 1:19-21
[8] WLC–Answer to Q3 "What is the Word of God?"
[9] Eph 2:20; Rev 22:18,19; Isa 8:20; Lk 16:29,31; Gal 1:8,9; 2Ti 3:15,16

JANUARY 4

THE WORD AND THE SPIRIT

We tend to overestimate our abilities. Because we can understand in part, we think we can also understand the whole. However, we are fallen creatures, and we do not have the ability to know God intimately or respond positively to his message unless our stony hearts are softened and our eyes are spiritually opened.[10]

The Scriptures manifest several things to us: that they are the Word of God and they show us God's attributes; they expose the darkness of our sin and show us our one hope in Christ.[11] However, the Scriptures require the Spirit of God to move in the hearts of men to make a full persuasion that they are the very word of God.[12]

Have you tested God's word? Are you convicted of sin in your life? Do you repent and seek the loving arms of a merciful Savior? Do you live in the hope of God's promises? If so, give thanks to God for performing a supernatural work in your heart by his Spirit. Our confession of true and saving faith is not from within ourselves, but it is a gift.[13]

In our prayer today, we ask to be humbled for thinking we can do any part of this Christian walk on our own. Let's also give our heavenly Father thanks for revealing himself to us.

---

[10] Ps 119:18; Ez 36:26; 2Cr 3:3
[11] Ac 18:28; Heb 4:12; Jas 1:18; Ps 19:79; Ro 15:4; Ac 20:32
[12] Jn 16:13,14; 1Jn 2:20,27; Jn 20:31–WLC Q4
[13] Ep 2:8-9; Mt 16:17; Jn 1:13

January 5

Scriptures and the Message

The Scriptures principally teach what man is to believe concerning God and what duty God requires of man.[14] We have the Scripture to teach us about God, but it's not about knowledge only. We are called to action, called to repent and believe in the Christ, and further to be and to make disciples.[15]

The scriptures make known what God is,[16] *the persons of the Godhead,*[17] *his decrees, and the execution of his decrees.*[18] This is everything we need regarding the knowledge of God and our relationship to him.

As large as the canon of the Bible is, it does not compare to the volumes written by fallen man on philosophy and psychology. However, these sciences, with their many words and expressed thoughts, will never scratch the surface relative to the straight forward and godly truth given to us in the Scriptures.

As secular man continues to look within himself for the answers of life, he will only further be frustrated as answers evade him. Yet the man of God, exposed to the Scriptures, allows light to disperse the darkness of his mind, and he shall find refuge in the Lord.

---

[14] 2 Ti 1:13–WLC Q5.
[15] A disciple is simply a "believing learner" of Jesus Christ.
[16] Heb 11:6
[17] 1 Jn 5:17
[18] Ac 15:14,15,18, 27,28–WLC Q6

JANUARY 6

WHAT IS GOD?

God is a Spirit, in and of himself infinite in being, glory, blessedness, and perfection: all-sufficient.[19] There is nothing of God that is outside of perfection. Although we are not capable of understanding this fully, we can see, examine, and test his character through the Scriptures. Furthermore, as his children, we have his transforming power working within us.

Far from the caricature as an old, wise man with long gray beard, *God is eternal, unchangeable, incomprehensible, everywhere present.*[20] Being limited ourselves, we must be careful not to place our limitations on God. We are created in his image, yet we often demonstrate that we believe the opposite, even praying at times that God would conform to *our* will. Consider the next set of Yahweh's characteristics:

We can be comforted that God is *almighty, knowing all things, most wise, most holy, most just, most merciful and gracious, long-suffering, and abundant in goodness and truth.*[21] There is nothing in our lives that God has not ordained and will use for our ultimate benefit and to his own immediate and ultimate glory.

Focus your prayer today on God's holy attributes.

---

[19] Jn 4:24; Ex 3:14; Job 11:7-9; Ac 7:2; 1Ti 6:15; Mt 5:48; Ge 17:1–WLC Q7
[20] Ps 90:2; Mal 3:6; Jas 1:17; 1Ki 8:27; Ps 139:1-13
[21] Rev 4:8; Heb 4:13; Ps 147:5; Ro 16:27; Isa 6:3; Rev 15:4; Dt 32:4; Ex 34:6

JANUARY 7

ARE THERE MORE GODS THAN ONE?

There is but one only, the living and true God.[22] Many would agree with the idea of *one God*, but would be quick to add that the many world religions all serve the *same* God. The common phrase is, *There are many paths to God.* However, the road of true religion is narrow and singular. Let's explore the fallacies.

There is a sense in which many paths lead to God holds true. If we speak of the different walks, lifestyles, and circumstances in a person's life that finally lead to them hearing[23] and responding in faith to the Gospel. But *that* faith is in itself singular. The more common idea is that *many paths* refers to *many religions*, and in this sense, the Bible speaks plainly—absolutely not.

What if we agree that there is One God and that Jesus Christ is the only way to him; are all Christian religions then true? What about the Mormons, Jehovah Witnesses, and others that place Christ at the head of their church? The answer is clear. If any testament about Christ is different than that which is revealed in Scriptures alone, this is not the same Christ nor the true Gospel.[24]

We must confess the God, the Father and the Son, who is the Christ of the Holy Scriptures, to have true and saving faith. Pray for the Holy Spirit to reveal false beliefs in your life that you might repent.

---

[22]   Dt 6:4; 1Co 8:4,6; Jer 10:10–WLC A7
[23]   Ro 10:17
[24]   Ga 1:6-10

JANUARY 8

THE GODHEAD

The Trinity, although not addressed as such, is plainly taught in the Scriptures. Trying to comprehend the Trinity is no easier than grasping the eternality of God. However, we are graced with glances at the majesty of each person and their corresponding relationships.

There are three persons in the Godhead: the Father, the Son, and the Holy Ghost, and these three are one true, eternal God, the same in substance, equal in power and glory, although distinguished by their personal properties.[25]

The personal relationship of the Godhead:[26] *It is proper to the Father to beget the Son,*[27] *and to the Son to be begotten of the Father,*[28] *and to the Holy Ghost to proceed from the Father and the Son from all eternity.*[29]

Give thanks today that we have a Father in heaven to whom we may cry *Abba* and a Son who came down from heaven to redeem us and the Holy Spirit who lives within us, constantly revealing to us the Father and Son. It is a grand and true mystery! One that includes all of creation, all of redemption, all of our sanctification, and all of our eternal hope in glory.

---

[25] 1 Jn 5:7; Mt 3:16,17; Mt 28:19; 2Co 13:14; Jn 10:30–WLC Q9
[26] WLC Q10
[27] Heb 1:5,6,8
[28] Jn 1:14,18
[29] Jn 15:26; Gal 4:6

January 9

Trilateral Equality

To embark on a journey of the Trinity will, along with its fascinating depth, show tremendous overlap in the three persons. For example: the Scriptures, at different times, assign both the creation and the resurrection to each of the persons of the Trinity. Distinct yet without separation from being one. It is impossible to adequately describe the Trinity.

The scriptures manifest that the Son and the Holy Ghost are God equal with the Father, ascribing unto them such names,[30] attributes,[31] works,[32] and worship[33] as are proper to God only.[34]

We do not abandon the Trinity because it's either impossible to understand or to difficult to define. These mysteries are found all over the Scriptures. Take the following examples: who authored the Scriptures, man or God? The answer is *yes* to both. How about, *who lives your Christian life, you or the Spirit?* Again, the answer is *yes*. We are responsible to be holy, yet it is God alone who sanctifies (makes us holy). It is here that we bow to the sovereignty of God and let the tension exist. God understands it, and that should give us total comfort.

---

[30] Isa 6:3,5,8 with Jn 12:41 and with Ac 28:25; 1Jn 5:20; Ac 5:3,4
[31] Jn 1:1; Isa 9:6; Jn 2:24,25; 1Co 2:10,11
[32] Col 1:16; Ge 1:2
[33] Mt 28:19; 2Co 13:14
[34] WLC A11

JANUARY 10

THE DECREES OF GOD

In life, a person may try to live by a certain moral standard. We set goals for education, career, and family, some short-term and others long. We contemplate life, its direction, our failures, and adjust to correct our path. However, God never changes.

In his eternal and omniscient existence, God does not contemplate the possible outcome or the paths taken to achieve a desired outcome. In his sovereign will, he speaks all things and their end into existence.

God's decrees are the wise, free, and holy acts of the counsel of his will,[35] whereby, from all eternity, he hath, for his own glory, unchangeably foreordained whatsoever comes to pass in time,[36] especially concerning angels and men.[37]

While man continues to form God into an image that suits his own desires at a given time, the true and eternal God is worthy to be feared and worshiped at every moment, now and in eternity. The person who knows the true, living God will be ultimately thankful for every difficultly as well as every blessing that comes in their life.[38]

We can give thanks for every event in our lives.

---

[35]   Eph 1:11; Ro 11:33; Ro 9:14,15,18
[36]   Eph 1:4,11; Ro 9:22,23; Ps 33:11
[37]   WLC A12
[38]   2 Co 12:10

January 11

Of Angels and Men (Part 1)

Of all creation, only angels and men live consciously above natural instinct. These two are also bound by God's eternal moral law. As God is perfect, so is his standard for angels and men. In service, worship, and accountability, angels and men are solely designated either to eternal glory or to eternal wrath.

God, by an eternal and immutable decree, out of his mere love, for the praise of his glorious grace, to be manifested in due time, hath elected some angels to glory[39] *and in Christ hath chosen some men to eternal life and the means thereof.*[40]

Some of us will hate what was just stated. Our disdain for election arises primarily from two points: our pride and our demand for what we perceive as fair. We also consider this a violation against free will. However, upon closer examination, we shall see that we truly do not want fairness, but mercy, and that prior to regeneration, our wills are in bondage to sin and we are haters and enemies of God.[41] We seek neither God[42] nor salvation. It is God who seeks,[43] and it is not by the will of man but of God that we are saved.[44]

We will explore our redemption deeper in future dates.

---

[39] 1 Ti 5:21
[40] Eph 1:4-6; 2Th 2:13,14
[41] Jer 17:9; Ro 1:30
[42] Ps 10:4; Ro 3:11
[43] Lu 19:10
[44] Jo 1:13

JANUARY 12

OF ANGELS AND MEN (PART 2)

God is under no obligation, except to his own character and eternal promises, to save any part of his creation. He is the potter and has full rights over the clay to use it as he wishes.[45] God has elected some angels and men to glory. He also passed by others to stand in righteous judgment.

God's election is *also, according to his sovereign power and the unsearchable counsel of his own will (whereby he extends or withholds favor as he pleases,) hath passed by and foreordained the rest to dishonor and wrath, to be for their sin inflicted, to the praise of the glory of his justice.*[46]

The fact that God grants eternal glory to even one who sins against him is a marvelous demonstration of his mercy and grace. Through his mercy, he is glorified. Just as well, he is glorified in his justice. It's all to God's glory. There is no unrighteousness in God.[47]

We tend to compare ourselves to those who are worse than us. The true standard of pass/fail is Jesus Christ, and God does not judge on a curve. All sin must be judged. God's judgment for his elect was not ignored, but the full fury of God's wrath was transferred to Jesus on our behalf.[48] Pray that you would better understand God's mercy.

---

[45]   Ro 9:21
[46]   Ro 9:17,18,21,22; Mt 11:25,26; 2Ti 2:20; Jude 4; 1 Pet 2:8; WLC A13b
[47]   Ro 9:14
[48]   Gal 2:20; Ro 5:8

JANUARY 13

GOD'S DECREES

God's ways are higher than our ways. We are not expected to know his purpose, but only to understand that he is sovereign and has purpose in all things, to his glory.[49]

God executes his decrees in the works of creation and providence, according to his infallible foreknowledge and the free and immutable counsel of his own will.[50]

Sometimes, God appears to be inconsistent in his handling of people in the Scriptures. God might take a faithful ruler of many years, like King Uzziah, and upon one recorded act of pride, afflict him with leprosy, execute him from his office, and have this be his only epitaph.[51] Then God appears so lenient on some of Israel's biggest enemies, who continually defame the name of God and persecute Israel.

Trusting God means leaning fully on him, whether or not we understand the deeper purpose, because we know he is worthy to be trusted.[52] There is nothing that happens that he does not allow, and in the life of a believer, there is no more comforting truth.[53]

Pray that you will be made more trusting of the One who has paid the highest price for your redemption.

---

[49] Is 55:9; Eph 1:9
[50] Eph 1:11 WLC Q14
[51] 2 Chron 26
[52] Pr 3:5, Eph 1:12
[53] Rom 8:31

January 14

Creation

That God created all things *ex nihilo* (out of nothing) is not likely to be contested by readers of this book. Yet there may be some of us, who have bought into academia's millions and millions of years of evolution. Evolution does seem to make sense at times, especially when evolutionists bash any who would claim science actually supports intelligent design and even more extraordinarily, a young earth.

The work of creation is that wherein God did in the beginning, by the word of his power, make of nothing the world, and all things therein, for himself, within the space of six days and all very good.[54]

If we choose to not take God at his word at this point, we bring the authority of his word into suspicion at other points; like Exodus 20:11, "For *in* six days the Lord made the heavens and the earth, the sea, and all that *is* in them, and rested the seventh day. Therefore the Lord blessed the Sabbath day and hallowed it." Here, we have God establishing a pattern for his people, based specifically on a literal six-day creation, then the Sabbath.

But perhaps the biggest test we face in creation is that God allowed for wickedness. Yes, good and bad, all things were made for himself. It is a difficult concept, but the allowance of wickedness does not necessitate a conflict of God's holiness. The alternative view that wickedness showed up without God's hand is much more frightening.

---

[54] Ge 1:1-31; Heb 11:3; Pr 16:4

JANUARY 15

DO ANGELS EARN THEIR WINGS?

As were all original entities that God created, angels were also created in a state that was fit for their designed purpose. Though the ranks of angels vary, it was not due to any merit of their own.

God created all the angels, spirits, immortal, holy,[55] *excelling in knowledge, mighty in power, to execute his commandments, and to praise his name*[56] *yet subject to change.*[57]

Lucifer ranked highly as a cherub,[58] yet through his five prideful claims,[59] he fell. Even further, it is stated that the devil was a murderer from the beginning.[60]

We see in the Scriptures that God creates angels that would remain holy and others that would fall and leave their first domain,[61] yet both sets completely comply with the bidding of God as he sees fit.[62]

What do you think is significant about God knowing that holy angels would fall? How does this relate to the fall of man?

---

[55] Col 1:16; Ps 104:4; Mt 22:30; Mt 25:31
[56] 2Sa 14:17; Mt 24:36; 2Th 1:7; Ps 103:20,21
[57] 2Pe 2:4 WLC Q16
[58] Ez 28:14-15
[59] Is 14:12-15
[60] John 8:44
[61] Jude 1:6
[62] Job 1:6-12

January 16

Mankind: Male and Female

Have you ever contemplated your belly button? There are two people who did not have them: Adam and Eve. Both were created fully mature by the hand of God. Created with incredible traits.

After God had made all other creatures, he created man: male and female, formed the body of the man of the dust of the ground and the woman of the rib of the man,[63] endued them with living, reasonable, and immortal souls[64]; made them after his own image, in knowledge, righteousness, and holiness;[65] having the law of God written in their hearts, and power to fulfill it[66] and dominion over the creatures yet subject to fall.[67]

There is nothing so deep as man with his heart, soul, mind, and strength.[68] So profound that Jesus used this four-dimensional way for man to love God. Furthermore, Jesus' love for us is described in another four dimensions.[69] When it comes to Jesus, love is superlative.

Man, being created in God's image, is an entrusting act by God, yet being subject to fall would require the humanly impossible act of redemption. Redemption was already in motion when man first breathed.

---

63 Ge 1:27; Ge 2:7; Ge 2:22
64 Ge 2:7 with Job 35:11 and Ecc 12:7 and Mt 10:28 and Lk 23:43
65 Ge 1:27; Col 3:10; Eph 4:24
66 Ro 2:14,15; Ecc 7:29
67 Ge 1:28; Ge 3:6; Ecc 7:29–WLC Q17
68 Mark 12:30
69 Ep 3:18

JANUARY 17

THE WORKS OF PROVIDENCE

I remember as a kid, hearing that God knew everything that was going to happen, and I would try to fake him out: raising my right hand instead of the left, blurting out a made-up word, etc. It was childish, but I would be assured that God's omniscience failed not.

The scene is painted more completely when we look at God's hand in the universe. At times, it seems the world is spinning out of control and man is getting away with brutal wickedness. We learn from the Scriptures that nobody is "faking out" God:

God's works of providence are his most holy, wise, and powerful preserving and governing all his creatures,[70] *ordering them, and all their actions, to his own glory.*[71]

God is not simply a deity that wound up the universe and let it spin on an open course of random chance, wherever that may lead. Rather, God's sustaining power holds every atom in place and directs every cell division. Furthermore, God's providence denies that anything takes place without his knowledge, his permission, or against his glory.

We may ask questions, but do not expect answers that will satisfy. We might be chastised for even asking.[72]

Pray that you will acknowledge God and trust his ways.

---

[70] Ps 145:17; Ps 104:24; Isa 28:29; Heb 1:3; Ps 103:19
[71] Mt 10:29,31; Ge 45:7; Ro 11:36; Isa 63:14–WLC Q18
[72] Job 38:1-42:17; Rom Ch 9

JANUARY 18

PROVIDENCE TOWARD ANGELS

Angels are not human, and because of this, we must be careful not to force our flesh upon them. They are God's creation and are purposed for his glory exactly as God has ordained.

God, by his providence, permitted some of the angels, willfully and irrecoverably, to fall into sin and damnation,[73] *limiting and ordering that and all their sins to his own glory*[74] *and established the rest in holiness and happiness,*[75] *employing them all*[76] *at his pleasure in the administrations of his power, mercy, and justice.*[77]

The first thing that may grab our attention is that when angels fell, there was no redemption. Should this trouble us? Not if we understand that God can handle his mercy and justice freely. It may also cause us concern about losing our redemption once we get to heaven. We cannot. What God has redeemed and adopted is eternal.

What we should be sure to take away from this doctrine is that both righteous and fallen angels are employed by God. What prideful act will ever stand against God? This is why humility is critical in our lives and why Jesus came as a humble servant.[78]

---

[73] Jude 6; 2Pe 2:4; Heb 2:16; Jn 8:44
[74] Job 1:12; Mt 8:31
[75] 1 Ti 5:21; Mk 8:38; Heb 12:22
[76] Ps 104:4
[77] 2 Ki 19:35; Heb 1:14 WLC Q19
[78] Phil 2:7

January 19

First Estate of Man

It is difficult, nay, impossible to comprehend life prior to the Fall. We have no experience of freedom from sinful nature. Yet Adam and Eve had no experience of sin or shame prior to their disobedience. How devastating it must have been when their direct access and communion with God was broken. What of their original estate?

The providence of God toward man in the estate in which he was created was the placing him in paradise, appointing him to dress it, giving him liberty to eat of the fruit of the earth; putting the creatures under his dominion and ordaining marriage for his help; affording him communion with himself; instituting the Sabbath;[79] entering into a covenant of life with him, upon condition of personal, perfect, and perpetual obedience, of which the tree of life was a pledge; and forbidding to eat of the tree of the knowledge of good and evil upon the pain of death.[80]

It is incredibly hard to fathom anyone giving up these original conditions. Yet every one of us would have done no differently. The only man that stood the test is the last Adam, Jesus Christ.[81]

Being prone to sin is no excuse for continued disobedience. Be prayerful that you walk in the Spirit, in the light of God's forgiveness.

---

[79] Ge 2:8,15,16; Ge 1:28; Ge 2:18; Ge 1:26,27,28,29; Ge 3:8; Ge 2:3
[80] Gal 3:12; Ro 10:5; Ge 2:9; Ge 2:17–WLC Q20
[81] 1 Cor 15:21-22, 45

January 20

First Estate Lost

Adam and Eve fell because their desire for the forbidden outweighed their capacity for obedience. They were most free without any blemish of a fallen nature. There is some mystery left in understanding where they tripped up.

Our first parents, being left to the freedom of their own will, through the temptation of Satan, transgressed the commandment of God in eating the forbidden fruit and thereby fell from the estate of innocence wherein they were created.[82]

It could be argued that they were tricked and unaware that the serpent was up to no good. While this is true of Eve, it is not with Adam. Look at the Scriptures, *Adam was not deceived, but the woman being deceived, fell into transgression.*[83] What does this mean? The most straightforward answer is that Adam, being aware of the situation, still proceeded to follow after her.

In either case, both of them broke free of their immediate protector; Eve's point of submission should have been to her husband, running to him to save her from the serpent's beguiling. In the same manner, Adam, knowing Eve had fallen, did not first seek the counsel of God, but willfully step into death with Eve.

Do you detest God's rules of submission or are you thankful?

---

[82] Ge 3:6,7,8,13; Ecc 7:29; 2Co 11:3–WLC Q21
[83] 1 Tim 2:14

JANUARY 21

HEIRS OF SIN

How can we who are depraved of innocence expect to make a better choice than the originally untainted wills of Adam and Eve? Many people want to argue for autonomy, yet we learn that our will is in bondage.[84]

The covenant being made with Adam as a public person, not for himself only, but for his posterity, all mankind descending from him by ordinary generation, sinned in him, and fell in that first transgression.[85]

Do not confuse free will with *moral agency*. We are free in the sense that we can make choices. However, we are only free to act according to our greatest desire at that given time. We have a bent for sin, and unless we are otherwise deterred, we will follow that desire as far as it will take us. Man only acts good because consequences might deter him from his satisfaction.

We do not have to teach children to be bad. Humans are born selfish and demanding and in need only for instruction and discipline. Until we feel moral accountability, we only obey the rules because of the ever-increasing punishment for continued sinful actions. Our basic rule of behavior is *how good am I going to be to avoid consequences that I do not want to face.*

We are all born as children of Adam. Our only hope is for rebirth as children of God where sin has no dominion over us.

---

[84]   Ro 6:16-22
[85]   Ac 17:26; Ge 2:16,17 with Ro 5:12-20 and with 1Co 15:21,22–WLC Q22

January 22

Les Miserables

What is more miserable than being dead in one's sin? Regardless of the seasons of fun and excitement that sin can generate, we all know that it does not last. Unfortunately, we continue to chase after temporary fulfillment until we have come to the end of ourselves or are dead.[86]

The fall brought mankind into an estate of sin and misery.[87] This is not the kind of inheritance that we dream of. We like the idea of a rich uncle leaving us a small fortune. Living the high life. Left to ourselves, our inherited sin leaves us bankrupt in this life and in eternity. But better than a rich uncle, believers have a heavenly Father who promises an inheritance that will never fade.[88]

In similar manner to an earthly last will and testament, God the Father leaves an inheritance to his children. The Father has one true Son, but he also adopts children whom are renewed by his Holy Spirit.[89] Through this adoption, we share in all the glorious eternal inheritance with Jesus Christ.

While we are brought into this world in a state of sin and headed for certain destruction, how could we complain when there is an inheritance beyond magnitude for those whom believe?

---

[86] Rom 1:24-32
[87] Ro 5:12; Ro 3:23–WLC Q23
[88] Ro 8:17, He 6:17, James 2:5
[89] Ro 8:14

January 23

Sin Defined

We have talked about sin for several days, yet without giving a complete definition of what it means for us to sin. I think it would be safe to say that we all have a general idea of what it means to sin against God. We might sum it up as breaking the Ten Commandments. We would be correct in stating so; however, there is more to this picture than we usually want to realize.

Sin is any want of conformity unto, or transgression of, any law of God, given as a rule to the reasonable creature.[90]

Working our way backward through this definition we see that this statement is limited to the reasonable creature. Therefore, at this time, we will not touch on the sin of infants, mentally challenged people, or those otherwise incapable of understanding wrongdoing, especially in offending the invisible and wise God.

We should easily recognize that any transgression of God's law is sin. However, the depths to what this means lies in the statement of one's *want of conformity*. It is here that the subtleties of our sins against God might be missed or even ignored. When at any moment we desire God to acquiesce to our own desires, we have transgressed against him. Do we think we have a better plan than God?

As you pray today, ask God to reveal areas of your life in which you sinned against him; repent and seek to be sensitive to his holiness.

---

[90] 1 Jn 3:4; Gal 3:10,12–WLC Q24

January 24

The Depth of Sin

Do you have your thinking caps on? This next statement of how far man is fallen is a massive sentence. Take your time to comprehend each segment between the commas and it will not be too overwhelming. Each segment builds upon the previous. Don't forget to read the supporting Scriptures in the footnotes.

The sinfulness of that estate wherein man fell consists in the guilt of Adam's first sin,[91] the want of that righteousness wherein he was created, and the corruption of his nature, whereby he is utterly indisposed, disabled, and made opposite unto all that is spiritually good and wholly inclined to all evil and that continually,[92] which is commonly called original sin and from which do proceed all actual transgressions.[93]

I trust that you were able to follow this statement. In summary, it shows us the depth of our sin and the areas of our being that it affects. This is known as *total depravity*. This is not saying that man is *utterly depraved* (as bad as he can possibly be at all possible times), but *totally*, in which there is not any part of our physical or spiritual existence is not affected by sin.

Total depravity is a far cry from being *generally good* as modern psychology would have us believe. Oh, the depths of our corruption! Thank God for the cleansing power of Christ's blood.

---

91 Ro 5:12,19
92 Ro 3:10-19; Eph 2:1-3; Ro 5:6; Ro 8:7,8; Ge 6:5
93 Jas 1:14,15; Mt 15:19–WLC Q25

January 25

Thanks for the Hand-Me-Downs

We have all heard someone tell us, "You look just like your father," or "You have your mother's eyes." How about this one? "You are a filthy sinner just like your parents." Although we would not likely hear this, it is a true statement.

Original sin is conveyed from our first parents unto their posterity by natural generation, so as all that proceed from them in that way are conceived and born in sin.[94]

Here is another one of those times when we want to scream, "That's not fair!" It is difficult to see why we should be accounted as sinners because it was inherited. But much in the same manner in which we do not have any say about our physically inherited traits, sin is also handed down through the natural process.

Take a deeper look at our criticism of God's fairness. Do we really think that we, being born into sin, should rebuke a holy God? Inherited sin is a biblical truth in which we might see God's holiness as far above the darkness of fallen man. Inherited sin does not stand alone, we also have to answer for our own unrighteous acts.

We have a terminal disease. It is both genetic and self-inflicted. We all test positive for the S-I-N virus. Do you possess the only cure? It is redemption by the blood of Christ.

---

[94] Ps 51:5; Job 14:4; Job 15:14; Jn 3:6–WLC 26

January 26

Watch That First Step

Relationships, which may take years to build up, can be torn down in a matter of moments. When the perfect relationship between God and Adam was broken, a lot more than feelings were hurt.

The fall brought upon mankind the loss of communion with God, his displeasure and curse; so as we are by nature children of wrath, bond slaves to Satan,[95] and justly liable to all punishments in this world, and that which is to come.[96]

This is quite the fall for one disobedient act. On the contrary because we have been sold to sin, we only know disobedience, living our unredeemed lives to fulfill the desires of the flesh. Even using the word "living" in the sentence above is a bit misleading. For we have not life, but are dead in trespasses and sins.[97]

Within the fallen condition, any moments of temporary peace, life, and happiness are purely mercies of God. If justice was not withheld by God's patience, our punishment would swift and proper. However, God prolongs some of our lives. Some will be storing up wrath through their disobedience, and some God will save, granting repentance and eternal life.

Do you have life in Christ? Give thanks to God that you have been purchased from being a slave of Satan.

---

[95]   Ge 3:8,10,24; Eph 2:2,3; 2Ti 2:26
[96]   Ge 2:17; La 3:39; Ro 6:23; Mt 25:41,46; Jude 7–WLC 27
[97]   Eph 2:1

JANUARY 27

PUNISHMENTS IN THIS WORLD

We are in our eighth day of focus on sin and its penalty. We should, by now, have a good sense of what the fall of man, as well as our own sin, has meant in terms of separation of our relationship with God. However, we have yet to plunge the depths of God's process in addressing our disobedience.

The punishments of sin in this world are either inward, as blindness of mind, a reprobate sense, strong delusions, hardness of heart, horror of conscience, and vile affections;[98] or outward, as the curse of God upon the creatures for our sakes, and all other evils that befall us in our bodies, names, estates, relations, and employments, together with death itself.[99]

The punishment is against our complete being. Inwardly, being our spiritual and mental purity and outwardly, of physical and emotional relationships with the world around us. There is no partial fall. We don't have poor vision, we are spiritually blind. We don't seek God, but we hate him and hide our sin. The hand of judgment hangs over our heads with only God's patience withholding his justice.

It is because of total depravity that we could only give full credit to the grace of God in our salvation. If we think that we participate to any degree in our own righteousness, we are not believing the fullness of grace and God is not receiving praise as he ought.

---

[98] Eph 4:18; Ro 1:28; 2Th 2:11; Ro 2:5; Isa 33:14; Ge 4:13; Mt 27:4; Ro 1:26
[99] Ge 3:17; Dt 28:15-18; Ro 6:21,23 WLC 28

January 28

Everlasting Punishment

Some people, even some who would call themselves Bible-believing Christians, do not believe in hell or eternal punishment. Certainly, they are not reading the Scriptures at face value, nor taking the words of Jesus as absolute truth. But God's Word is true regardless of one's interpretation. Universal truths stand because of God's design. They do not fail or change because we don't like them.

The punishments of sin in the world to come are everlasting separation from the comfortable presence of God and most grievous torments in soul and body without intermission in hellfire forever.[100]

I am not good at enduring suffering. I can hardly bear the twenty-four-hour flu, let alone a weeklong ailment. When I consider eternity in hell, I can sympathize with those who banish such thoughts. But we stand on God and his truth alone. Therefore, we know that everlasting consciousness exists. We also know that there are only two destination possibilities: heaven with its eternal peace or hell with its eternal punishment.

For those who do not fear the One who can cast our bodies and souls into hell, it is a clear indication on just how darkened they have become. We all would do well to grasp the deeper reality of hell. If we did, we would give an endless effort to warn those around us.

Lord, give us a sense of urgency in this matter.

---

[100] 2 Th 1:9; Mk 9:43,44,46,48; Lk 16:24—WLC Q29

January 29

Where Is the Hope?

After several days of learning about the sin of man, the misery that he brought upon himself, and the just punishment he has in this world and the next, we may feel we are without hope. Certainly, God acts justly when he punishes sin and condemns men to hell. However, this is not a one-sided plan of God.

God does not leave all men to perish in the estate of sin and misery,[101] *into which they fell by the breach of the first covenant, commonly called the Covenant of Works,*[102] *but of his mere love and mercy delivers his elect out of it and brings them into an estate of salvation by the second covenant, commonly called the Covenant of Grace.*[103]

It is a blessing beyond compare that God does not leave all men to perish in their sins. He would be perfectly justified to do so. Furthermore, his glory would not be in any way diminished. But *God, by an eternal and immutable decree, out of his mere love, for the praise of his glorious grace has chosen some men to eternal life.*[104]

We wrestle with this thought of God's sovereignty in salvation of only some. However, we must always keep in mind that we have already agreed that *all* men stand justly condemnable. Now enters grace, of which God may show mercy to whomever he chooses.

---

[101] 1 Th 5:9
[102] Gal 3:10,12
[103] Tit 3:4-7; Gal 3:21; Ro 3:20-22–WLC Q30
[104] Eph 1:4-6; 2Th 2:13,14–WLC Q13 revisited

January 30

Let's Make a Covenant

When God, by his mercy and grace, saves some men from eternal punishment, it is not without justice being served. Because the wages of sin is death,[105] the elect's sin still requires payment. In the case of those who are redeemed, we have a substitute that took our death penalty upon himself.

The covenant of grace was made with Christ as the second Adam and in him, with all the elect as his seed.[106]

The best example I can give is in the manner of our court system. If I were to break the law, I might end up in court. The judge could say something like the following, "Sir, you have broken the law, your penalty is one thousand dollars or sixty days in jail."

If I cannot pay, an advocate may step forward and make the payment on my behalf. The judge would then proclaim, "This court is satisfied. Payment is made in full. Case dismissed. You may go free." Those who believe in Jesus Christ have such an advocate. He has paid the death penalty on our behalf, never to be judged again.

The covenant of grace is similar to the above example. Father God demands justice for sins. However, Christ has stepped forward according to their eternal covenant of behalf of the elect, that is, all whom would ever believe.

---

[105] Rom 6:23
[106] Gal 3:16; Ro 5:15-21; (John 17:2) WLC Q31

JANUARY 31

HOW IT WORKS

The covenant of grace is not a flippant last-minute thought of God to get him out of a pickle because we were unable to live up to his standard. This covenant was made in eternity between God the Father and the Son who would pay the ransom for all believers.

The grace of God is manifested in the second covenant, in that he freely provides and offers to sinners a Mediator,[107] and life and salvation by him and requiring faith as the condition to interest them in him, promises, and gives his Holy Spirit to all his elect to work in them that faith, with all other saving graces,[108] and to enable them unto all holy obedience, as the evidence of the truth of their faith and thankfulness to God, and as the way which he has appointed them to salvation.[109]

The covenant of salvation is much deeper than trying to resolve man's sin issue. Our falleness is complete, penetrating into every part of our being. Therefore, the extent to which we need God to act within us is all encompassing. We cannot act on our own, for dead men cannot move toward God. It is all God; he begins the work of salvation in us, and he also completes it.[110]

Give thanks to the Lord that his promise of salvation in you is complete from beginning to end. There is no God like our God.

---

[107] Ge 3:15; Isa 42:16; Jn 6:27
[108] 1 Jn 5:11,12; Jn 3:16; Jn 1:12; Pr 1:23; 2Co 4:13; Gal 5:22,23
[109] Eze 36:27; Jas 2:18,22; 2Co 5:14,15; Eph 2:18 WLC Q32
[110] Phil 1:6

FEBRUARY 1

COVENANTS: OLD AND NEW

We sometimes look at the Old Covenant (the Law) and the New Covenant (Grace in Christ) as two different means of salvation. However, we should note that both are resolved at the cross. While the Old points forward to the cross, the New looks back upon Jesus' sacrifice. Righteousness in both cases is through faith.[111]

The covenant of grace was not always administered after the same manner, but the administration of it under the Old Testament were different from those under the New.[112]

Over the next couple of days, we will see that the Old and New Testaments are only different administrations of the same Covenant of Grace. The plan of salvation has not changed. It is not as if God tried the Law and its continuous sacrificial system for several millennia, then decided that it did not work and devised a back-up plan.

A couple of things to keep in mind: (1) the sacrifices of the Old Covenant never forgave a single sin,[113] and (2) the purpose of the Law was to show us that it was impossible for us keep it and further, to expose our sin.[114]

The Covenant of Grace in both the Old and New Covenants has always been that salvation comes only by faith.

---

[111] Rom 4:1-5
[112] 2 Co 3:6-9–WLC Q33
[113] Heb 10:4; Gal 3:11
[114] Rom 5:20; Gal 3:19-24

FEBRUARY 2

GRACE ADMINISTERED: OT

The Old Testament saints kept strict rules and performed countless sacrifices to show the obedience of their faith. All the while, they looked forward to the One who would bring full redemption.

The covenant of grace was administered under the Old Testament, by promises, prophecies, sacrifices, circumcision, the Passover,[115] and other types and ordinances, which did fore-signify Christ then to come, and were for that time sufficient to build up the elect in faith in the promised Messiah,[116] by whom they then had full remission of sin and eternal salvation.[117]

The Scriptures tell us that many Old Testament saints were aware that Messiah to come would suffer for his people. Yet by the time that Jesus walked the earth, the religious were full of pride and the zealots wanted only to usher in a new king to supplant Caesar. But there were some meek and humble who would recognize Jesus as the One who was promised.[118]

Have you ever wondered if you would have been faithful under the Old Testament Law? The answer is that righteousness always comes by faith to those who have ears to hear. God's gift of grace is timeless. Offer praise to the God who saves all generations by Christ.

---

[115] Ro 15:8; Ac 3:20,24; Heb 10:1; Ro 4:11; 1Co 5:7
[116] Heb Chapters VIII, IX and X; Heb 11:13
[117] Gal 3:7,8,9,14–WLC Q34
[118] John 1:26-30, 40-41, 11:27; Mt 16:6

FEBRUARY 3

GRACE ADMINISTERED: NT

The New Testament is distinguished in several ways from the Old. Perhaps the largest factor is that the daily sacrifice ceased. There is no more blood to be shed for the remission of sins. Christ shed the only blood that ever forgave sin. He paid the price once, for all.[119]

Under the New Testament, when Christ the substance was exhibited, the same covenant of grace was and still is to be administered in the preaching of the word and the administration of the sacraments of baptism and the Lord's Supper[120] *in which grace and salvation are held forth in more fullness, evidence, and efficacy to all nations.*[121]

Jesus Christ brought forth the culmination of Old Testament's Law. He fulfilled all righteousness,[122] and God's Covenant of Grace was now to be administered in a new manner.

We, who now live in the New Testament period, have the benefit of looking back and seeing many mysteries of the Old Testament revealed. By this, we can live free from the guilt of sin, knowing that Jesus has paid the penalty on our behalf. We also can walk in the newness of this redeemed life.

Consider today, the cost of your redemption.

---

[119] Rom 6:10; Heb 7:27, 9:12, 10:10
[120] Mk 16:15; Mt 28:19,20; 1Co 11:23,24,25
[121] 2 Co 3:6-18; Heb 8:6,10,11; Mt 28:19–WLC Q35
[122] Mt 3:15, 5:17

FEBRUARY 4

CHRIST THE MEDIATOR

So many religions, so many paths to God. Unfortunately, this is the opinion of so many people, including some who attend Christian assemblies. In a simple biblical comment, they are wrong.

The only Mediator of the covenant of grace is the Lord Jesus Christ,[123] who, being the eternal Son of God, of one substance and equal with the Father,[124] in the fullness of time became man and so was and continues to be God and man in two entire distinct natures and one person forever.[125]

Is it unfair for God to make only one way of salvation? How about the earnest people who only believe what they've been taught their whole lives? At first blush, it may seem like a valid argument. The better question is, why would we expect truth to operate differently in religion than it does in other areas of life?

If a child was raised to believe 2 + 2 = 5 or that gravity is just an illusion, would it be okay to leave him uncorrected just because of their sincerity? Of course not. Just as contradictory statements cannot both be correct, we cannot have opposing views of religion both be true. Either Jesus is the only path to God or he is not.[126]

Embrace Christ and lovingly expose false religion.

---

[123] 1 Ti 2:5
[124] Jn 1:1,14; Jn 10:30; Php 2:6
[125] Gal 4:4; Lk 1:35; Ro 9:5; Col 2:9; Heb 7:24,25–WLC Q36
[126] Jn 14:6

FEBRUARY 5

SON OF GOD, SON OF MAN

Yesterday, we determined that contradictory statements cannot both be true. Specifically in that Christ is the only mediator between God and man. There are times when a paradox exists, but it is does not violate logic.

Christ, the Son of God, became man by taking to himself a true body and a reasonable soul,[127] *being conceived by the power of the Holy Ghost in the womb of the Virgin Mary, of her substance, and born of her,*[128] *yet without sin.*[129]

Apparent paradoxes exist throughout the Scriptures. For example: who is responsible for authoring the book of Romans? Paul, right? Oh, hold on, it was the Holy Spirit. There it says: 100 percent Paul and 100 percent Holy Spirit. The same tension lies in the reality of the Trinity or the eternal existence of God. For things we cannot humanly understand, but the Scripture says are true, we must simple yield to our limitations.

The son of God did not come into existence on the day of his birth. He was, at that time, manifest in the flesh of man. Fully God, fully man, and there we must once again let the tension rest for God's ways are higher than our ways. For this, I am glad, that God has it all under control. Praise God if you can rest in this knowledge.

---

[127] Jn 1:14; Mt 26:38
[128] Lk 1:27,31,35,42; Gal 4:4
[129] Heb 4:15; Heb 7:26–WLC Q37

FEBRUARY 6

CHRIST MUST BE GOD

We easily comprehend Jesus, the man. Hearing the stories of Jesus walking amidst his people and communing with them. We might even understand his miracles to the degree that God worked his power through Jesus. But where we may initially fail in our comprehension is where Jesus, at every moment, was fully God.

It was requisite that the Mediator should be God, that he might sustain and keep the human nature from sinking under the infinite wrath of God and the power of death;[130] give worth and efficacy to his sufferings, obedience, and intercession;[131] and to satisfy God's justice, procure his favor, purchase a peculiar people, give his Spirit to them,[132] conquer all their enemies, and bring them to everlasting salvation.[133]

No man, regardless how disciplined, would ever be able to meet the requirements of the mediatory between God and the rest of humanity. One reason is that the mediator must not only be able to lay his life down for the sins of God's people, but he must also be able to raise himself from the grave. Jesus said, "I lay it (my life) down of myself. I have power to lay it down, and I have power to take it again." This statement from John 10:18 is God's power over death.

---

[130] Ac 2:24;,25; Ro 1:4; Ro 4:25; Heb 9:14
[131] Ac 20:28; Heb 9:14; Heb 7:25-28
[132] Ro 3:24,25,26; Eph 1:6; Mt 3:17; Tit 2:13,14; Gal 4:6
[133] Lk 1:68,69,71,74; Heb 5:8,9; Heb 9:11-15–WLC Q38

FEBRUARY 7

CHRIST MUST BE MAN

We will never understand the depth of humility of God's Son. That he would step from his heavenly realm and lower himself to the status of a poor servant is beyond our comprehension. Nonetheless, by one act of righteousness, showed the extent of love.

It was requisite that the Mediator should be man that he might advance our nature, perform obedience to the law, suffer and make intercession for us in our nature,[134] have a fellow-feeling of our infirmities that we might receive the adoption of sons and have comfort and access with boldness unto the throne of grace.[135]

Jesus coming down to earth would be akin to a man coming in the form of an ugly mutt to save a bunch of purebred, yet rabid, golden retrievers. Oh, our shame that was placed on him! Then to top it off, we receive his righteousness and are adopted as children of God and joint heirs with Christ.[136]

We are very good at feeling sorry for ourselves when things drift from our plan. What about the man whose life of perfect obedience was met with misery, slander, torment, and death?

Take some time today to consider the cost of your redemption. Is there any request of us that would be too bold for him to ask?

---

[134] Heb 2:16; Gal 4:4; Heb 2:14; Heb 7:24,25
[135] Heb 4:15; Gal 4:5; Heb 4:16
[136] Ro 8:15-17–LWC Q39

FEBRUARY 8

CHRIST THE GOD-MAN

We have learned over the past couple of days that it was required that Christ be God and that Christ be man. It follows that for both of these to be true, they must be true at the same time.

It was requisite that the Mediator, who was to reconcile God and man, should himself be both God and man, and this in one person that the proper works of each nature might be accepted of God for us[137] *and relied on by us as the works of the whole person.*[138]

As we dig into the mysteries of God's Word, we will have moments of clarity, understanding certain principles behind the Scriptures. However, we will always be left wanting as we cannot attain to the omniscient mind of God.

The more you study the Word, the more God enlightens his mysteries. The more you understand about Jesus, the more you know about God. Jesus said, "I and my Father are one, and he who has seen me has seen the Father." We study Christ to know God.

If our Mediator was not God incarnate, the offering for sins would have been made void by the inherited sin from Adam. Give God thanks for sending his Son who fulfilled all righteousness. Ask Jesus to reveal himself that you might see the Father.

---

[137] Mt 1:21,23; Mt 3:17; Heb 9:14
[138] 1   Pe 2:6–WLC Q40

FEBRUARY 9

HIS NAME SHALL BE JESUS

Jesus…There's just something about that Name. Master! Savior! Jesus! Let all heaven and earth proclaim! Kings and kingdoms will all pass away, but there's something about that Name.

—Gaither

Our Mediator was called Jesus because he saves his people from their sins.[139]

For the believer, this is the whole purpose of Christ. No matter what history remembers about Jesus, if he is not the Savior, then all is in vain. The healings, the feeding of thousands, the rebuke and restoration of Peter, the carrying of the cross, all for show without eternity being purchased. He is Savior.

Names in biblical times, often held more meaning than simple identification: from Adam (man), to Isaac (laughing), to Joshua (the Hebrew version of Jesus (Savior), to finally our Savior, Jesus. As a Christian, it should be impossible to separate the name of Jesus from his work on the cross.

Are you saved? It's only because of the name that you claim. Jesus who paid your debt. Jesus who conquered the grave. Jesus who sits at the right hand of the Father and will judge every person based on their relationship with his name and all that it represents.

Pray and pray earnestly, knowing it's heard in Jesus' name.

---

[139] Mt 1:21–WLC Q41

FEBRUARY 10

JESUS THE CHRIST

Christ (Greek) in the New Testament and Messiah (Hebrew) in the Old Testament both mean *anointed*.

Our Mediator was called Christ because he was anointed with the Holy Ghost above measure and so set apart and fully furnished with all authority and ability[140] to execute the offices of prophet, priest, and king of his Church[141] in the estate both of his humiliation and exaltation.

There are many men of the Scriptures that are labeled as anointed. Kings and priests were anointed as servants of God. There was even a pagan king, Cyrus, anointed of God for his purpose.[142] But there is only one who was *the* Anointed and promised One to fulfill all righteousness.

> O Lord God, do not turn away the face of Your Anointed; Remember the mercies of Your servant David.
>
> 2 Chronicles 6:42

> The kings of the earth set themselves, And the rulers take counsel together, Against the Lord and against His Anointed.
>
> Psalm 2:2

Remember that Christ is anointed above all. Spend time today meditating on the meaning of Jesus as anointed.

---

[140] Jn 3:34; Ps 45:7; Jn 6:27; Mt 28:18,19,20
[141] Ac 3:21,22; Lk 4:18,21; Heb 5:5,6,7; Heb 4:14,15; Ps 2:6; Mt 21:5; Isa 9:6,7; Php 2:8-11–WLC Q42
[142] Is 45:1

FEBRUARY 11

JESUS THE PROPHET

There are many who claim to not believe in Jesus as the Christ, but do recognize him as a prophet and teacher. Although they are lost without knowing him as their Savior, they cannot deny his earthly office. Jesus' role as prophet is significant in showing he was, in the very least, approved of God and therefore a revealer of truth.

Christ executes the office of a prophet in his revealing to the church in all ages by his Spirit and word and in diverse ways of administration[143] *the whole will of God in all things concerning their edification and salvation.*[144]

Prophets of God were different from the so-called *prophets* of pagan kings. God's standard for his prophets' claim success is 100 percent fulfillment. If a false prophet was discovered, his sentence was death. This is why Nostradamus has no right to be considered as prophet.

There is no room for fortune tellers in the life of a believer. The Bible speaks strongly against flirtation with horoscopes, séances, and anything else that takes our trust from him and his holy Word.

Jesus gave dozens of prophecies about events that would take place both short-term and long-term. The perfect fulfillment of these are just one of the supports that confirm him as the Son of God.

Give thanks today that your faith is confirmed through prophecy.

---

[143] Jn 1:18; 1Pe 1:10,11,12 ; Heb 1:1,2
[144] Jn 15:15; Ac 20:32; Eph 4:11,12,13; Jn 20:31–WLC Q43

FEBRUARY 12

JESUS THE PRIEST

The priesthood was a God-appointed sect of men, from the tribe of Levi, whose responsibility was to perform the daily sacrifices in the temple. The endless string of sacrifices were acts of obedience by God's people, which showed that there was no forgiveness without the shedding of innocent blood.

Christ executes the office of a priest in his once offering himself a sacrifice without spot to God[145] to be a reconciliation for the sins of his people[146] and in making continual intercession for them.[147]

All of the sacrifices prior to Jesus' death, as the Lamb of God, were only symbolic and set as remembrance of the wages of sin. Those thousands upon thousands of sacrifices never forgave one sin.[148] But Jesus was able to stand in the place of sinful man and take our sin upon himself. Both Old and New Testaments saints are forgiven at the cross.

Furthermore, by his resurrection, he reigns in heaven, where he continues to represent us through eternity. The need for a priesthood ended at Calvary. To continue in ritualistic sacrifices is to deny the Savior's statement from the cross, "It is finished."[149]

---

[145] Heb 9:14,28
[146] Heb 2:17
[147] Heb 7:25–WLC Q44
[148] Heb 10:4
[149] John 19:30

FEBRUARY 13

JESUS THE KING

It is no wonder that Israel so anxiously awaited the Messiah. They were correct in understanding what the final salvation of their nation meant: Christ as King.

Christ executes the office of a king in calling out of the world a people to himself[150] and giving them officers, laws, and censures by which he visibly governs them;[151] in bestowing saving grace upon his elect, rewarding their obedience, and correcting them for their sins, preserving, and supporting them under all their temptations and sufferings,[152] restraining and overcoming all their enemies,[153] and powerfully ordering all things for his own glory, and their good; and also in taking vengeance on the rest, who know not God and obey not the gospel.[154]

Because Israel ignored the other side of the Messianic prophecies, those which showed Messiah to be a *suffering servant*, they were blinded by their own narrow vision and by the religious leaders of the day who were more interested in their own high positions.

Pray that, as we serve God, we are not missing his important details because we are dwelling on self-interests.

---

[150] Ac 15:14,15,16; Isa 55:4,5; Ge 49:10; Ps 110:3
[151] Eph 4:11,12; 1Co 12:2; Isa 33:22; Mt 18:17,18; 1Co 5:4
[152] Ac 5:31; Rev 22:12; Rev 2:10; Rev 3:19; Isa 63:9
[153] 1 Co 15:25; Ps 110:1,2 (See the Psalm throughout)
[154] Ro 14:10,11; Ro 8:28; 2Th 1:8,9; Ps 2:8,9 -WLC Q45

FEBRUARY 14

CHRIST'S HUMILIATION

We will be spending the next several days looking into the humiliation of Jesus Christ. What is his humiliation and how was it manifest in his life? First off, let look at what it entails.

The estate of Christ's humiliation was that low condition wherein he for our sakes, emptying himself of his glory, took upon him the form of a servant in his conception and birth, life, death, and after his death until his resurrection.[155]

Jesus, pre-existing in eternity as the most holy second person of the Trinity, stepped into position of lowest possible stature. Without fear of holding on to his high position, the king became slave.

Only God, who has absolutely nothing to threaten his omnipotence, could lower himself without interference of pride. Unlike Lucifer, though created highest ranked among the angels, was not satisfied with his role and fell to pride.[156]

We must not allow pride to take over lest we also sin against God. He has given us a very good and perfect gift, how shall we say it is not enough? Consider Christ's humility. Consider his purpose for lowering himself that we might share in the riches of his inheritance.

Redemption was not cheap; it cost Christ everything.

---

[155] Php 2:6,7,8; Lk 1:31; 2Co 8:9; Ac 2:24–WLC Q46
[156] Is 14:12-14

FEBRUARY 15

HUMILIATION IN A STABLE

Our most celebrated holiday is the birth of Christ. It is the only time left when you will hear the proclamation "Christ, the Savior is born!" ringing throughout the streets and shopping centers. Although I think that commercialism has gone too far with music in November; perhaps it's God's way of saying he wants more time of public worship.

Christ humbled himself in his conception and birth in that being from all eternity the Son of God, in the bosom of the Father, he was pleased in the fullness of time to become the son of man, made of a woman of low estate, and to be born of her with diverse circumstances of more than ordinary abasement.[157]

While we sing "Newborn King," we read of much humility in his birth. Although only a few have knowledge of this child being the Christ, some shepherds, some wise men, and the parents, the rest of the world sees only a poor family and bad timing to give birth in a stable. God, however, was most glorified in his perfect plan.

Although we are correct to see the humility of Jesus' birth, we also have Scriptural insight that this pleased the Father. God only allows, at every possible moment, for things to be most glorifying to himself. How this happens is beyond our comprehension, but the next time we look at the Nativity scene, we know why we sing, "Glory to God in the highest and peace to his people on earth."[158]

---

[157] Jn 1:14,18; Gal 4:4; Lk 2:7–WLC Q47
[158] Lk 2:14

FEBRUARY 16

A LIFETIME OF HUMILIATION

Humility expresses itself in diverse ways. We have all experienced times when we thought we were absolutely sure of ourselves only to be embarrassed by our error. However, for Jesus, it was not a matter of being shown up, for pride never got in his way. His humility was manifest in a life of meekness through defining moments.

Christ humbled himself in his life by subjecting himself to the law, which he perfectly fulfilled, [159] *and by conflicting with the indignities of the world, temptations of Satan,* [160] *and infirmities in his flesh, whether common to the nature of man or particularly accompanying that his low condition.* [161]

Picture a bar of pure gold. Now place this bar into a lifetime of testing where it is continually subjected to fire. Because it truly is gold, it will pass every test without any impurities. In the same manner, Jesus was tested and tempted, and because he was truly God, he never failed a test or bended to any sin.

You may think Jesus spoke with pride when he rebuked his mother or the religious authorities. But speaking words of knowledge is not in itself a display of pride. Truth spoken simply exposes error. How should we expose error?

Give thanks to Christ who shines his light into darkness. [162]

---

[159] Gal 4:4; Mt 5:17; Ro 5:19
[160] Ps 22:6; Heb 12:2,3; Mt 4:1-12; Lk 4:13
[161] Heb 2:17,18; Heb 4:15; Isa 52:13,14–WLC Q48
[162] Jn 1:5

FEBRUARY 17

HUMILIATION IN DEATH

As many times as I have watched the passion event of various movies, I always tell myself that I do not even know the half of it. Jesus' arrest and condemnation was the biggest act of injustice of all time.

Christ humbled himself in his death in that having been betrayed by Judas, forsaken by his disciples, scorned and rejected by the world,[163] condemned by Pilate, and tormented by his persecutors,[164] having also conflicted with the terrors of death and the powers of darkness, felt and borne the weight of God's wrath, he laid down his life an offering for sin,[165] enduring the painful, shameful, and cursed death of the cross.[166]

What is more amazing still is that Christ did all of this for me and everyone who would believe in his name. So every lash of the whip, every thorn that lodged in his head, every harsh word and each drop of spittle, and finally each of the three nails were deserved, but by us. Yet Christ took it all upon himself and stated, "Father, forgive them, for they know not what they do."[167]

Jesus' expression of ultimate love was demonstrated that day. He laid his life down willingly for our sake and he did so in the most humble way.

---

[163] Mt 27:4; Mt 26:56; Isa 53:2,3
[164] Mt 27:26-50; Jn 19:34
[165] Lk 22:44; Mt 27:46; Isa 53:10
[166] Php 2:8; Heb 12:2; Gal 3:13–WLC Q49
[167] Lk 23:34

FEBRUARY 18

HUMILIATION AFTER HIS DEATH

Jesus hung on that cross, naked for the world to look upon and mock. He took his last breath and gave up his spirit at the moment of the noramally sacrificed Passover lamb. His substitutionary death on behalf of his people was complete. Yet his humiliation continued.

Christ's humiliation after his death consisted in his being buried[168] and continuing in the state of the dead and under the power of death till the third day,[169] which hath been otherwise expressed in these words, He descended into hell.[170]

The Jewish traditions that were followed for the burial of Jesus were observed. His expedient removal from the cross and burial in the tomb would have made the event business like. I wonder what the somber mood was like when everyone returned to their homes. There were many different relationships with Jesus. They must have all been thinking, *What now?*

We might understand Mary's emptiness as she just lost her child. But how about John, who now was entrusted with the care of Mary above Jesus' other siblings? And what about the disciples, whose entire lives had been altered to follow Jesus? What do they do now that he is gone? The agony and questions would be short-lived: just three days.

Death of a loved one brings change. How profound.

---

[168] 1Co 15:3,4
[169] Ps 16:10; Ac 2:24,25,26,27,31; Ro 6:9; Mt 12:40
[170] TWLC–Q50

FEBRUARY 19

LET HIM BE EXALTED

We have made it through the humiliation of Christ, and now, we will focus on celebration, discussing his triumph after his death.

The estate of Christ's exaltation comprehends his resurrection, ascension, sitting at the right hand of the Father,[171] and his coming again to judge the world.[172]

Without the resurrection of Jesus Christ, there is no salvation. If Christ dies on the cross, but does not defeat death, then sin still fulfills its purpose of separating both the Son and the believer from the Father. Paul states this most clearly when he comments that, "If Christ not be risen, we are of all men most miserable."[173]

Christ's resurrection was not for an immediate earthly reign. Through his ascension, we know he has retained his proper place as the king of heaven. We have insight into this fact when we read of Jesus' prayer before his death: *And now, O Father, glorify Me together with Yourself, with the glory which I had with You before the world was.*[174]

Finally, the exalted Christ will return again as judge over all the world. For those who are in Christ, our judgment is his righteousness.

---

[171] 1Co 15:4; Mk 16:19; Eph 1:20
[172] Ac 1:11; Ac 17:31–WLC Q51
[173] 1Co 15:17-19
[174] Jn 17:5

FEBRUARY 20

EXALTED AT HIS RESURRECTION

The following is a fairly extensive statement for a daily devotional reading. Since there is hardly a more important doctrine that the resurrection of Christ, it is worth our time to understand its contents and all that was accomplished through it.

Christ was exalted in his resurrection in that not having seen corruption in death (of which it was not possible for him to be held) and having the very same body in which he suffered, with the essential properties thereof (but without mortality and other common infirmities belonging to this life), really united to his soul, he rose again from the dead the third day by his own power;[175] whereby he declared himself to be the Son of God, to have satisfied divine justice, to have vanquished death and him that had the power of it, and to be Lord of quick and dead:[176] all which he did as a public person, the head of his Church, for their justification,[177] quickening in grace, support against enemies, and to assure them of their resurrection from the dead at the last day.[178]

The totality of Christ's resurrection will not be known by us until we join him in glory. We live by confidence in him because of what he accomplished by his death and through his resurrection.

---

[175] Ac 2:24,27; Lk 24:39; Ro 6:9; Rev 1:18; Jn 10:18
[176] Ro 1:4; Ro 8:34; Heb 2:14; Ro 14:9
[177] 1Co 15:21,22; Eph 1:20,22,23; Col 1:18; Ro 4:25
[178] Eph 2:1,5,6; Col 2:12; 1Co 15: 25,26,27; 1Co 15:20–WLC Q52

FEBRUARY 21

THE ASCENSION

The testimony of our faith in Christ's ascension is stated best in Paul's first letter to Timothy when he concluded about the great mystery of godliness. Completely sure of this truth, he states that it is without controversy that Christ was *received up in glory.*[179]

Christ was exalted in his ascension in that having after his resurrection often appeared unto and conversed with his apostles, speaking to them of the things pertaining to the kingdom of God, and giving them commission to preach the gospel to all nations, forty days after his resurrection, he, in our nature, and as our head, triumphing over enemies,[180] *visibly went up into the highest heavens, there to receive gifts for men,*[181] *to raise up our affections thither, and to prepare a place for us, where himself is, and shall continue till his second coming at the end of the world.*[182]

We may be able to envision ourselves walking at the time of Jesus' ministry on earth. However, imagining the forty days during his resurrected presence is a tough one. They could hear him and touch him, yet he was able to transcend our spatial laws. He walked through walls and appeared out of nowhere.

The most spectacular event must be the few who witnessed his ascension into the heavens. One day, we too will know.

---

[179] 1 Tim 3:16
[180] Ac 1:2,3; Mt 28:19,20; Heb 6:20; Eph 4:8
[181] Ac 1:9,10,11; Eph 4:10; Ps 68:18
[182] Col 3:1,2; Jn 14:3 ; Ac 3:21–WLC Q53

FEBRUARY 22

ON HIS THRONE

Some question if Jesus is truly on his throne because they see that he allows wickedness to continue without immediate justice. However, the plan of those who are yet to be redeemed would be cut short by such an action. The Lord is allowing time for those who would be pulled from their lives of misery into the kingdom by the conversion of their hearts by the Holy Spirit.

Christ is exalted in his sitting at the right hand of God in that as God-man, he is advanced to the highest favor with God the Father, with all fullness of joy, glory,[183] and power over all things in heaven and earth[184] and does gather and defend his church and subdue their enemies, furnishes ministers and people with gifts and graces,[185] and makes intercession for them.[186]

It is because of Christ's reign that we stand without fear of ultimate destruction. We know that persecution may come, but our pain pales in comparison to the glory we shall have with him in heaven.[187]

The world hates this messages. Even some who would claim to be Christians hate it. For only those who truly belong to Christ love his every Word, his law, and the promises that it brings to his glory alone.

---

[183] Php 2:9; Ac 2:28 with Ps 16:11; Jn 17:5
[184] Eph 1:22; 1Pe 3:22
[185] Eph 4:10,11,12; Ps 110:1 (see the Psalm throughout)
[186] Ro 8:34–WLC Q54
[187] Php 3:8

FEBRUARY 23

ON OUR BEHALF

Yesterday, we were challenged to test our faith. Do we believe every Word that proceeds from the mouth of God? Do we love that Word? If we do, then we have nothing to fear that this world can bring. We have God's answer and we hold all truth through the Scriptures. We have a Savior that represents us with iron-clad redemption, destroying any and every accusation.

Christ makes intercession by his appearing in our nature continually before the Father in heaven in the merit of his obedience and sacrifice on earth, declaring his will to have it applied to all believers,[188] answering all accusations against them, and procuring for them quiet of conscience, notwithstanding daily failings,[189] access with boldness to the throne of grace, and acceptance of their persons and services.[190]

The answer to every sin is Christ's blood. The answer to every accusation is Christ's obedience. The means of both of these is imputation. Our sins were imputed (accounted) to Christ and his righteousness is imputed to us. When God looks at us, he sees Christ in us. If anyone is not in Christ, they do not belong to him.[191]

Give thanks today that you do not stand condemned to one day face the judgment on your own. He stands for you, if you believe.

---

[188] Heb 9:12,24; Heb 1:3; Jn 3:16; Jn 17:9,20,24
[189] Ro 8:33,34; Ro 5:1,2; 1Jn 2:1,2
[190] Heb 4:16; Eph 1:6; 1Pe 2:5–WLC Q55
[191] Ro 8:9

FEBRUARY 24

HERE COMES THE JUDGE

Just as assuredly as Jesus walked the earth two thousand years ago, there will be a second coming of Christ. Only this time, every eye will see him. There will be great rejoicing for those who believe, but there will be nowhere to run for those who stand condemned.

Christ is to be exalted in his coming again to judge the world in that he, who was unjustly judged and condemned by wicked men,[192] shall come again at the last day in great power and in the full manifestation of his own glory and of his Father's, with all his holy angels,[193] with a shout, with the voice of the archangel, and with the trumpet of God[194] to judge the world in righteousness.[195]

I would be counted among those who deserve judgment if I were to face him on my own. In fact, I know that if at any moment his grace was removed from me, I would surely stand without excuse.

This is the righteousness of God: that sin cannot stand before him. The whole world has sinned and the whole world will be judged in righteousness. Those whose sins were not paid for at the cross will pay their own wages.[196] If you happen to be one who thinks you are *good person* and that you will make it to heaven on your own, you will not. Repent and believe. Salvation is in Christ and none other.

---

[192] Ac 3:14,15
[193] Mt 24:30; Lk 9:26; Mt 25:31
[194] 1Th 4:16
[195] Ac 17:31- WLC Q56
[196] Ro 3:23

FEBRUARY 25

IS THERE A MEDIATOR IN THE HOUSE?

It is common in the court system to have a mediator come between two parties to work through their differences.

Christ, by his mediation, hath procured redemption,[197] with all other benefits of the covenant of grace.[198]

In society, we work to earn wages. In the spiritual realm, we are at odds with a righteous God. If we face God on our own, we shall receive the just wages of our sin: death. However, for those of us to whom redemption has come, we have Christ's righteousness.

Every sin by every person will be paid for. Those without Christ will pay in everlasting punishment. With Christ as our mediator, we have One that goes between us and God. Jesus, having paid the penalty for the sins of the elect, has wiped the slate clean, and by his righteousness, we have entered into everlasting fellowship with God.

Those who have Christ as their mediator also receive the promised blessings in this life and the next. The promises we receive are not temporal health, wealth, and prosperity. No, our blessings are much deeper than that. That we may glorify God, even in our suffering, that whatever trials may come, they pale in comparison to the eternal glories that we will have in eternity.

Give thanks to Jesus for going to the cross on your behalf.

---

[197] Heb 9:12
[198] 2Co 1:20–WLC Q57

FEBRUARY 26

GOD'S WORK IN US

There are so many pastors telling people how to join the God's family. Whether it is repeating a prayer, going down to the altar, inviting Jesus into your heart, or being baptized, these have no effect on one's position as lost or saved.

We are made partakers of the benefits, which Christ hath procured, by the application of them unto us,[199] *which is the work especially of God the Holy Ghost.*[200]

Being saved is not something that we do, but something that Christ has done for us and is realized in us when the Holy Spirit opens our hearts to the Gospel. The work of Christ through the power of the Holy Spirit.

Likewise, it is by the power of God that we receive all his benefits.[201] The prayer of repentance and one's baptism is the result of regeneration. There is no formula for converting ourselves to Christ. The work is done in us by the Holy Spirit, and it is all God's grace.

We must be careful how we evangelize. If we give people a formula, we can lead them into false assurance of their salvation. Think about how many say, "Yep, I'm going to heaven. I went to the altar when I was eight," or "I was baptized so I'm all good." There is no brute evidence of conversion, only a heart changed by God.

---

[199] Jn 1:11-13
[200] Tit 3:5-7–WLC Q58
[201] Ps 103:1-4

FEBRUARY 27

PARTAKERS OF REDEMPTION

Although we may be uncertain that a profession of faith is true, we are assured that everyone who is regenerated by the Holy Spirit possesses authentic faith.

Redemption is certainly applied and effectually communicated to all those for whom Christ hath purchased it,[202] who are in time by the Holy Ghost enabled to believe in Christ according to the gospel.[203]

Because salvation is fully of God, those whom he saves, receive the Gospel, believe upon it, and are come into the family of God. They further are sealed by the Holy Spirit, never to be forsaken. If Christ has purchased us, the Spirit guarantees the purchase eternally.

Salvation is the perfect work of the Triune God. The Father eternally chooses believers as a gift to the Son. The Son purchases the elect and raises them up on the last day. The Holy Spirit regenerates the heart and seals the transaction. No believer slips God's fingers.

Because this is fully the work of God, there is nothing that we can do to obtain it. We cannot even boast in our faith since it is a gift of God. He begins the work in us, and he completes it until Jesus returns. We have nothing to boast in except Christ.[204]

---

[202] Eph 1:13,14; Jn 6:37,39; Jn 10:15,16
[203] Eph 2:8; 2Co 4:13,14—WLC Q59
[204] Phil 1:6, Ro 3:27

FEBRUARY 28

SAVED WITHOUT THE GOSPEL?

This is perhaps the most resisted doctrine among Christians: the fact that there may be some who never hear the Gospel and yet cannot be saved without it. This brings up many questions of the fairness of God. However, God never claims to be fair. He is perfectly righteous and exercises his mercy and grace on his terms.

They who, having never heard the gospel, know not Jesus Christ[205] and believe not in him cannot be saved;[206] be they never so diligent to frame their lives according to the light of nature or the laws of that religion which they profess;[207] neither is there salvation in any other, but in Christ alone, who is the Savior only of his body, the church.[208]

Their primary question is typically framed in this manner: *What about the innocent natives of deep Africa who has never heard the gospel? Are you telling me God will send them to hell?* The answer to that question is no. God will never send an innocent person to hell. However, there are no *innocent* people, only sinners who fall short of the glory of God.

Nobody slips through the cracks in God's sovereign world. Yet faith only comes by the hearing of the Gospel. So the tougher question to ask ourselves is, *What do we do for those who have not yet heard?*

---

[205] Ro 10:14; 2Th 1:8,9; Eph 2:12; Jn 1:10-12
[206] Jn 8:24; Mk 16:16
[207] 1Co 1:20-24; Jn 4:22; Ro 9:31,32; Php 3:4-9
[208] Ac 4:12; Eph 5:23 WLC Q60

MARCH 1

THE INVISIBLE CHURCH

Whether a person just started attending church or they have claimed to be a Christian their whole life, one's salvation is solely dependent on their spiritual condition. Have they been born again? Have they received the Gospel? Do they believe in Jesus?

All that hear the gospel and live in the visible church are not saved, but they only who are true members of the church invisible.[209]

Because we are dealing with conditions of the heart, it is impossible to know for certain who is saved. There are many who play the part very well: regular attendance, volunteering, teaching, etc., but, looking like a Christian is not equal to being a Christian. There are also some who look hard and callous on the outside, but their heart is true to the Gospel of Christ. Only God knows the earnest heart.

The true church is the congregation of saved people. Because we cannot necessarily see who the true believers are, we call this the invisible church. This mystery gives us a grand responsibility in how we treat everyone around us. The goal is to be Christ-like without prejudice.

Christian love is love in action. The invisible church is the body of Christ and is animated by faith in action. We are his hands and feet. Many different spiritual gifts all working together to make disciples.

Make it your prayer today to put your love into action. Let everything you do be done to the glory of God.

---

[209] Jn 12:38-40; Ro 9:6; Mt 22:14; Mt 7:21; Ro 11:7–WLC Q61

MARCH 2

THE VISIBLE CHURCH

In contrast to the invisible church, the visible church is what the world sees as those who claim the Christian faith. As such, the visible church is made up of both saved and unsaved professors of the faith.

The visible church is a society made up of all such as in all ages and places of the world do profess the true religion[210] *and of their children.*[211]

A sampling of the visible church is all who would stand amidst the congregation to state that they believe in the Gospel. Although we could not make a determination to the authenticity of any of their professions, we do live under authentic assumption. God handles the matters of the heart. However, the leadership of the church disciplines unbecoming actions as Jesus outlined for us in Matthew 18.

The Lord works in his own timing and in his own sweet way. We do not know at what moment he will open the ears of those to hear his Word. The work of regeneration is the Lord's. Only God can raise a dead man or give sight to the blind. The day when we are renewed by the Spirit is when we truly receive the lordship of Jesus Christ.

As true believers, we should make every effort that the Gospel preached on Sunday is lived by us throughout the week. Are we making ourselves available to confirm the saving and sanctifying message?

---

[210] 1Co 1:2; 1Co 12:13; Ro 15:9-12; Rev 7:9; Ps 2:8; Ps 22:27-31; Ps 45:17; Mt 28:19,20; Isa 59:21

[211] 1Co 7:14; Ac 2:39; Ro 11:16; Ge 17:7–WLC Q62

MARCH 3

PRIVILEGES WITHIN THE BODY

I can remember a time when I dreaded going to church. I was bored, the pastor did not communicate the Bible well, and the people all went through the motions of rote prayer and tradition. Before and after service, there was little, if any, fellowship within the congregation. What a difference when we began attending a church who lived their beliefs.

The visible church has the privilege of being under God's special care and government;[212] of being protected and preserved in all ages, notwithstanding the opposition of all enemies,[213] and of enjoying the communion of saints, the ordinary means of salvation,[214] and offers of grace by Christ to all the members of it in the ministry of the gospel, testifying, that whosoever believes in him shall be saved, and excluding none that will come unto him.[215]

What a stark contrast the true fellowship of a body of believers that live out their faith with biblical instruction. All who enter are welcome to receive all the benefits within. The church is not just sixty minutes on Sunday. It is a community of believers living and breathing Christ and his mission to draw all people to himself.

Give thanks if you are a member of a living church. If you are not, pray about making this a priority in your life.

---

[212] Isa 4:5,6; 1Ti 4:10
[213] Ps 115:1,2,9; Isa 31:4,5; Zec 12:2,3,4,8,9
[214] Ac 2:39,42
[215] Ps 147:19,20; Ro 9:4; Eph 4:11,12; Mk 16:15,16; Jn 6:37–WLC Q63

MARCH 4

THE INVISIBLE CHURCH

Have you ever looked around at the sea of people in a sports arena or shopping mall or even at your church and wondered which ones are going to heaven and which ones might be spending eternity in hell?

The invisible church is the whole number of the elect that have been, are, or shall be gathered into one under Christ, the head.[216]

There is no way to tell, by external means, who the true believers are. Someone asked Charles Spurgeon why he preaches to everyone, knowing that all are not number among the elect. Spurgeon replied, "If you will just lift up the back of their shirts to see if they're marked with a big E, I'll preach just to them."

As mentioned before, the invisible church resides within the visible church. The invisible church is composed solely of true believers. These are separate because they not only hear the gospel, but they also believe and obey it. Jesus says, "If you love me, you will keep my commands."[217] This he said just after he confirmed them to be believers.

The invisible church is composed of true disciples of Christ. A disciple is follower of Jesus. Even further, a disciple is a learning, believing, and persevering child of God.

Take regular time to confirm the sincerity of your belief.[218]

---

[216] Eph 1:10,22,23; Jn 10:16; Jn 11:52–WLC Q64
[217] Jn14:15
[218] 2Pe 2:10

March 5

Fellowship with Christ

Although the visible church enjoys fellowship within the body, only true believers have fellowship with Jesus Christ. These alone are kept by the power of the Holy Spirit, sealed until the day of redemption.

The members of the invisible church by Christ enjoy union and communion with him in grace and glory.[219]

Privileges enjoyed by the unsaved community of the visible church pale in comparison to the riches of the regenerate. The depth of God's love poured out in life-changing aspects of regeneration include a new nature, assurance of salvation, revelation of God's Word, the mind of Christ, and true fellowship between believers. The invisible church is also the only party able to offer viable worship to God. Jesus tells us in John 4 that God is Spirit and those who worship him must worship him in spirit and truth.

Those who are part of the invisible church, through the regeneration of the Holy Spirit, have been made alive, together with Christ. Our future bodily resurrection is considered a done deal and we are *now* citizens of heaven. All of this is has taken place while we are yet sinners. This, my dear friends, is grace defined. Nothing of ourselves, just Jesus.

In your prayers today, take some time to consider that your salvation is only of God's goodness and that you are now, even at this moment, members of the eternal family of Jesus Christ.

---

[219] Jn 17:21; Eph 2:5,6; Jn 17:24- WLC Q65

MARCH 6

UNION WITH CHRIST

One reason that divorce is such an ugly and sinful event is because it destroys the pattern and imagery that has been established in all godly unions. What God has joined together, man should protect at every expense. Thankfully, the union that God grants to us by his Son is not held by man's power.

The union which the elect have with Christ is the work of God's grace,[220] whereby they are spiritually and mystically, yet really and inseparably, joined to Christ as their head and husband,[221] which is done in their effectual calling.[222]

Most people do not understand the concept of becoming "one flesh". Therefore, to them, divorce is not much different than breaking up with a high school sweetheart. If we more thoroughly taught to our children that godly unions are supernatural covenants, perhaps the process leading up to marriage would be taken more seriously.

The church is expressed as the bride of Christ. The marriage of Jesus to his bridesmaid is one mystery of the *already/not yet*, where we are already inseparably joined to Christ, but our final realization of this union will be at the end of time.

Do you wait, with great anticipation, the day when we will celebrate with Jesus at the Marriage Supper of the Lamb?

---

[220] Eph 1:22; Eph 2:6-8
[221] 1Co 6:17; Jn 10:28; Eph 5:23,30
[222] 1Pe 5:10; 1Co 1:9–WLC Q66

MARCH 7

CALLED WITHOUT FAIL

Christ will someday join together with his bride. His bride was chosen before the foundation of the world. Jesus calls his sheep and they follow.

Effectual calling is the work of God's almighty power and grace,[223] whereby (out of his free and special love to his elect and from nothing in them moving him thereunto[224]) he does, in his accepted time, invite and draw them to Jesus Christ, by his word and Spirit,[225] savingly enlightening their minds,[226] renewing and powerfully determining their wills,[227] so as they (although in themselves dead in sin) are hereby made willing and able freely to answer his call, and to accept and embrace the grace offered and conveyed therein.[228]

There are two basic *calls* of the Gospel. The effectual call of God to his elect, as defined above. There is also the general call, which is the outward call of the Gospel offering grace to everyone who would freely come. This call is refused by the wicked and hardened hearts of all until such a time when they might be enabled by the Holy Spirit.

Are you thankful that God raises the dead, makes the blind to see, and opens the ears of the deaf? Do you know your Master's voice?

---

[223] Jn 5:25; Eph 1:18-20; 2Ti 1:8,9
[224] Tit 3:4,5; Eph 2:4,5,7,8,9; Ro 9:11
[225] 2Co 5:20 compared with 2Co 6:1,2; Jn 6:44; 2Th 2:13,14
[226] Ac 26:18; 1Co 2:10,12 (See WLC Q12)
[227] Eze 11:19; Eze 36:26,27; Jn 6:45
[228] Eph 2:5; Php 2:13; Dt 30:6–WLC Q67

MARCH 8

A CALL SPECIFIC

The general or outward call of the gospel is rejected by many. It is often-times attractive to many, but only for a season. We see this example in Jesus' parable of the sower and the seed, where some received the Word with initial gladness, but they never experienced a true conversion, and eventually, they returned to their stony hearts.

All the elect, and they only, are effectually called; although others may be, and often are, outwardly called by the ministry of the word[229] and have some common operations of the Spirit[230] who, for their willful neglect and contempt of the grace offered to them, being justly left in their unbelief, do never truly come to Jesus Christ.[231]

There is a difficult truth that comes with the doctrine of election. That truth is that some are passed over and are not converted. However, regardless of one's position, unless there was a universal salvation, we are all left with some souls going to hell. We do not teach double election, i.e., God does not choose some to go to hell. People are bound for hell because of their own sin and unbelief.

Just as God chose Israel unto himself for his own purposes, and we do not fret about that, God can and does choose individuals for salvation. Everything that God does is just and right and for his glory. We have no right to question God. It is right only to worship.

---

[229] Ac 13:48; Mt 22:14
[230] Mt 7:22; Mt 13:20,21; Heb 6:4-6
[231] Jn 12:38-40; Ac 28:25-27; Jn 6:64,65; Ps 81:11,12—WLC Q68

MARCH 9

BELIEVERS' COMMON GROUND

What God shares with his elect are all saving benefits of his grace. The outpouring of his saving power to both begin and complete our salvation, granted without fail and without outside influence.

The communion in grace which the members of the invisible church have with Christ is their partaking of the virtue of his mediation, in their justification, adoption, sanctification, and whatever else, in this life, manifests their union with him.[232]

There are times when I let pride get the best of me. I have sat in a church service and smugly thought that I was deserving of the grace I received. Thinking like the publican who thanked God that he was not like the other sinners while the reality is that I could share in the title as the Chief of Sinners. Thankfully, God will not let us maintain that mind-set, but will chasten us unto humility, in love.

Shall I think the work that God has begun in me is now up to me to complete? By no means! For it is God who completes that which he has started.[233] We are partakers of every function of salvation, and therefore, we share together in these virtues, for God is no respecter of persons.

Pray for a proper attitude in your salvation, then spend time in thanksgiving for the manifestation of his grace in your life.

---

[232] Ro 8:30; Eph 1:5; 1Co 1:30–WLC Q69
[233] Phil 1:6

MARCH 10

RIGHTEOUSFIED

I know it's not a word, but sometimes, the English language falls short of having a good direct interpretation of Greek. When we think of justice, we think of proper legal action. However, when it comes to being justified by God, it goes much deeper than this.

Justification is an act of God's free grace unto sinners[234] in which he pardons all their sins, accepts and accounts their persons righteous in his sight,[235] not for anything wrought in them or done by them, but only for the perfect obedience and full satisfaction of Christ by God imputed to them[236] and received by faith alone.[237]

We have the righteousness of Christ accounted to us. Our account was bankrupt, yet the full righteousness of Jesus was transferred to us. Furthermore, it is a double transfer where all of our unrighteousness, our sin, our shame, our storehouse of impurity, are also transferred to Christ. He took it all, nailed it to the cross on our behalf, cancelled our debt, and made us joint heirs as sons of God.[238]

The realization of this total purchase of our lives, despite our wickedness, is the most humbling doctrine. This humility should lead to our obedience to our Lord. Make today a day of thanksgiving for your justification, and ask the Holy Spirit to teach obedience.

---

[234] Ro 3:22,24,25; Ro 4:5
[235] 2Co 5:19,21; Ro 3:22,24,25,27,28
[236] Tit 3:5,7; Eph 1:7; Ro 5:17-19; Ro 4:6-8
[237] Ac 10:43; Gal 2:16; Php 3:9–WLC Q70
[238] Col 2:13,14; Ro 8:16,17

MARCH 11

GOD'S FREEDOM TO GIVE

Partaking in being justified by God is not following a formula of mustering up any effort on our part. This includes conjuring up faith within ourselves. Just as grace is a gift freely given by God, so is the saving faith with which we trust him.

Although Christ, by his obedience and death, did make a proper, real, and full satisfaction to God's justice in the behalf of them that are justified,[239] yet in as much as God accepts the satisfaction from a surety, which he might have demanded of them and did provide this surety, his own only Son,[240] imputing his righteousness to them and requiring nothing of them for their justification but faith, which also is his gift, their justification is to them of free grace.[241]

God is always previous. The clearer we see this, the more properly aligned our position with God becomes. Salvation is not a lifeline that we hold on to; rather, it is the rescued sinner, double-embraced in the loving hands of the Father and Son with full assurance.[242]

With this understanding that God freely rescues us from the dead, how much more shall we have confidence in his ability to sustain us, to sanctify us, and ultimately to glorify us. God's salvation is always and without exception eternal. If you're his, you're his forever!

---

[239] Ro 5:8-10,19
[240] 1Ti 2:5,6; Heb 10:10; Mt 20:28; Da 9:24,26; Isa 53:4,5,6,10,11,12; Heb 7:22; Ro 8:32; 1Pe 1:18,19
[241] 2Co 5:21; Ro 3:24,25; Eph 2:8; Eph 1:7–WLC Q71
[242] Jo 10:25-30

MARCH 12

JUSTIFYING FAITH

Yesterday, we examined the Scriptural support that saving faith is a gift from God. So, does the believer lose his claim to his own faith in Christ? Absolutely not! Saving faith is personally exercised by a regenerated will that has been set free by the power of the Holy Spirit through the hearing of the Word.

Justifying faith is a saving grace,[243] *wrought in the heart of a sinner by the Spirit and word of God,*[244] *whereby he, being convinced of his sin and misery, and of the disability in himself and all other creatures to recover him out of his lost condition,*[245] *not only ascends to the truth of the promise of the gospel, but receives and rests upon Christ and his righteousness, therein held forth, for pardon of sin, and for the accepting and accounting of his person righteous in the sight of God for salvation.*[246]

There is nothing contradictory about one's saving faith being a gift of God. Personal wisdom is of no value to God. Man cannot aspire to know God through education or philosophy. In fact, God will often blind the eyes of such self-reliance. True wisdom begins with the fear of the Lord.

God, less of me and more of you. Thank you, Father, for rescuing me from the pit of destruction. Please engrave your Word on my heart.

---

[243] Heb 10:39
[244] 2Co 4:13; Eph 1:17-19; Ro 10:14,17
[245] Ac 2:37; Ac 16:30; Jn 16:8,9; Ro 5:6; Eph 2:1; Ac 4:12
[246] Eph 1:13; Jn 1:12; Ac 16:31; Ac 10:43; Php 3:9; Ac 15:11–WLC Q72

MARCH 13

HOW DOES IT WORK?

We have learned what justification is and from whom it comes, but how is it that we are justified in the eyes of God? How does it work?

Faith justifies a sinner in the sight of God, not because of those other graces that do always accompany it, or of good works that are the fruits of it,[247] *not as if the grace of faith or any act thereof were imputed to him for his justification,*[248] *but only as it is an instrument by which he receives and applies Christ and his righteousness.*[249]

If you were to gaze upon a beautiful sculpture, you would not likely ask about which chisel the artist used. We understand that the artist is the genius behind the sculpture and the chisel is just an instrument used by the artist. Saving faith is the instrument that God gives to those whom he effectually calls. Saving faith is always partnered with a redeemed heart, which has been set free by God's grace.

Let's take one more example. When we turn the handle on our faucet, we have faith that water is going to pour out. Our faith neither produces the water or the pump pressure to push it out. We similarly exercise faith in Christ, not to produce salvation, but because our heart has been changed by the hearing the Word and now freely believes. Who will you thank for your faith, yourself or God?

To God alone be the glory, both now and forever!

---

[247] Gal 3:11; Ro 3:28
[248] Ro 4:5; Ro 10:10
[249] Jn 1:12; Php 3:9; Gal 2:16—WLC Q73

MARCH 14

CHILDREN OF GOD

Many people have adopted children throughout history. It is often said that a parent's love for their adopted child is indistinguishable from one which is naturally born. How much more so for those who are adopted through the perfect love of the heavenly Father?

Adoption is an act of the free grace of God, in and for his only Son Jesus Christ, whereby all those that are justified are received into the number of his children,[250] have his name put upon them, the Spirit of his Son given to them, are under his fatherly care and dispensations,[251] admitted to all the liberties and privileges of the sons of God, made heirs of all the promises and fellow-heirs with Christ in glory.[252]

Once a child is adopted into a loving home, they receive all the benefits of life with that family. All the more for those adopted as children of God. The promise of adoption is a binding contract to which God freely subjects himself.

Another aspect of adoption is its immediate effect. Adoption initiates immediately upon regeneration. We are *now* the children of God. We *now* have a Father in heaven. We *now* are sealed by the Holy Spirit. We wait only for the revealing of our eternal benefits.

Pray that the Lord will reveal adoption's deeper understanding.

---

[250] 1Jn 3:1; Eph 1:5; Gal 4:4,5; Jn 1:12
[251] 2Co 6:18; Rev 3:12; Gal 4:6; Ps 103:13; Pr 14:26; Mt 6:32
[252] Heb 6:12; Ro 8:17–WLC Q74

MARCH 15

SANCTIFICATION

I want to be a better person. Who hasn't thought this before? And what difference separates this statement when it is made by a Christian? The secular person might strive for higher morals through self-improvement, but the Christian's goal is a life of holiness.

Sanctification is a work of God's grace, whereby they whom God hath, before the foundation of the world, chosen to be holy, are in time, through the powerful operation of his Spirit[253] applying the death and resurrection of Christ unto them, renewed in their whole man after the image of God; having the seeds of repentance unto life, and all other saving graces, put into their hearts,[254] and those graces so stirred up, increased and strengthened,[255] as that they more and more die unto sin, and rise unto newness of life.[256]

Christians are a work in progress. We are saved now; that is a historic event upon our regeneration. We were freed from the bondage of sin; however, our flesh remains and the Spirit works within us, through obedience to the Word of God, to a closer reflection of holiness of God. We sin less, but we hate that sin more.

Because we love God, we make every effort to be obedient children. If you are living with a remaining sin, throw off the broken chains, repent, and believe that God is working in you unto holiness.

---

[253] Eph 1:4; 1Co 6:11; 2Th 2:13
[254] Ro 6:4-6; Eph 4:23,24; Ac 11:18; 1Jn 3:9
[255] Jude 20; Heb 6:11,12; Eph 3:16-19; Col 1:10,11
[256] Ro 6:4,6,14; Gal 5:24–WLC Q75

MARCH 16

REPENTANCE UNTO LIFE

Yesterday, we looked at "Sanctification," understanding it to be an ever-increasing holy life, by the power of the Holy Spirit, who leads us to obedience of God's Word. The pursuit of holiness is reflected in a new life that loves God and hates sin. What does this life look like?

Repentance unto life is a saving grace, wrought in the heart of a sinner by the Spirit and word of God,[257] *whereby out of the sight and sense, not only of the danger, but also of the filthiness and odiousness of his sins,*[258] *and upon the apprehension of God's mercy in Christ to such as are penitent, he so grieves for and hates his sins, as that he turns from them all to God,*[259] *purposing and endeavoring constantly to walk with him in all the ways of new obedience.*[260]

The wicked person does not hate sin, even though they might hate the consequences of sin. However, those whom are regenerated are given a new heart, a heart which desires a godly life. Although a desire for sin still remains, the believer now understands how sin hampers the God/man relationship.

The Scriptures state that a believer will not continue in their sin. However, because of their new nature, they will repent by turning away from it. Believers long for a strong relationship with God, and such a relationship is not possible when they are stuck in habitual sin.

---

[257] 2Ti 2:25; Zec 12:10; Ac 11:18,20,21
[258] Eze 18:28,30,32; Lk 15:17,18; Hos 2:6,7; Eze 36:31; Isa 30:22
[259] Joel 2:12,13; Jer 31:18,19; 2Co 7:11; Ac 26:18; Eze 14:6; 1Ki 8:47,48
[260] Ps 119:6,59,128; Lk 1:6; 2Ki 23:25–WLC Q76

MARCH 17

JUSTIFICATION AND SANCTIFICATION

We are likely to hear quite a bit more, from the pulpit, on justification than sanctification. However, having a full understanding of both and how they work in the believer's life are equally important.

Although sanctification be inseparably joined with justification, yet they differ, in that God in justification imputes the righteousness of Christ, in sanctification his Spirit infuses grace, and enables to the exercise thereof;[261] in the former, sin is pardoned; in the other, it is subdued.[262] the one doth equally free all believers from the revenging wrath of God, and that perfectly in this life, that they never fall into condemnation;[263] the other is neither equal in all, nor in this life perfect in any, but growing up to perfection.[264]

Because justification is where we find salvation and forgiveness of sin, we understand the depths that grace has gone to determine us as righteous in God's eyes. Okay, we're saved and that is great, but what are we doing with our salvation now? Sanctification is the work of grace in us for the rest of our lives; we do well to understand it as God's children.

The command to *be holy because I am (God is) holy* is for which we strive. Although we will not attain perfection in this lifetime, we are to be *growing up to perfection* until we are called to our eternal home. Not just act your age, but act your position in Christ.

---

[261] 1Co 6:11; 1Co 1:30; Ro 4:6,8; Eze 36:27
[262] Ro 3:24,25; Ro 6:6,14
[263] Ro 8:33,34
[264] 1Jn 2:12-14; Heb 5:12-14; 1Jn 1:8,10; 2Co 7:1; Php 3:12-14—WLC Q77

MARCH 18

ALREADY, NOT YET

It has been twenty-five years since I first understood that my salvation was by grace alone. Up until that time, although I loved God and understood that Jesus died for me, I still felt that it was up to me to hold on to God to remain saved. Little did I know that my efforts were not only ineffective, but were actually sinful, due to the pride behind them because I was trying to add to what God had accomplished.

The imperfection of sanctification in believers arises from the remnants of sin abiding in every part of them, and the perpetual lustings of the flesh against the spirit; whereby they are often foiled with temptations and fall into many sins[265] are hindered in all their spiritual services,[266] and their best works are imperfect and defiled in the sight of God.[267]

True believers hate sin, yet we are burdened by the unredeemed flesh that remains. We are perplexed by God allowing us to fail, knowing that it was sin that originally separated us from him. However, God's purposes are higher than our knowledge, and we have the promise that his plan is perfect.

Therefore, we have confidence that his allowance for our weak flesh is for our benefit. Not because we now have a license to sin, but because through our weakness, we are made strong by him. He keeps our reliance upon him, so that our pride will not again overtake us.

---

[265] Ro 7:18,23; Mk 14:66-72; Gal 2:11,12
[266] Heb 12:1
[267] Isa 64:6; Ex 28:38–WLC Q78

MARCH 19

GOD NEVER LETS GO

If it is sin that originally separated us from God, how is it that salvation is not severed upon sinning again? What's different?

True believers, by reason of the unchangeable love of God, and his decree and covenant to give them perseverance,[268] *their inseparable union with Christ, his continual intercession for them, and the Spirit and seed of God abiding in them*[269] *can neither totally nor finally fall away from the state of grace, but are kept by the power of God through faith unto salvation.*[270]

When Christ died at the cross, every sin which had been or ever would be committed by believers was paid for in full. That atonement (the covering of our sins) is applied at the moment we believe. For sin to separate us once again is for the atonement to fail, which is impossible.

Besides the plethora of Scriptures that clearly state the eternal work on the cross, if a single sin was not already covered, Jesus would once again have to pay the price. From Jesus' own lips, he states *Tetelastai*, meaning *Paid in full*, which is the end of all debt.

Whom God has justified (made righteous) while yet sinners would be contradictory for him to not sustain because of sin. If salvation is 100 percent by grace, then how would sustaining it be by anything more. We can trust God to finish the work he began in us. Praise him!

---

[268] Jer 31:3; 2Ti 2:19; Heb 13:20,21; 2Sa 23:5
[269] 1Co 1:8,9; Heb 7:25; Lk 22:32; 1Jn 3:9; 1Jn 2:27
[270] Jer 32:40; Jn 10:28; 1Pe 1:5–WLC Q79

MARCH 20

CONFIDENCE IN CHRIST (PART 1)

How is it possible to have assurance that our faith will not fail? What about those who appear to fall completely away from their faith?

Such as truly believe in Christ and endeavor to walk in all good conscience before him[271] may, without extraordinary revelation, by faith grounded upon the truth of God's promises, and by the Spirit enabling them to discern in themselves those graces to which the promises of life are made,[272] and bearing witness with their spirits that they are the children of God, be infallibly assured that they are in the estate of grace, and shall persevere therein unto salvation.[273]

There are four possible positions for a person's assurance. First, a person can be saved and be fully assured of their faith. Next, a person can be saved, yet have no confidence in it. Then, there are some who think they're saved, but are truly lost. Finally, there are some who are lost and know they're lost.

People who are lost but think they're going to heaven are probably in the most dangerous position. This is because their pride is in the way of letting them see their need for Christ's blood alone. They think they are saved because they go to church or have Christian parents or are simply "good enough," passing the curve on which God grades humanity. These people need to have God give them ears to hear about their truly depraved position and need of rescue. Pray for the lost.

---

[271] 1Jn 2:3
[272] 1Co 2:12; 1Jn 3:14,18,19,21,24; 1Jn 4:13,16; Heb 6:11,12
[273] Ro 8:16; 1Jn 5:13–WLC Q80

MARCH 21

CONFIDENCE IN CHRIST (PART 2)

Yesterday, we look at those who are lost but think they're saved. But what about true believers who struggle with assurance?

Assurance of grace and salvation not being of the essence of faith,[274] true believers may wait long before they obtain it[275] and, after the enjoyment thereof, may have it weakened and intermitted, through manifold distempers, sins, temptations, and desertions,[276] yet are they never left without such a presence and support of the Spirit of God as keeps them from sinking into utter despair.[277]

True believers have the promise of the Word and the Holy Spirit who bears witness within them, that they are indeed God's children. However, assurance is accumulated over time as believers have these promises written on their hearts. The testing of our faith and our trials are actually granted by God to add confidence to our faith, not weaken it. It is through these events that we learn to lean on God's faithfulness and not our own. We have assurance of our faith not because we are strong, but because we know God will not fail us.

Whether you are in a valley of doubt or experiencing full confidence in your salvation, why not take some time to thank God for never failing you. Repent of your doubt and ask the Holy Spirit to help your unbelief. To have assurance, we must place our eyes on God.

---

[274] Eph 1:13
[275] Isa 1:10; Ps 88:1,2,3,6,7,9,10,13,14,15
[276] Ps 77:1-12; SS 5:2,3,6; Ps 60:8,12; Ps 31:22; Ps 22:1
[277] 1Jn 3:9; Job 13:15; Ps 73:15,23; Isa 54:7-10–WLC Q81

MARCH 22

AFTER OUR LAST BREATH

Regardless of the degree of pain and suffering the lost may suffer in this world, they are now living their best days. On the other hand, regardless of the degree of joy and prosperity the invisible church may enjoy in this world, we are experiencing our very lowest times.

The communion in glory that the members of the invisible church have with Christ, is in this life,[278] immediately after death,[279] and at last perfected at the resurrection and day of judgment.[280]

As believers, we have communion with Christ both now and forever. However, for the reprobate, they are void of communion both now and forever, facing eternal punishment without relief.

If we understand the coming judgment, our sense of urgency for sharing the Gospel to the lost world will take priority. For this reason, we study God's Word, to have it written on our hearts, so that we are ready to give an answer of the faith that saves. Furthermore, we prepare to teach and convince a dying world.

The Christian life is one of worship; through congregational worship, yes, but ever more so in preparing ourselves to know God and his Son, Jesus Christ, and to enjoy communion with him. You may recall our highest tenant, the chief end of man: *to glorify God and fully to enjoy him forever.* All of this is perfected upon our resurrection.

---

[278] 2Co 3:18
[279] Lk 23:43
[280] 1Th 4:17–WLC Q82

MARCH 23

BEFORE OUR LAST BREATH

As only true believers are members of the invisible church, these alone will share in specific promises of the indwelling Spirit in this life and the glory that awaits them in heaven.

The members of the invisible church have communicated to them in this life the first fruits of glory with Christ, as they are members of him their head, and so in him are interested in that glory which he is fully possessed of[281] and, as an earnest thereof, enjoy the sense of God's love,[282] peace of conscience, joy in the Holy Ghost, and hope of glory.[283]

There are many reasons to spend time in the Scriptures. We learn of God and his attributes. We learn the history of mankind: those of faith who please God, and those of pride who reap God's wrath. We can count the fulfilled prophecies showing Jesus as Messiah. We watch the Messiah in action as he displays his sinless life and power over sin. But our biggest benefit in knowing Scripture is learning and understanding the promises directed to all believers.

The Bible tells us that all things in him are guaranteed. Our biggest mistake would be not to trust this. What if we lived out that which we say we believe? Would not our lives reflect the One whom we confess? Would we not be his hands and feet in this world, doing his work as disciples? Possess peace and do not hold back!

---

[281] Eph 2:5,6
[282] Ro 5:5 compared with 2Co 1:22
[283] Ro 5:1,2; Ro 14:17—WLC Q83a

MARCH 24

WOE UNTO THOSE OF UNBELIEF

As only true believers are members of the invisible church, only these will share in specific promises of the indwelling Spirit in this life and the glory that awaits them in heaven.

On the contrary, sense of God's revenging wrath, horror of conscience, and a fearful expectation of judgment are to the wicked the beginning of their torments, which they shall endure after death.[284]

I repeated the starting paragraph from yesterday in order to show the believer's contrast to those who are perishing. It is bone-chilling to consider the weight of this matter. Reread the catechism statement above, consider these judgments contemplatively.

- God's revenging wrath
- horror of conscience
- fearful expectation of judgment

These are just the *beginning of their torments*. Oh, the fear is mind-bending. The judgment of God is not something that can be recanted of in eternity. The consequences of unbelief in this life are eternal.

It is our call to share the gospel with every nation.[285] We allow the truth of God's Word to speak for us and the Holy Spirit will work in the hearts of the elect. We are not here to moralize our nation, but to be heralds of Good News, even if it means proclaiming God's judgment.

---

[284] Ge 4:13; Mt 27:4; Heb 10:27; Ro 2:9; Mk 9:44–WLC Q83b
[285] Mt 28:18-20

MARCH 25

ONCE TO DIE

One cliché says that this world only brings two certainties: death and taxes. Although we typically dread the latter for most of our lives, it is certainly no comparison to our limited lifespan and eternity that follows.

Death being threatened as the wages of sin,[286] it is appointed unto all men once to die[287] for that all have sinned.[288]

I am always amazed at the accomplishments some people achieve in their lifetime. I tend to want to believe that they somehow have more hours in their day than the rest of us. When the fact of the matter is that they work more practically toward their goals.

As Christians, regardless of our busy schedules, we have one vocation to pursue, i.e., to make disciples. This is the short descriptive, yet very important part of how we live out our lives. I would say that, in this regard, Satan has got us right where he wants us. For we tend to spend all of our time focused on everything regarding our Christian lives except witnessing to those around us.

This is a tough pill to swallow, but now is the time to wash it down with the Living Water of our life in Christ and truly become obedient to his most important instruction to us. The self-fulfilled Christian life is an oxymoron. Take up your cross and follow Jesus.

---

[286] Ro 6:23
[287] Heb 9:27
[288] Rom 3:23; Ro 5:12–WLC Q84

MARCH 26

DELIVERED FROM DEATH?

The wages of sin is death. Why are not the righteous delivered from death, seeing all their sins are forgiven in Christ?

The righteous shall be delivered from death itself at the last day and even in death are delivered from the sting and curse of it[289] so that although they die, yet it is out of God's love,[290] to free them perfectly from sin and misery[291] and to make them capable of further communion with Christ, in glory, which they then enter upon.[292]

If our ultimate destination was simply a life rescued from physical death, we would have to carry our natural faculties with us forever. The physical resurrection promises so much more than we could ever enjoy in our current bodies.

It is a mystery that our spirit has been freed, but our flesh remains temporarily unredeemed. We have victory over sin, but our flesh wrestles with our worldly desires. God's purposes in leaving us in this state is not fully known, but there is at least one long lesson for us. We learn, through our own continued weakness to fully rely upon God's sustaining power in our salvation. God began this work in us, and it is only God who completes the work. It is a pride-shattering life we lead until our final redemption. Stand fast in God's power. Our glorification awaits us at the final resurrection. Then we shall behold our God!

---

[289] 1Co 15:26,55,56,57; Heb 2:15
[290] Isa 57:1,2; 2Ki 22:20
[291] Rev 14:13; Eph 5:27
[292] Lk 23:43; Php 1:23–WLC Q85

MARCH 27

IN GLORY WITH CHRIST (PART 1)

Death shall indeed come to us all in this life. However, the sufferings we face in this life are not worthy to be compared with glories that await us in heaven.[293]

The communion in glory with Christ, which the members of the invisible church enjoy immediately after death, is in that their souls are then made perfect in holiness[294] and received into the highest heavens,[295] where they behold the face of God in light and glory,[296] waiting for the full redemption of their bodies, which even in death continue united to Christ.[297]

Death for the believer should not hold any fear, only joy. We may have some anxiety over the unknowns that await us, but we should not fear judgment. We have assurance in Christ, knowing he has paid our debt at the cross, never to be paid again.

With this confidence, we anticipate the glories which await. Can you imagine living in perfection? No body aches, never a cold, no stress, no anger to manage, no temptation to resist, just the joy of a holy life with our Savior.

Take some time to meditate on your reunion with Christ. What glories shall you behold as you gaze upon his magnificent face?

---

[293] Rom 8:18
[294] Heb 12:23
[295] 2Co 5:1,6,8; Php 1:23 compared with Ac 3:21 and Eph 4:10
[296] 1Jn 3:2; 1Co 13:12
[297] Ro 8:23; Ps 16:9; 1Th 4:14–WLC Q86a

MARCH 28

In Glory with Christ (Part 2)

Our souls shall be with Christ immediately upon our death, but we will wait for the final resurrection where we shall be given new bodies that shall never know corruption. Not true for the unbeliever.

The bodies of the redeemed rest in their graves as in their beds,[298] till at the last day they be again united to their souls.[299] Whereas the souls of the wicked are at their death cast into hell, where they remain in torments and utter darkness, and their bodies kept in their graves, as in their prisons, till the resurrection and judgment of the great day.[300]

All humans will have their bodies resurrected. Both the redeemed and those cast into hell will be given new bodies that will last for eternity. While the Church experiences unsurpassed joy, the souls of the wicked remain in torment, then face judgment where they will be found guilty of their sin, their hatred and rejection of God and his righteousness. They shall bow their knee, confess his Lordship, and then be cast into the eternal lake of fire.

Yes, all creation will confess Jesus as Lord, some in this lifetime, the rest at judgment. The sense of urgency to share the Gospel is overwhelming. How many family members and friends have heard us proclaim the saving grace of God which is freely offered to all? We cannot save anyone, but we can warn them of judgment.

---

[298] Isa 57:2
[299] Job 19:26,27
[300] Lk 16:23,24; Ac 1:25; Jude 6,7–TWLC Q86b

MARCH 29

RESURRECTION TO LIFE

Knowledge is power? Not completely. The fear of the Lord is the beginning of wisdom.[301] Wisdom includes knowledge with God's perspective. God has given us his Word that we may know his command and his promises. Knowledge of this life and the next.

We are to believe that at the last day, there shall be a general resurrection of the dead, both of the just and unjust:[302] when they that are then found alive shall in a moment be changed and the self-same bodies of the dead that were laid in the grave, being then again united to their souls forever, shall be raised up by the power of Christ.[303]

If it is in the Word, it is there for our edification. Therefore, we are to read, understand, and believe the promises of this life and what awaits in the next. We therefore know that there is not only a heaven that awaits the redeemed, but there is a hell for those who reject God.

Many people take liberty to accept heaven, yet reject hell. However, this is purely unbelief. The Scriptures are not there for us to pick and choose what is true. In fact, what part of man thinks that his own beliefs actually alter reality? Can a man fall out of a tree and float safely to the ground simply because he chooses to believe gravity is optional? What God has established remains unshaken.

---

[301] Pr 1:7; Ps 111:10; Job 28:28; Is 33:6
[302] Ac 24:15
[303] 1Co 15:51-53; 1Th 4:15-17; Jn 5:28,29—WLC Q87a

MARCH 30

RESURRECTION TO DEATH

Just as a man cannot believe gravity out of reality, he cannot unbelieve the punishment of hell out of judgment. There is no reincarnation nor does a man simply go out of existence as his body returns to dust.

The bodies of the just, by the Spirit of Christ and by virtue of his resurrection as their head, shall be raised in power, spiritual, incorruptible, and made like to his glorious body;[304] and the bodies of the wicked shall be raised up in dishonor by him as an offended judge.[305]

The Atheists will face the one true God whom they have rejected their whole lives. They will have admit that they always knew God existed and that his laws were fixed by his holiness. As well, every other person who denies the revelation of God as truth will stand without excuse and in full accountability of their sin and its wages.

How nonsensical to say, "You believe your truth and I'll believe mine." There is only one truth. However, I will grant you that *many paths lead to God.* In fact, every path will get you a front row seat to God. However, only the righteous, narrow path through Jesus Christ leads to heaven. All other paths condemn you at the Great White Throne Judgment. The Lord will proclaim their guilt and cast them into the very hell they denied.

---

[304] 1Co 15:21-23,42-44; Php 3:21
[305] Jn 5:27-29; Mt 25:33–WLC Q87b

MARCH 31

RESURRECTION ANTICIPATION

Knowing that the Bible holds the answers to all things to which the Lord would have us to believe, we get some insight to the eternity that awaits us.

Immediately after the resurrection shall follow the general and final judgment of angels and men;[306] the day and hour whereof no man knows, that all may watch and pray, and be ever ready for the coming of the Lord.[307]

In the month ahead, we will take a closer look at what the Judgment of God shall bring to both the righteous and the wicked. We will also look into the laws that God has given to us. The Law which is a guide to living a godly life and to show us its usefulness as it pertains to all men. The Law that forces us to rely on God for all righteousness.

Today, we see our proper demeanor as we wait for eternity. We know the promise of heaven, yet we are to pray in anticipation. Although we cannot know the Day of Christ's return, we are to be ready in waiting. Eternity is to be always at the front of our minds.

The second coming of Jesus is our hope. We have life in Christ now, but our vision is blurry. But at that day, we shall see him with the veil lifted from our eyes and we shall know him as he truly is!

In a moment, in the twinkling of an eye, we shall be like him.[308]

---

[306] 2Pe 2:4; Jude 6,7,14,15; Mt 25:46
[307] Mt 24:36,42,44; Lk 21:35,36–WLC Q88
[308] 1Cor 15:50-58; 1Jn 3:2-3

APRIL 1

JUDGMENT DAY FOR THE WICKED

This is not an April Fool's Day joke. There is, in fact, nothing more serious than the judgment of all men at the throne of God. If we truly believe Jesus, we must also believe when he says that many go by the wide path of unbelief that leads to destruction.

At the day of judgment, the wicked shall be set on Christ's left hand and, upon clear evidence and full conviction of their own consciences,[309] shall have the fearful but just sentence of condemnation pronounced against them[310] and thereupon shall be cast out from the favorable presence of God and the glorious fellowship with Christ, his saints, and all his holy angels, into hell, to be punished with unspeakable torments, both of body and soul, with the devil and his angels forever.[311]

Jesus went on to say that there will be many who will be judged as wicked, thinking that they we among the believers.[312] This can be a scary thought: *Am I among those who will be surprised that I did not make it into heaven?* There is comfort for true believers. God has promised the Holy Spirit as One who testifies within us.

However, the reprobate have no such internal testimony, and all of their efforts are full of pride and wickedness. If you think that you are *good enough* to make it into heaven, repent and seek Christ's mercy.

---

[309] Ro 2:15,16
[310] Mt 25:33; Mt 25:41-43
[311] Lk 16:26; 2Th 1:8,9–WLC Q89
[312] Mt 7:21-23

APRIL 2

JUDGMENT DAY FOR BELIEVERS
(PART 1)

Believers will enter into judgment with the promise of Christ's righteousness imputed to them. We know that in ourselves there is no goodness (according to God's standard) and that all of our self-effort is filthy in his eyes. Believers have been rescued from the pit, and we look forward to the day when we will cast off these bodies.

At the day of judgment, the righteous, being caught up to Christ in the clouds,[313] shall be set on his right hand, and there openly acknowledged and acquitted, shall join with him in the judging of reprobate angels and men[314] and shall be received into heaven, where they shall be fully and forever freed from all sin and misery, filled with inconceivable joys.[315]

Unlike the wicked, it is not likely that the righteous in Christ will fear the unknown when ushered to God's Judgment. We have many comforting promises knowing our Master. We further have the promise of being changed immediately upon our resurrection, into the image of Christ.[316] If we are made like him, what shall we fear?

The reprobate will fear both God and the saints to whom authority is granted. The capacity of our judgment over wicked men and angels, I do not know, but we can be sure that we will only judge by the righteous wisdom granted to us by Jesus Christ. It's all Jesus.

---

[313] 1Th 4:17
[314] Mt 25:33; Mt 10:32; 1Co 6:2,3
[315] Mt 25:34,46; Eph 5:27; Rev 14:13; Ps 16:11–WLC 90a
[316] 1Jn 3:2

APRIL 3

JUDGMENT DAY FOR BELIEVERS (PART 2)

I have been blessed with many good days in this life. Days filled with fun, great relationships, activities, and family. However, nothing comes close to what we shall experience in heaven.

Made perfectly holy and happy both in body and soul, in the company of innumerable saints and holy angels,[317] *but especially in the immediate vision and fruition of God the Father, of our Lord Jesus Christ, and of the Holy Spirit to all eternity.*[318] *And this is the perfect and full communion, which the members of the invisible church shall enjoy with Christ in glory at the resurrection and day of judgment.*

We look forward to the day where we shall experience no more sorrow or pain. No low points, no boredom, no regrets, just great joy and perfect relationships with our Savior and heavenly family.

Heaven will be much more than the best of what we know in this life. We can imagine seeing the brightest colors, hearing the heavenly music, and tasting the most flavorful fruits, but we cannot even glimpse living beyond these four dimensions of space and time. The best we can do is get a taste from those who have visited the throne room, like Isaiah and John.[319]

Our inspiration for living a godly life in this world is the knowledge of the unsurpassing joy, which is to come in the next. For this, we endure our trials with joy, knowing God is glorified.

---

[317] Heb 12:22,23
[318] 1Jn 3:2; 1Co 13:12; 1Th 4:17,18–WLC Q90b
[319] Is 6:1-7; Rev 1:9-18

APRIL 4

CALL OF DUTY

He has shown you, O man, what is good; And what does the LORD require of you But to do justly, To love mercy, And to walk humbly with your God.

Micah 6:8

The duty, which God requires of man, is obedience to his revealed will.[320]

This seems simple enough. However, we realize that a life of obedience to God is anything but easy. In fact, it is an impossible task, to which we must constantly repent and bring our conduct back in step with the Spirit.

There is a reason why we are unable to live perfectly obedient. The Scriptures tell us that our inability drives us toward dependency on God. We see our sin as being exceedingly sinful. Our pride is vanquished and we learn humble obedience. Yet the weakness of our flesh does not exempt us from the requirement of obedience.

As believers, our lives generally progress closer in step with the Spirit of God. We sin less often and less grievously, and at the same time, we hate our sin more intensely. Our lives more closely represent Christ and yet our dependency on him is even greater.

We keep his commands because we love God. We love God because he first loved us.[321] Walking in his Spirit, we are obedient.

---

[320] Ro 12:1,2; Mic 6:8; 1Sa 15:22–WLC Q91
[321] 1Jn 4:19

APRIL 5

THE MORAL LAW

God's requirement for obedience began before Adam's fall. In his original state, Adam was given specific instruction to obey God.

The rule of obedience revealed to Adam in the estate of innocence, and to all mankind in him, besides a special command not to eat of the fruit of the tree of the knowledge of good and evil was the moral law.[322]

The moral law: the command to do what is right in the eyes of the Lord. The portal that Satan often uses to tempt us is our eyes. *So when the woman (Eve) saw that the tree was good for food, that it was pleasant to the eyes, and a tree desirable to make one wise, she took of its fruit and ate. She also gave to her husband with her, and he ate.*[323] The New Testament also speaks of the lust of the eyes and lust of the flesh resulting from the sinful world.[324]

It is given to every person to have God's moral law written on their hearts. Once we are mature enough to understand right from wrong, we become accountable to obedience. How early can you remember that stealing a piece of candy was wrong? It is amazing how quickly God stamps his moral law into our hearts.

Jesus sums up the whole of the Law with two commandments. To love God and to love others. If we keep these, we keep them all.

---

[322] Ge 1:26,27; Ro 2:14,15; Ro 10:5; Ge 2:17–WLC Q92
[323] Ge 3:6
[324] 1Jn 2:16

APRIL 6

THE DEPTH OF THE MORAL LAW

We mentioned yesterday that our eyes are the portals Satan uses to tempt us. On the contrary, God uses our ears to communicate his commands and his Word of life; faith comes by hearing.

The moral law is the declaration of the will of God to mankind, directing and binding everyone to personal, perfect, and perpetual conformity and obedience thereunto, in the frame and disposition of the whole man, soul and body,[325] and in performance of all those duties of holiness and righteousness, which he owes to God and man:[326] promising life upon the fulfilling and threatening death upon the breach of it.[327]

The Law of God is neither ambiguous nor slack; rather, it is precise and binding. God, being perfect, must demand perfection; anything short of perfection is deemed as sin. You may be thinking, *Isn't this an impossible requirement for fallen man?* To which the answer is, *Yes, it is.*

This why God sent his only Son. Through the virgin birth, Jesus was born without inherited sin to fulfill all righteousness and to die on behalf of the elect. Therefore, any idea that man can achieve a merit of righteousness on his own is in itself a sin. Perhaps it is the most grievous sin because it is full of pride and denies what God has done for us. This denial can be interpreted as nothing less than unbelief.

---

[325] Dt 5:1-3,31,33; Lk 10:26,27; Gal 3:10; 1Th 5:23
[326] Lk 1:75; Ac 24:16
[327] Ro 10:5; Gal 3:10,12–WLC Q93

APRIL 7

THE MORAL LAW TODAY

Adam, in his original state of innocence, failed to keep the law. What use is the moral law for mankind today?

Although no man, since the fall, can attain to righteousness and life by the moral law,[328] yet there is great use thereof, as well common to all men, as peculiar either to the unregenerate or the regenerate.[329]

We will explore the particular use of the moral law in the days ahead. In general, the law was established before the fall, not because God felt the need to establish some ground rules, but because the moral law simply reflected what preexisted in the character of God.

With God comes all of his holiness, glory, righteousness, and the perfection thereof. God's moral law exists intrinsically with him. It was the moral law that Lucifer broke when his pride sought a position equal with his Creator.[330] It is this same righteous law that was broken in the garden. We want to be our own god.

We must handle the moral law with caution. If we conclude: *since no man is able to keep God's law, then why try at all?* we shall not see redemption. The Law does not allow us to attain righteousness. The Law exposes our sin. It is by the Law that we have recognition of our inability and are driven to our knees to beg for mercy.

---

328 Ro 8:3; Gal 2:16
329 1Ti 1:8–WLC Q94
330 Is 14:12-14

APRIL 8

MORAL LAW FOR ALL MEN

As a kid, if I knew I could get away with something, I pretty much did it. The primary resistance to my disobedience was my fear of the consequences of getting caught. Sometimes, I ignored the consequences and did it anyway. The Law is purely good, but man's heart is deceivingly wicked. The Law always points to a holy God.

The moral law is of use to all men, to inform them of the holy nature and will of God,[331] and of their duty, binding them to walk accordingly;[332] to convince them of their disability to keep it, and of the sinful pollution of their nature, hearts, and lives;[333] to humble them in the sense of their sin and misery, and thereby help them to a clearer sight of the need they have of Christ, and of the perfection of his obedience.[334]

The moral law is not simply a guideline for maintaining peace and order in a fallen world. It is obligatory for man to live accordingly. Ignorance is not freedom. In fact, ignorance of the law is impossible. In a general sense of knowing right from wrong, God has written his law on the heart of every man.

We hate the Law of God until the Holy Spirit gives us a new heart. Our renewed spirit agrees with his Spirit that we are his children. From this moment, we are free from bondage and enabled to obey.

---

[331] Lev 11:44,45; Lev 20:7,8; Ro 7:12
[332] Mic 6:8; Jas 2:10,11
[333] Ps 19:11,12; Ro 3:20; Ro 7:7
[334] Ro 3:9,23; Gal 3:21,22; Ro 10:4–WLC Q95

APRIL 9

LAW FOR THE UNREGENERATE

Nobody ever fished off the pier of a tiny resort until the management posted a "No Fishing" sign. I wonder how much longer it would have taken Adam and Eve to investigate the forbidden fruit had Satan not questioned the prohibition. People who ignore instructions eventually find themselves face-to-face with consequences.

The moral law is of use to unregenerate men, to awaken their consciences to flee from wrath to come,[335] and to drive them to Christ[336] or, upon their continuance in the estate and way of sin, to leave them inexcusable[337] and under the curse thereof.[338]

The moment they ate of the fruit, they experienced shame. Running, hiding and covering themselves. Their act drove them away from God and left them expecting justice. This is a common experience for all mankind. The questions is, *What do we do with our guilt?*

The purpose of the law is much more than abiding by a set of rules to keep the peace. The deeper purpose is to show our inability to live to God's standard and to expose our sinfulness. There are two reactions to our sin. First, our shame makes us run away, and we are left without excuse in front of a holy God. The other: our spirit is enabled to agree with God and we recognize our inability to live sinless and we are driven into the Savior's arms to be rescued by the blood of the Righteous One.

---

[335] 1Ti 1:9,10
[336] Gal 3:24
[337] Ro 1:20; Ro 2:15
[338] Gal 3:10–WLC Q96

APRIL 10

BELIEVERS AND THE LAW (PART 1)

We have seen the purpose of the Law in convicting man of his sinfulness. We further understand that the Law can drive a man toward the Savior or leave him inexcusable and under the curse. But what takes place after one's conversion? What is the effect of the law?

Although they that are regenerate and believe in Christ be delivered from the moral law as a covenant of works,[339] so as thereby they are neither justified[340] nor condemned.[341]

For those who have been redeemed by God, who have faith in his Son, these are no longer under the curse of the Law. God's perfect Law has performed its duty by exposing sin and driving those who would be redeemed to the cross. As regeneration is solely of grace, our works account for nothing.

When the blood of Jesus covers our sin, our sin can no longer condemn us. Forgiven, as far as east is from west, sin is destroyed. Furthermore, since it is by Christ's righteousness alone, our good works have no merit in our justification. This eliminates both sides of the equation for the moral law in one's justification or condemnation.

Believers tend to think that now that they are saved, they must sustain their faith through keeping the law. Regardless of good intent, this is really a slap in Jesus' face. Shall we try to add to grace?

---

[339] Ro 6:14; Ro 7:4,6; Gal 4:4,5
[340] Ro 3:20
[341] Gal 5:23; Ro 8:1–WLC Q97a

APRIL 11

BELIEVERS AND THE LAW (PART 2)

Yesterday, we learned that believers have been delivered from the moral law. We know that it is not our efforts, but Jesus who began a good work in us and he will complete it.[342] His perfect work should not be diminished by our efforts to maintain righteousness through the Law. However, the law does have benefits for the regenerate.

Yet besides the general uses (of the moral law) common to them with all men, it is of special use to show them how much they are bound to Christ for his fulfilling it and enduring the curse thereof in their stead and for their good[343] and thereby to provoke them to more thankfulness[344] and to express the same in their greater care to conform themselves thereunto as the rule of their obedience.[345]

Just because believers have been delivered from the Law does not mean that the Law is sin.[346] Furthermore, our deliverance from the Law does not mean that we need not live according to its standard.

The believer moves from being an opponent of the Law to living harmoniously alongside of it . As God's children, we love his law. We experience its benefits through the righteous life in God. Because our spirit agrees with his Spirit, our lives are transformed as our minds are renewed through knowledge of his Word and Law.

---

[342] Ph 1:6
[343] Ro 7:24,25; Gal 3:13,14; Ro 8:3,4
[344] Lk 1:68,69,74,75; Col 1:12,13,14
[345] Ro 7:22; Ro 12:2; Tit 2:11-14–WLC Q97b
[346] Ro 7:7

APRIL 12

GOD'S SUMMARY OF HIS LAW

We have spent several days discussing God's moral law and its effectiveness on every man. Now, we shall take at look at the Law itself. What is it? To whom does it pertain? And what duties are specified?

The moral law is summarily comprehended in the Ten Commandments, which were delivered by the voice of God upon Mount Sinai and written by him in two tables of stone[347] *and are recorded in the twentieth chapter of Exodus. The four first commandments containing our duty to God and the other six our duty to man.*[348]

The Law is the command of God. It is binding to all mankind. It describes both general and specific laws that are easily comprehended as the moral rules for man's responsibilities to God and each other.

The first thing that we should recognize is that the law is not something man invented to improve the governance of a community. The Law was both spoken by God in a personal manner, then it was literally inscribed in stone by his own finger. Where God is clear and direct, man creates confusion.

Jesus said the sum of the Law is contained in only two commands: *to love God and to love others.* The natural man resists God and envies his neighbor. Although God's guidelines are simple, they are not without depth. Have you let God's law penetrate your heart?

---

[347] Dt 10:4; Ex 34:1-4
[348] Mt 22:37-40–WLC Q98

APRIL 13

RULES FOR PROPER UNDERSTANDING

For the proper understanding of the Ten Commandments, these rules are to be observed:

1. That the law is perfect and binds everyone to full conformity in the whole man unto the righteousness thereof and unto entire obedience forever, so as to require the utmost perfection of every duty and to forbid the least degree of every sin.[349]

The first thing we must understand is that God is true and his Law is righteous. For God to be a God of Love, we must also accept his judgment of evil. One does not come without the other. Therefore, as God's creatures, we are held to the standard he sets. Simply put, what he calls sin is sin. There are no white lies in the eyes of God.

To be cavalier with sin because it may not fit a capital punishment in our society is nothing less than trampling the blood of Christ underfoot in the eyes of God. For that little sin requires payment, and for the regenerate, it was purchased at Calvary. For those without a Redeemer, they will pay in their own eternal death.[350]

Do you think *that* judgment is harsh? It sure is! But God is gracious. Life in Christ is freely offered to all who would receive it. Man resists God and his ways, and those who do not repent and believe will find themselves facing their due and just penalty. In their pride, they blame God for their own fall. But his law remains perfect.

---

[349] Ps 19:7; Jas 2:10; Mt 5:21,22—WLC Q99a
[350] Ro 3:23, 6:23

APRIL 14

THE LAW IS SPIRITUAL

2. That it is spiritual and so reaches the understanding, will, affections, and all other powers of the soul as well as words, works, and gestures.[351]

Jesus shows us in the Scriptures referenced in the footnotes that the Law is spiritual. The physical restrictions of the law are rooted in our evil intentions—equating hatred with murder, and lust with adultery. To God, our sin is first exposed in the heart.

Our whole being is under examination of the Law. This is because we exist in God's world, which is subject to his perfect standard. He will not let his creation be exonerated by good behavior alone and allow vile thoughts to be winked at. We are told that all sin is first conceived in the heart before it brings forth sinful action. The Scriptures more often point to the condition of the heart, exposing the root of fallen man's issue.

Our most effective behavior change in avoiding sin is to have God's Word written our hearts. First, because the fear and knowledge of God is where wisdom is found. Second, because God tells us that actions follow the heart, so when our heart is seeking God, it is not seeking wickedness.

Focus on purifying your heart through the reading of God's Word. The Word inscribed on your heart shall bring a holy life.

---

[351] Ro 7:14; Dt 6:5 compared with Mt 22:37-39 & Mt 5:21-44–WLC Q99b

APRIL 15

DO THIS, DON'T DO THAT

3. That one and the same thing, in diverse respects, is required or forbidden in several commandments.[352]

God's Law contains both requirements in honoring him and restrictions against offending him. An example of the former is *Honor thy mother and father*, where any failure to do so is a sin against God. An example of a restriction is the prohibition of lying.

We all understand that doing something we are not supposed to do is sin. But how about when we do not do something we are commanded to do? These are called *sins of omission*, and they are just as dishonoring in God's eyes.

The thing about it is these are not often preached from the pulpit, and they certainly are not considered important by the public. There was a time, not too long ago, when commerce was not allowed on Sundays in honor of keeping the Sabbath Day holy. Regardless that Saturday is by definition the Sabbath, Sunday was observed by the church. Rest was practiced, and it was law in most communities.

How quickly the memory of such things are vanquished. The only remnant of such a law is the forbidding sale of alcohol before noon on Sunday. I am certain that once this law is removed, there will be barely a ripple of knowledge on why such a law ever existed. Ask the Holy Spirit to reveal any wicked ways within you. It may be more difficult to find out what we are *not doing* to honor our Lord.

---

[352] Col 3:5; Am 8:5; Pr 1:19; 1Ti 6:10–WLC Q99c

APRIL 16

ONE COIN, TWO SIDES

4. That as, where a duty is commanded, the contrary sin is forbidden,[353] and where a sin is forbidden, the contrary duty is commanded;[354] so where a promise is annexed, the contrary threatening is included,[355] and where a threatening is annexed, the contrary promise is included.[356]

God's Law is extremely deep in principle but very simplistic in logic. That is to say that although God's righteousness is profoundly limitless, even a child can understand the rules to govern our lives.

We understand that where God's law is broken, there is a consequence. However, we do not often look at the blessings promised to us when we are obedient. Many view God as a cosmic killjoy, forbidding anything pleasurable. They see the curse and ignore the blessing. All the while, God is longing to bless those who would serve him.

On the other hand, people sometimes trade their obedience for short-term pleasures, leaving themselves threatened with judgment. God knows exactly what each person needs in the way of punishment or mercy. Why only some people are punished in this life is a mystery. Other times, God turns men over to their sinful behavior. Wickedness will face final judgment for every ungodly thought and deed. Is God purging the sin in your life? Seek his correction.

---

[353] Isa 58:13; Dt 6:13 compared with Mt 4:9,10; Mt 15:4,5,6
[354] Mt 5:21-25; Eph 4:28
[355] Ex 20:12 compared with Pr 30:17
[356] Jer 18:7,8; Ex 20:7; Ps 15:1,4,5; Ps 24:4,5–WLC Q99d

APRIL 17

SEMPER FI

5. That what God forbids is at no time to be done;[357] what he commands, is always our duty;[358] and yet every particular duty is not to be done at all times.[359]

The US Marine Corp's motto "Semper Fi" is stands for "Always Faithful." This is God's requirement of his followers: we are to be faithful at every point of his Law, at all times, and without excuse.

God, being perfectly good and righteous himself, complies with his character. This means that the standard for people to please him must be perfection. Today's devotion is not so much about the solution to our failure to uphold this standard, but just to realize that this is, in fact, the standard to which we are to be dutiful.

Man's inability to comply with God's perfect standard is no excuse for ignoring it altogether. Rather, this unattainable standard should drive man to seek refuge in his Savior's arms. Because of his righteousness, Jesus' blood satisfied God's wrath for everyone who believes. Outside of Jesus, the sinner faces judgment on his own.

Every particular duty is not to be done at all times. This is simply saying that the time for righteous living is perpetual, but particular laws are seasonal; we cannot observe the Sabbath every day. Pray that you will be sensitive to a godly standard. Then live out that lifestyle.

---

[357] Job 13:7,8; Ro 3:8; Job 36:21; Heb 11:25
[358] Dt 4:8,9
[359] Mt 12:7–WLC Q99e

APRIL 18

UMBRELLA POLICY

6. That under one sin or duty, all of the same kind are forbidden or commanded together with all the causes, means, occasions, and appearances thereof and provocations thereunto.[360]

The US Tax Code has increase from thousands of words to nearly 6 million words. This is equal to about 80,000 pages of red tape. This is seven times the number of words in the Bible, where only a small portion of this total is dedicated to the Law. The Bible is clear and precise where it needs to be, and God expects common sense to fill in the blanks. Reason and logic coupled with godly wisdom are sufficient.

The book of Romans says that fallen man professes to be wise but becomes foolish.[361] The statement carries a lot of insight. The main point being that when man ignores the plain things of God, his corruption is deepened. Further, when a person tries to find loopholes in God's moral law, their intent is selfishly sinful.

The believer is comforted with the Law rather than burdened. We know that the Spirit leads us into all righteousness and warns us when we start to stray. We delight in the Law of God. We know that we glorify him when we walk according to his ways and not our own. By the Holy Spirit, we abide in Jesus Christ, just as branches produce fruit according to the vine in which they abide. What stage of your walk with God are you in? Are you burdened by his commandment? Or do you delight in his Law?

---

[360] Mt 5:21-28; 15:4-6; Heb 10:24,25; 1Th 5:22; Jude 23; Gal 5:26; Col 3:21–
    WLC Q99f
[361] Ro 1:22

APRIL 19

BOUND BY ASSOCIATION

7. That what is forbidden or commanded to ourselves, we are bound, according to our places, to endeavor that it may be avoided or performed by others, according to the duty of their places.[362]

My parents did not drink or smoke, but when I was growing up, I did not understand why their standards should apply to me. The idea was that if I was living under their roof, I was expected not to defame our good name. In the same manner, those who live in a God-fearing household are expected to live according the biblical standard. It goes further than just expectations. We are bound to it.

Our responsibility goes beyond avoiding those things that are prohibited. It includes performing duties that are commanded. The commands of God are to be a blessing a person's life. Unbelievers also benefit by observing the moral law. One example is our legal system in America. Our law is established to protect all people from the harmful actions of lawbreakers. In a similar fashion, a nonbeliever who honors their parents will benefit in that relationship.

We should also be careful not to look at just the moral aspects of the Law of God. We will always want to remember that the final purpose of the Law is to drive us toward the Redeemer.[363] We cannot be justified by keeping the Law, for it is impossible to do so perfectly at all times and in all aspects. God, on our behalf, has fulfilled the perfect Law through Jesus Christ. Have you been perfected through him?

---

[362] Ex 20:10; Lev 19:17; Ge 18:19; Josh. 24:15; Dt 6:6,7–WLC Q99g
[363] Ro 5:20,21; Gal 3:24

APRIL 20

HE AIN'T HEAVY

8. That in what is commanded to others, we are bound, according to our places and callings, to be helpful to them[364] and to take heed of partaking with others in what is forbidden them[365].

Laws vary from state to state and country to country. Visitors to a region are bound, not by the laws from where they reside, but by the laws of land they are presently in. Being in his world, we are obligated to his law and also responsible to hold others accountable, assisting them in areas of which they may be ignorant.

For unbelievers, this may not make sense to them. After all, why should they be obligated to another's religion? The answer is because God's Law is not a "pick your poison" type of religion. God's moral law is universal, and therefore, everyone is absolutely accountable to it.

While a good portion of the moral law, like stealing, lying, and murder are upheld by all communities around the world, other sins, like envy or dishonoring one's parents, might not be understood. Therefore, it is in such areas as these in which we are to educate and hold each other accountable.

God's Law is to be a delight to his people. We benefit from our obedience to it. Finally, through our inability to keep it perfectly, we are shown the perfect work of Christ on our behalf that we might partake in his imputed righteousness, just as he took upon himself our guilt.

---

[364] 2Co 1:24
[365] 1Ti 5:22; Eph 5:11–WLC Q99h

APRIL 21

THE TEN COMMANDMENTS

We have discussed several general responsibilities to God's Law. Now, we move deeper into its details. What special things are we to consider in the Ten Commandments?

We are to consider, in the Ten Commandments, the preface, the substance of the commandments themselves, and several reasons annexed to some of them, the more to enforce them.[366]

Because it is impossible to describe the infinite, it may leave us thinking that we cannot know anything of Almighty God. Just because we cannot know all things does not mean we cannot know anything. God manifests himself to us by his character. His character is manifest to us through the Holy Scriptures, specifically through his commandments and the interactions with his creation.

As we focus our attention on the Ten Commandments, we will be well served to look beyond the rules and explore the perfect attributes of God as they are developed progressively for us. The proper understanding of biblical attributes provide a holy image of God for us. Furthermore, they eliminate any false pretense we may have. Our false beliefs about God are idolatry and considered blasphemous in his sight.

I trust that you, like me, are desiring to know God in a closer, personal, and more biblical way. If so, make an extra effort to learn his commandments in a fresh way with the Holy Spirit as your guide.

---

[366] Westminster Larger Catechism Question 100 (WLC–Q100)

APRIL 22

THE PREFACE (PART 1)

It's often stated that if you do not understand the fundamentals, you will not truly understand the finer points. This will never be more true than when studying the Word of God. We must know that God is, and that he makes himself known through his creation and by his Word.

The preface to the Ten Commandments is contained in these words," I am the Lord thy God, which have brought thee out of the land of Egypt, out of the house of bondage."[367] Wherein God manifests his sovereignty, as being Jehovah, the eternal, immutable, and Almighty God,[368] having his being in and of himself,[369] and giving being to all his words and works.[370]

There is one proper worldview. It all begins with the biblical God. The scriptures declare both his being and his character. As God is the creator of this universe, our universe, the only worldview that can possibly work is the one that begins with this foundation.

God was not created, but is eternal. He is the Ancient of Days, yet it is not proper to say he is old. God exists outside of time. He is before all things. Through his eternal being and his omnipotence, he has provided the exact universe in which he wants his creation to exist. We will do well to pay close attention to his instruction.

---

[367] Ex 20:2
[368] Isa 44:6
[369] Ex 3:14
[370] Ex 6:3 WLC Q19, Ac 17:24,28—WLC Q101a

APRIL 23

THE PREFACE (PART 2)

Since there is but one true God, we should be pleased to know of his benevolence. God, betrayed continuously by prideful beings and having every right to enact the immediate penalty for our sin, shows his people longsuffering mercy.

And that he is a God in covenant, as with Israel of old, so with all his people,[371] who, as he brought them out of their bondage in Egypt, so he delivers us from our spiritual thralldom[372] and that therefore we are bound to take him for our God alone and to keep all his commandments.[373]

There will be many who will resent having any obligation to God or his law. Yet if they are not bound to the one true God, they are bound as slaves to the lusts of this world. We are all slaves to one master, either this sinful world, or the One who redeems us out of it.

There is a godly call that beckons all men to freely come and drink the water of life. However, most will flex their sinful pride and die at the river's edge. They think that they are good, yet they only compare to those who might be worse around them. God has set his standard in his law, our failure at any point in thought or deed destroys the perfect obedience he requires. Let us gaze upon the pure goodness of Christ, who did fulfill the law. Then, let us be covered by his blood that he spilled on behalf of those whom he redeems. We are bound.

---

[371] Ge 17:7 compared with Ro 3:29
[372] Lk 1:74,75
[373] 1Pe 1:15-18; Lev 18:30; Lev 19:37 WLC Q101b

APRIL 24

OUR DUTY TO GOD

If we agree that the God of the Bible is the One True God, then we are ready to believe that his commands are worthy to followed. Our first set of obligations is to worship him as he declares himself to us.

The sum of the four commandments containing our duty to God is to love the Lord our God with all our heart and with all our soul and with all our strength and with all our mind.[374]

Although one might expect the fear of the Lord to produce tyrannical obedience, we find that it is anything but forced for those whom serve the living God. Our primary duty is not fear, but love. Love in a wholesome and totalitarian manner.

With all our heart: The biblical heart is the center of all spirituality and being. It's not based on emotion, but on conviction.

With all our soul: The soul can be defined as the life of the inner man. The life of the soul continues after the death of the body. The soul is the true being of man and the body is just its dwelling.

With all our strength: Just as is states, we are to give our best effort at all times to serve God. We demonstrate our love by keeping his commandments. When we fail, we were weak in love.

With all our mind: Serving and loving God comes from a proper understanding of who he is. We know him through the Scriptures.

---

[374] Lk 10:27–WLC Q102

APRIL 25

THE FIRST COMMANDMENT

We are now going to begin to look at these commandments on a detailed level. Do not expect boredom as we dig into these otherwise basic laws of God. If our desire is to love God in the manner that he asks us, we must understand these laws deeply.

The first commandment is "Thou shalt have no other gods before me."[375]

The simplicity of this first command might catch us off guard. But what is it saying? Are there other gods? Do we have a choice of various gods and just pick one that best suits us?

The duties required in the first commandment are the knowing and acknowledging of God to be the only true God and our God.[376]

There is only one God. Anything we place in priority, at any given time, above honoring the true God, is like putting another god first. There is no other God, yet we often place the Lord subservient to our own wants. When we put other things ahead of God, it exposes the idols yet remaining in our world. How quickly we can deceive ourselves.

In our fallen state, our pride often wins out. We fail when we allow the flesh to overcome our spirit. Our redeemed spirit seeks to be true to God, our flesh pulls us away. This is why we are to love him with all of our heart, soul, strength, and mind; to fail not.

---

[375] Ex 20:3–WLC Q103
[376] 1Ch 28:9; Dt 26:17; Isa 43:10; Jer 14:22–WLC Q104a

APRIL 26

FIRST COMMANDMENT DUTIES

So what does it look like to have "no other gods before Him"? We can attribute our obedience to this command by these duties:

To worship and glorify him accordingly by thinking, meditating, remembering,[377] highly esteeming, honoring, adoring, choosing, loving,[378] desiring, fearing of him, believing him, trusting, hoping, delighting,[379] rejoicing in him, being zealous for him, calling upon him, giving all praise and thanks, and yielding all obedience and submission to him with the whole man,[380] being careful in all things to please him and sorrowful when in anything he is offended and walking humbly with him.[381]

There should be nothing here that surprises us. These are godly traits of obedience in love. We find it easy to ignore these traits at times. Our flesh still cries out to get its own way. Temptations are subtle and attractive. We are easily tempted by the fun factor of sin. However, what at first seems harmless is often our spit in the Lord's face.

It says that we must *be careful in all things to please him.* This means that we must be aware not to be flippant in our actions. Failure to walk humbly opens us to pride. Obedience requires effort.

---

[377] Ps 95:6,7; Mt 4:10; Ps 29:2; Mal 3:16; Ps 63:6; Ecc 12:1
[378] Ps 71:19; Mal 1:6; Isa 45:23; Josh. 24:15,22; Dt 6:5
[379] Ps 73:25; Isa 8:13; Ex 14:31; Isa 26:4; Ps 130:7; Ps 37:4
[380] Ps 32:11; Ro 12:11 with Num. 25:11; Php 4:6; Jer 7:23; Jas 4:7
[381] 1Jn 3:22; Jer 31:18; Ps 119:136; Mic 6:8–WLC Q104b

APRIL 27

FIRST COMMANDMENT SINS (PART 1)

We have discussed our duties as Christ's followers. We have also talked about the sinful omissions by failing to keep these requirements. Today, we will move into the other side, the things that God prohibits.

The sins forbidden in the first commandment are atheism, in denying or not having a God;[382] idolatry, in having or worshipping more gods than one or any with or instead of the true God;[383] the not having and avouching him for God and our God.[384]

I have witnessed to atheists before. When asked about their guilt of rejecting God's existence, they simply respond that, "There is no guilt because there is no God." I go on to tell them that their denial of God does not nullify his existence, just as the denial of gravity does not allow you step off a cliff without consequence. It about this time they get uneasy as they realize that denying God's existence is as impossible as the denial of physical laws.

The Scriptures tell us that every man knows there truly is a God, but that they suppress this truth in unrighteousness. They deny their Creator with corrupt and foolish hearts. Furthermore, in an absurd follow up to their denial, they will then move to manufacture their own gods. Anything but the true God for these fools. Beliefs contrary to the existence of the One True God is idolatry and is the foremost of all sin.

---

[382] Ps 14:1; Eph 2:12
[383] Jer 2:27,28 compared with 1Th 1:9
[384] Ps 81:11—WLC Q105a

APRIL 28

FIRST COMMANDMENT SINS (PART 2)

Further sins forbidden in the First Commandment are:

The omission or neglect of anything due to him required in this commandment: ignorance, forgetfulness,[385] *misapprehensions, false opinions, unworthy and wicked thoughts of him,*[386] *bold and curious searching into his secrets.*[387]

We have discussed the sin of omission (not doing what we ought to do), but how about missing something that is not on our mind? The Lord holds us responsible to know all areas in which we are to be obedient; ignorance is not a free pass. Nor is forgetfulness. To forget the things we once knew of God and our service to him shows insincerity and disrespect. We are to delight in his law, not disregard it.

God is not to be figured out. His ways are infinitely above ours. We have no comprehension of the hidden things of God and to try and determine the things he keeps hidden from us is sin. That being said, we are to search out the matters to which he reveals to us. Our efforts in discovering the deep spiritual truths of the Bible are commended, but we shall not try to determine the why and how of the secret things of God.

We know that God has established his plan for salvation. We trust his plan, learn all we can, and leave the mysteries to him.

---

[385] Isa 43:22,23,24; Jer 4:22; Hos 4:1,6; Jer 2:32
[386] Ac 17:23,29; Isa 40:18; Ps 50:21
[387] Dt 29:29–WLC Q105b

APRIL 29

FIRST COMMANDMENT SINS (PART 3)

Still further:

All profaneness, hatred of God, self-love, self-seeking,[388] and all other inordinate and immoderate setting of our mind, will, or affections upon other things, and taking them off from him in whole or in part;[389] vain credulity, unbelief, heresy, misbelief, distrust, despair, incorrigibleness,[390] and insensibleness under judgments, hardness of heart, pride, presumption, carnal security.[391]

We should really be feeling the breadth of prohibitive actions and attitudes of God's first command. You may be thinking, *Enough already. I get it!* But by giving these independent sins a closer look, perhaps you will find, as I do, some things that need to be addressed in our lives. Some things that we barely give much thought. This is the value of searching out the supporting Scriptures.

Today's section is perhaps the most revealing because it contains pride as a specified sin. Pride itself is really the root attitude of all sin. It is pride that sets our affection of ourselves above God. It is pride that demands self-fulfillment regardless of who it affects. If we allow the Holy Spirit to convict us at the moment pride is revealed, we will avoid a whole host of things that grieve God. Pray for conviction.

---

[388] Tit 1:16; Heb 12:16; Ro 1:30; 2Ti 3:2; Php 2:21
[389] 1Jn 2:15,16; 1Sa 2:29; Col 3:2,5
[390] 1Jn 4:1; Heb 3:12; Gal 5:20; Ac 26:9; Ps 78:22; Ge 4:13; Jer 5:3
[391] Isa 42:25; Ro 2:5; Jer 13:15; Ps 19:13; Zeph 1:12–WLC 105c

APRIL 30

FIRST COMMANDMENT SINS (PART 4)

The following sins might be described as deceitfully deceitful:

Tempting of God; using unlawful means, and trusting in unlawful means; carnal delights and joys;[392] *corrupt, blind, and indiscreet zeal; lukewarmness and deadness in the things of God; estranging ourselves and apostatizing from God;*[393] *praying or giving any religious worship to saints, angels, or any other creatures;*[394] *all compacts and consulting with the devil and hearkening to his suggestions; making men the lords of our faith and conscience.*[395]

What do I mean by *deceitfully deceitful?* I mean that the majority of the sins listed above contain an element of preemptive deceit. These are sinful paths that are paved with good intensions. In others, we ignore the conscious check of the Spirit, proceeding from one level of sin to the next. Picture an extramarital affair: how many sins are left in their path as they finally reach the bedroom? Flirtation. Perhaps drunkenness. Deception in three different ways: self, spouse, target. Relocation to a private place. Then, when they get caught, they will say, "I don't know, it just happened," with the long trail blazed.

Oh! The deceitfulness of unchecked pride and unrepented sin! Commit yourself to obedience in a penitent life. Walk in his light.

---

[392] Mt 4:7; Ro 3:8; Jer 17:5; 2Ti 3:4

[393] Gal 4:17; Jn 16:2; Ro 10:2; Lk 9:54,55; Rev 3:16; Rev 3:1; Eze 14:5; Isa 1:4,5

[394] Ro 10:13,14; Hos 4:12; Ac 10:25,26; Rev 19:10; Mt 4:10; Col 2:18; Ro 1:25

[395] Lev 20:6; 1Sa 28:7,11; 1Ch 10:13,14; Ac 5:3; 2Co 1:24; Mt 23:9–WLC Q105d

MAY 1

FIRST COMMANDMENT SINS (PART 5)

This final list of sins do not require a long, distinguished path to their demise. Rather, these sins are immediate denials of the True God, his Spirit, and his leadings in the ways of righteous living.

Slighting and despising God and his commands; resisting and grieving of his Spirit,[396] *discontent and impatience at his dispensations, charging him foolishly for the evils he inflicts on us;*[397] *and ascribing the praise of any good we either are, have, or can do, to fortune, idols, ourselves, or any other creature.*[398]

God's ways are always holy, always righteous, and always perfectly placed in time. In other words, he is never wrong or out of control with any aspect of our lives or this world in which we live. Furthermore, any credit given to chance, luck, or anything but God for the good in our lives is a denial of God's sovereignty and control.

There are many lessons and examples given to us in the Scriptures. Perhaps none of these is more clearly demonstrated than in the life of Job. Job, who by God's own admission lived his life in an upright and penitent manner, was used as *the* case study of all time to the sovereignty of God. Regardless of Job's pain, suffering, and innocent confusion, he did not have any right to questions God's motives. We learn near the end of the book that God's ways are righteous and never to be second-guessed. A tough life lesson for us all.

---

[396] Dt 32:15; 2Sa 12:9; Pr 13:13; Ac 7:51; Eph 4:30
[397] Ps 73:2,3,13,14,15,22; Job 1:22
[398] 1Sa 6:7,8,9; Da 5:23; Dt 8:17; Da 4:30; Hab 1:16—WLC 105e

MAY 2

NO GODS BEFORE ME

The sum of all cognizant sin is when God is not honored for the God whom he is: the I *am who I AM*—YAHWEH. We are to have no gods before him.

These words "before me" or "before my face" in the first commandment teach us that God, who sees all things, takes special notice of, and is much displeased with the sin of having any other God: that so it may be an argument to dissuade from it and to aggravate it as a most impudent provocation[399] as also to persuade us to do as in his sight, whatever we do in his service.[400]

We have nearly exhausted the prohibited sins under the umbrella of the First Commandment. Now, we simply confirm that all sin is the dishonoring of the True God and his supreme authority.

Although *before me* could refer to Almighty God taking a backseat to any other god, this is not the way it is used here. The point is that, in God's omniscience, there is nothing that takes place without his intimate knowledge of the event nor the attitude behind the event. Therefore, we cannot simply move God down just one notch on the totem pole. We conceptually displace him from his rightful throne altogether.

God is not first on list of ten gods. He is first on a list of one. One Lord, One Truth, One Faith, One Savior, none other.

---

[399] Eze 8:5,6; Ps 44:20,21
[400] 1Ch 28:9–WLC Q106

MAY 3

THE SECOND COMMANDMENT

The second commandment is:

Thou shall not make unto thee any graven image, or any likeness of anything that is in heaven above, or that is in the earth beneath, or that is in the water under the earth: Thou shall not bow down thyself to them, not serve them: for I the Lord thy God am a jealous God, visiting the iniquity of the fathers upon the children unto the third and fourth generation of them that hate me, and showing mercy unto thousands of them that love me, and keep my commandments.[401]

You may be thinking to yourself, *Didn't we just cover this commandment?* In a sense, we have. But since God has specifically set this second command apart from *no other gods before me*, let's investigate it deeper.

This command details warnings of worshipping false gods through prohibition of creation and use of images or idols. This makes perfect sense. This is an act of worship of the creation over the creator. Or even worse, the worship of the work of one's own hands.

God will have none of this. We are to worship him as the God he presents to us. If we breech our one true belief, we have effectively not believed in God at all.

---

[401] Ex 20:4,5,6–WLC Q107

MAY 4

SECOND COMMANDMENT DUTIES
(PART 1)

Some say, "I do not need to go to church to be saved." While this does not violate our *faith alone* doctrine, I would counter by stating, "Once you are saved, you need the Church."

The duties required in the second commandment are the receiving, observing, and keeping pure and entire all such religious worship and ordinances as God hath instituted in his word,[402] particularly prayer and thanksgiving in the name of Christ;[403] the reading, preaching, and hearing of the word,[404] the administration and receiving of the sacraments.[405]

What many continue to misunderstand is the definition of the Church. The Church is the body of believers, not the chapel, cathedral, or other building. Thus wherever two or more believers are gathered, we have an assembly of the Church of Christ. It is here the assembly observes its responsibilities in making disciples and edifying God. The Church then goes into to the world to share the Gospel.

Because the Body consists of many members, each of varying spiritual gifts, we do rely on each other to honor the second commandment. We guard each other from false worship and instruct each other in the tenants of the faith as God shows us in his Word.

---

[402] Dt 32:46,47; Mt 28:20; Ac 2:42; 1Ti 6:13,14
[403] Php 4:6; Eph 5:20
[404] Dt 17:18,19; Ac 15:21; 2Ti 4:2; Jas 1:21,22; Ac 10:33
[405] Mt 28:19–WLC Q108a

MAY 5

SECOND COMMANDMENT DUTIES (PART 2)

The warnings of idolatry are to the congregation as well as to the individual follower of God. Therefore, the corporate church is responsible to regulate proper worship and rebuke the false. The remaining second commandment duties are:

Church government and discipline;[406] the ministry and maintenance thereof;[407] religious fasting; swearing by the name of God and vowing unto him:[408] as also the disapproving, detesting, opposing, all false worship;[409] and according to each one's place and calling, removing it, and all monuments of idolatry.[410]

These disciplines of proper worship may appear a bit *Old Testament*, and therefore, we might brush over them without much consideration. However, all of these are still relevant today. We are to worship in spirit and in truth. Where this is violated, sin crouches at the door.

When we fast, do we tell everyone the hunger pains we suffer? Do we emphasize our promises to people by saying, "I swear to God, this is true," rather than just letting our yes be yes? We should regularly reflect on our worship to be sure we are walking biblically with the Lord. The Church holds us accountable.

---

[406] Mt 18:15-17; Mt 16:19; 1Co 5 throughout; 1Co 12:28
[407] Eph 4:11,12; 1Ti 5:17,18; 1Co 9:7-15
[408] Joel 2:12,13; 1Co 7:5; Dt 6:13; Isa 19:21; Ps 76:11
[409] Ac 17:16,17; Ps 16:4
[410] Dt 7:5; Isa 30:22–WLC Q108b

MAY 6

SECOND COMMANDMENT SINS
(PART 1)

We have covered our duties to this commandment. We will now begin to look into the sins we are to avoid. Open your heart to be checked by the Spirit.

The sins forbidden in the second commandment are all devising, counseling, commanding, using, and any wise approving, any religious worship not instituted by God himself;[411] *tolerating a false religion;*[412] *the making any representation of God, of all or of any of the three persons, either inwardly in our mind, or outwardly in any kind of image or likeness of any creature whatsoever;*[413] *all worshipping of it, or God in it or by it.*[414]

The rules of obeying this portion of the Second Commandment will likely find most of us with some form of resistance. Being raised Roman Catholic, statues of the holy family and saints were commonplace. Even most of the crosses have the image of Jesus hanging upon it. Although the Catholics would not call this idolatry, but only a remembrance of their heritage, the warning of worshipping a physical likeness is clear.

Although the Protestant faiths have an empty cross, pointing toward the finished work, we should be careful not to attribute any power in the cross itself. For all power rests in God alone.

---

[411] Nu 15:39; Dt 13:6-8; Hos 5:11; Mic 6:16; 1Ki 11:33; 1Ki 12:33; Dt 12:30-32
[412] Dt 13:6-12; Zec 13:2,3; Rev 2:2,14,15,20; Rev 17:12,16,17
[413] Dt 4:15-19; Ac 17:29; Ro 1:21-23,25
[414] Da 3:18; Gal 4:8; Ex 32:5–WLC 109a

MAY 7

SECOND COMMANDMENT SINS (PART 2)

The Second Commandment sins continue as:

The making of any representation of feigned deities and all worship of them or service belonging to them;[415] all superstitious devices, corrupting the worship of God, adding to it, or taking from it, whether invented and taken up of ourselves,[416] or received by tradition from others, though under the title of antiquity, custom, devotion, good intent, or any other pretence whatsoever;[417] simony; sacrilege; all neglect, contempt, hindering,[418] and opposing the worship and ordinances which God hath appointed.[419]

I would say one area where immature Christians are ignorantly offending God is the area of astrology. *What's your sign?* is a common question in the dating world. In the same manner, many people check their horoscope for a little fun.

The problem is that these are not just novelties. On the contrary, although they may look harmless, they are truly portals to the demonic realm. Satan is crafty. Posing as a sheep, the wolf awaits his prey. Once a person opens themselves up to his influence, they may be heading on a controlled path to destruction. Ask the Lord to reveal any areas of your life that you have not recognized as idolatrous and repent.

---

[415] Ex 32:8; 1Ki 18:26,28; Isa 65:11
[416] Ac 17:22; Col 2:21-23; Mal 1:7,8,14; Dt 4:2; Ps 106:39
[417] Mt 15:9; 1Pe 1:18; Jer 44:17; Isa 65:3-5; Gal 1:13,14; 1Sa 13:11,12; 1Sa 15:21
[418] Ac 8:18; Ro 2:22; Mal 3:8; Ex 4:24-26; Mt 22:5; Mal 1:7,13; Mt 23:13
[419] Ac 13:44,45; 1Th 2:15,16–WLC 109b

MAY 8

WHY THE SECOND COMMANDMENT?

For I the Lord thy God am a jealous God, visiting the iniquity of
the fathers upon the children unto the third and fourth generation of them that hate me; and showing mercy unto thousands of
them that love me, and keep my commandments.

Exodus 20:5-6

*The reasons annexed to the second commandment the more to enforce it are:
besides God's sovereignty over us and propriety in us,[420] his fervent zeal for
his own worship[421] and his revengeful indignation against all false worship as being a spiritual whoredom,[422] accounting the breakers of this commandment such as hate him and threatening to punish them unto diverse
generations[423] and esteeming the observers of it such as love him and keep
his commandments and promising mercy to them unto many generations.[424]*
God sits above his creation. It is good that he desires and commands
worship. To place pride or arrogance into God's character is to not consider his sovereignty. Because God is righteousness, he cannot exercise
maligned traits. He is perfectly deserving of worship, and since we are
his creatures, we are righteously obligated to respond honorably. When
every good gift is from above, every life-giving breath we take, how
could we possibly not worship the Lord God? We battle with sinful
flesh, so we must submit ourselves to righteousness.

---

[420] Ps 45:11; Rev 15:3,4
[421] Ex 34:13,14
[422] 1Co 10:20-22; Jer 7:18-20; Eze 16:26,27; Dt 32:16-20
[423] Hos 2:2-4
[424] Dt 5:29–WLC 110

May 9

The Third Commandment

The third commandment is:

Thou shall not take the name of the Lord thy God in vain: for the Lord will not hold him guiltless that takes his name in vain.[425]

This is likely the most violated commandment pertaining to our relationship with God. Although this warning is much deeper than using the names of God as curse words, we can start there. Hollywood, in its purely secular way, has been utterly successful in using the terms *God damn* and *Jesus Christ* as the coarsest form of cursing. Although there are expletives that we consider worse to use in public, none carry the guilt associated with the flippant use of God's holy name.

Perhaps on the dark side of irony, a person using his name in vain is actually recognizing the True God. For they do not curse by the name of any other so-called deity. I often hear atheists use these terms. Do they subconsciously acknowledge the very God that they deny exists? God will not be mocked forever. One day, every knee will bow and every tongue will confess of the true God.[426] The mocking shall cease, and they will find themselves facing the damnation they called down so loosely in prior days.

As we enter into the particulars of this third commandment, let us repent of our mishandling of God's name and his character.

---

[425] Ex 20:7–WLC Q111
[426] Is 45:23

MAY 10

REQUIREMENTS OF THE THIRD (PART 1)

We glanced at this commandment yesterday with the most common violations. Before we dig deeper into the forbidden portions of this command, let us explore our duties to it.

The third commandment requires proper honor to the name of God, his titles, attributes,[427] ordinances, the word, sacraments,[428] prayer, oaths, vows, lots, his works,[429] and whatsoever else there is whereby he makes himself known.

Our first priority to keeping this commandment is to know the fullness that God's name includes. It is every portion of his being, creation, and instruction to which his name is attached. God is the first cause for all things. Which part of this universe does not include God's dominion?

We are not left guessing as to our expected duties to this matter. As in all things God, the answers are detailed in the Scriptures. He has revealed the honor he expects as well as the manner in which we should execute it. Although Christ has fulfilled the Old Covenant traditions, we still honor God in our bodies that are now the temple in which his Spirit dwells and reigns. Therefore, we continue to have the highest duty to honor his holy name.

God, your name is worthy of our most careful worship.

---

[427] Mt 6:9; Dt 28:58; Ps 29:2; Ps 68:4; Rev 15:3,4
[428] Mal 1:14; Ecc 5:1; Ps 138:2; 1Co 11:24,25,28,29
[429] 1Ti 2:8; Jer 4:2; Ecc 5:2,4,5,6; Ac 1:24,26; Job 36:24—WLC Q112a

MAY 11

REQUIREMENTS OF THE THIRD (PART 2)

We are required to handle the attributes of God's name to:

Be holily and reverently used in thought, meditation, word, and writing[430] by a holy profession and answerable conversation to the glory of God[431] and the good of ourselves and others.[432]

These are the how-to responses of honoring God's name. As should be readily noticeable, they encompass our entire life and our relationships with God, ourselves, and others. If we keep God first in all things, the natural response will be respectful to ourselves and others. It always begins with God. This is the manner in which Jesus summed up the whole of the Law.

When we confess the God of the Bible, our actions follow our profession. Righteous actions react to a converted heart. One believes with the heart first, then confession is made unto righteousness.[433] The converted believer intends to honor God.

Once true profession is made, we are futher enabled by the Spirit to honor God through obedience. The reading of the Word, our thoughts, prayers, and meditations lead us to properly worship God and his great name. Honor him!

---

[430] Mal 3:16; Ps 8:1,3,4,9; Col 3:17; Ps 105:2,5; Ps 102:18
[431] 1Pe 3:15; Mic 4:5; Php 1:27; 1Co 10:31
[432] Jer 32:39; 1Pe 2:12–WLC Q112b
[433] Ro 10:10

MAY 12

SINS OF THE THIRD COMMAND
(PART 1)

When it comes to sinning against the holy name of God, we may be surprised at just how many ways we can fall short.

The sins forbidden in the third commandment are the not using of God's name as is required.[434]

We will be taking a detailed look at a long list of Scripturally supported sins of taking the Lord's name in vain. Today, we begin with the general idea that we are to understand these biblical requirements and keep them. We receive a very plain warning in Titus. As Paul states, "They profess *to know* God, but in works they deny Him, being abominable, disobedient, and disqualified for every good work."[435]

One cannot be a child of God and not expect to keep his commandments. The above Scripture shows clearly that disobedience is the action of denial of his law. It further states that the areas in which we might keep his law are nullified by these other areas of disobedience. It's like driving the speed limit, but running a stop sign. The judge will not give any weight to your obedience of the speed limit, but will certainly convict you of breaking the other law in and of itself.

Do we bargain with ourselves, trading unrighteous behavior against our stockpile of obedience? There's no such thing. There is just the denial of our profession of faith left in the wake of our sin.

---

[434] Mal 2:2–WLC Q113a
[435] Titus 1:16

MAY 13

SINS OF THE THIRD COMMAND
(PART 2)

The sins forbidden in the third commandment are not honoring God's name as required:

And the abuse of it in an ignorant, vain, irreverent, profane,[436] superstitious,[437] or wicked mentioning, or otherwise using his titles, attributes,[438] ordinances, or works by blasphemy, perjury,[439] all sinful cursing.[440]

We have previously covered cursing using God's name. The uses of the Lord's name in a profane manner has been so abused that it has become commonplace in our society. Just because we are numb to it does not mean that God takes any less offense.

In this section, take note that the offense includes every demeaning use of all characteristics and functions tied to his name. Whether we say God will not fulfill his promise or that he will perform a duty that is against his character, these are vain uses of his name. How about lying under oath? How many actually swear into their testimony with full conviction? Lying is its own sin, but it is exacerbated when tied to the Lord's name.

Lord, we beg forgiveness for our blasphemy against you.

---

[436] Ac 17:23; Pr 30:9; Mal 1:6,7,12; Mal 3:14

[437] 1Sa 4:3,4,5; Jer 7:4,9,10,14,31; Col 2:20-22

[438] 2Ki 18:30,35; Ex 5:2; Ps 139:20

[439] Ps 50:16,17; Isa 5:12; 2Ki 19:22; Lev 24:11; Zec 5:4; Zech 8:17

[440] 1Sa 17:43; 2Sa 16:5–WLC Q113b

MAY 14

SINS OF THE THIRD COMMAND (PART 3)

Today, we continue to explore the depth of blasphemy. Do we realize the offenses we commit against God? We sin when we break our

Oaths, vows,[441] and lots;[442] violating of our oaths and vows, if lawful; and fulfilling them, if of things unlawful;[443]

Perhaps one of the most important promises we make in the name of the Lord is on our wedding day. The marriage vows are not only a commitment to our spouse, but they are a verbal confirmation of a God-ordained union. *What God has joined together, let no man separate.* Divorce, outside of God's accepted reasons (such as adultery), is something that is a strong blasphemy of God's name. It is like saying, "God, I know what is better for me than you do."

Blasphemy shows a distrust of God and an arrogant trust in our selves. The humble person understands their fleshy wickedness and pride. They are certain to test all things with the Spirit, knowing that they would be deceived by trusting in only themselves.

God's Word is substantiated by his name. His promises can never fail because he has sworn by his own name and will do well to protect his holy name at all cost. Regardless of our circumstances, his name is worthy to be exalted.

Father, I have been so quick to guard my own pride when I should be glorifying you. Strengthen your servants.

---

[441] Jer 5:7; Jer 23:10; Dt 23:18; Ac 23:12,14
[442]) Esth. 3:7; Esth. 9:24; Ps 22:18
[443] Ps 24:4; Eze 17:16,18,19; Mk 6:26; 1Sa 25:22,32,33,34–WLC 113c

MAY 15

SINS OF THE THIRD COMMAND
(PART 4)

Sometimes, we find ourselves in situations that leave us with many questions. Questions are perfectly normal and acceptable when we do not have the answers we are looking for. However, we must be extremely careful not to turn our questions into accusations of God or changing his word to fit our circumstance. Such sins of blasphemy against God's holy name include:

Murmuring and quarrelling at, curious prying into,[444] and misapplying of God's decrees and providences,[445] misinterpreting, misapplying, or any way perverting the word or any part of it[446] to profane jests.[447]

The most common reaction to not agreeing with the plain Word of God is to give it a spin to fit our purposes. We try to justify our sin by saying, "God made me this way." We misapply the Cross by thinking we can follow through with our sin and ask forgiveness later. We are right, and therefore, God must be wrong.

God has plainly spoken. Sin is the breach of his perfection. We do not get any relief through ignorance or misinterpretation. There is one God, and we are not him. We worship him in spirit and truth; this is nonnegotiable. Ask God to align your heart and mind with his. He will not withhold his truth from an earnest and contrite seeker.

---

[444] Ro 9:14,19,20; Dt 29:29
[445] Ro 3:5,7; Ro 6:1,2; Ecc 8:11; Ecc 9:3; Ps 39 throughout
[446] Mt 5:21 to end; Eze 13:22; 2Pe 3:16; Mt 22:24-31
[447] Isa 32:13; Jer 33:34,36,38–WLC 113d

MAY 16

SINS OF THE THIRD COMMAND (PART 5)

This next section may sound like petty crimes. Why name such nonessentials? Because in God's economy, there is no such thing. Sin, in any form, was enough to require the death of Christ. Therefore, we are careful to examine all areas that defame God's name. Such as:

Curious or unprofitable questions, vain janglings, or the maintaining of false doctrines;[448] *abusing it, the creatures, or anything contained under the name of God, to charms*[449] *or sinful lusts and practices.*[450]

To clarify my comment on nonessentials, this is not say that every portion of Scripture is doctrinally of the same importance. In fact, as it states above, spending time mingling in the nonessentials is a violation of this very commandment. We should defend the plain truths of God's Word being careful not to spend hours in idle controversy.

We are not to participate in fortune telling. This includes horoscopes, astrology, or divination, which are those who communicate beyond this world. To enlighten this further, nobody communicates with your dead relative. They could be a total farce or it could be the dark reality of demonic luring. Satan's bait is enticing.

Lord, today I commit to follow your holy name alone. May your Spirit guide my conscience in the light of your Word. Amen.

---

[448] 1Ti 1:4,6,7; 1Ti 6:4,5,20; 2Ti 2:14; Tit 3:9
[449] Dt 18:10-14
[450] 2Ti 4:3,4; Ro 13:13,14; 1Ki 21:9,10; Jude 4–WLC Q113e

MAY 17

SINS OF THE THIRD COMMAND (PART 6)

The final section describing ways in which we take the Lord's name in vain are fairly self-explanatory. These blasphemies include:

The maligning, scorning, reviling,[451] or any wise opposing of God's truth, grace, and ways;[452] making profession of religion in hypocrisy, or for sinister ends;[453] being ashamed of it, or a shame to it, by unconformable, unwise, unfruitful,[454] and offensive walking, or backsliding from it.[455]

What if we agree with God's Word on every point, save one? It would be evident that we have only confirmed our point of unbelief; for where we have contention with the Word, we have contention with God who defines truth and righteousness. Just as sinning at one point in the Law makes us guilty of all of the whole, distrust in only one area of God's name brings reasonable doubt of the balance into question.

This moves us into the area of the authenticity of our faith. Paul calls this *having a form of godliness but denying the power thereof.* James calls our faith without works *dead.* Jesus calls our vanity *hypocrisy.* The third commandment sums it up as *taking the Lord's name in vain,* or *blasphemy.* The picture should now be crystal clear.

---

451 Ac 13:45; 1Jn 3:12; Ps 1:1; 2Pe 3:3; 1Pe 4:4
452 Ac 13:45,46,50; Ac 4:18; Ac 19:9; 1Th 2:16; Heb 10:29
453 2Ti 3:5; Mt 23:14; Mt 6:1,2,5,16
454 Mk 8:38; Ps 73:14,15; 1Co 6:5,6; Eph 5:15,16,17; Isa 5:4; 2Pe 1:8
455 Ro 2:23,24; Gal 3:1,3; Heb 6:6–WLC Q113f

MAY 18

WHY THE THIRD COMMANDMENT?

The reasons annexed to the third commandment, in these words, "The Lord thy God" and "For the Lord will not hold him guiltless that takes his name in vain[456]" are because he is the Lord and our God; therefore, his name is not to be profaned or any way abused by us,[457] especially because he will be so far from acquitting and sparing the transgressors of this commandment as that he will not suffer them to escape his righteous judgment,[458] albeit many such escape the censures and punishments of men.[459]

The above statement summarizes the importance that God holds for his name. The statement is made in the negative: *the Lord will not hold him guiltless.* This manner of speaking intensifies the seriousness of God compared to the cavalier demeanor of the person who justifies their actions. God is saying more than "You are guilty." He is also saying, "You are without excuse."[460]

Sure, we might escape justice while we walk this earth. In fact, who is going to convict us of blasphemy in this day and age? But we escape nothing in eternal matters. We live our secret lives in the uninhibited view of God. What sin we hide in the darkness is in the spotlight on the open stage of God. As his children, this is a good thing, for we know the importance of a godly life. We are refined by his rebuke.

---

[456] Ex 20:7
[457] Lev 19:12
[458] Eze 36:21,22,23; Dt 28:58,59; Zec 5:2,3,4
[459] 1Sa 2:12,17,22,24; 1Sa 3:13–WLC Q114
[460] Rom 1:20

MAY 19

THE FOURTH COMMANDMENT

The fourth commandment is:

Remember the Sabbath day to keep it holy. Six days shalt thou labor and do all thy work, but the seventh day is the Sabbath of the Lord thy God: in it, thou shalt not do any work, thou, nor thy son, nor thy daughter, thy man-servant, nor thy maid-servant, nor thy cattle, nor thy stranger that is within thy gates. For in six days the Lord made heaven and earth, the sea, and all that in them is, and rested the seventh day: wherefore the Lord blessed the Sabbath day, and hallowed it.[461]

The word *sabbath* is the Hebrew word for *cease*. Sometimes, we see it translated *rest*, as in "On the seventh day, God rested." However, this may give us imagery of God needing to rest to recoup some energy, which is contrary to God's omnipotence. Rather, this command is given to us because God has established a pattern for man to follow. We are to cease from working, one day per week.

The Sabbath is a holy day. This is to say that it is set apart from the rest of the week. It is consecrated to the worship of God. In the next few days, we will break down the details of this command. We will see the areas of our life that are influenced by its observance.

Lord, you have named your Sabbath day as holy. Help us to understand the importance of its observance and its significance.

---

[461] Ex 20:8-11–WLC Q115

MAY 20

REQUIREMENTS OF THE FOURTH

You might be thinking that the Church has not done a very good job at keeping Saturday, the seventh day, set apart for God. The fact is that the Church began observing the first day of the week, Sunday, as its holy day in honor of the Resurrection.

The fourth commandment requires of all men the sanctifying or keeping holy to God such set times as he hath appointed in his word, expressly one whole day in seven; which was the seventh from the beginning of the world to the resurrection of Christ, and the first day of the week ever since, and so to continue to the end of the world, which is the Christian Sabbath[462] and in the New Testament called the Lord's day.[463]

To have a day other than Saturday (the seventh day) be a Sabbath is not a new concept. Sabbaths can take place on more than one day per week. In the Old Testament, many holy days were set apart and observed as Sabbath days. These are mostly referred to as the feast-days of Israel. For example, the observance of Passover, the Feast of Trumpets, the Feast of Unleavened Bread, and many others were holidays that were observed on any day of the week in which they happened to fall.

This commandment is designated specifically for a weekly pattern, but it is not limited to such. It is all about rest and worship.

---

[462] Dt 5:12-14; Ge 2:2,3; 1Co 16:1,2; Ac 20:7; Mt 5:17,18; Isa 56:2,4,6,7
[463] Rev 1:10–WLC Q116

MAY 21

THE LORD'S DAY SET APART

How is the Sabbath or the Lord's Day to be sanctified?

The Sabbath or Lord's day is to be sanctified by an holy resting all the day,[464] *not only from such works as are at all times sinful, but even from such worldly employments and recreations as are on other days lawful.*[465]

This is bound to rub people the wrong way. Are we not to be living in a continual Sabbath rest since Christ eliminated the daily sacrifice? The answer is *yes*. We no longer have to perform the endless and tedious act of blood sacrifice. Christ's blood has covered our sins once and for all. However, the Sabbath was given to man for his benefit and God's word remains active that we shall *cease from work* that we might dedicate ourselves to his worship.

A generation ago, all commerce was closed on Sundays. Today, there is barely a memory of such a thing. After thousands of years of observance, it only took a short time to quit honoring the Lord's Day in the public eye. We should not be surprised that the world chose money over God.

The world is all about the obliteration of everything that is holy. The Church has lost her voice in the community; not so much because of the lack of numbers, but due to a lack of conviction. In what ways do you keep the Sabbath?

---

[464] Ex 20:8,10
[465] Ex 16:25-28; Ne 13:15-22; Jer 17:21,22–WLC Q117a

MAY 22

SET APART FOR WHAT?

Jesus rebuked the Pharisee's over-observance of the Sabbath Law. He states that, "The Sabbath was made for man and not man for the Sabbath." The idea is not to simply obey rules for the sake of keeping rules, but to physically rest and honor God spiritually.

And making it our delight to spend the whole time (except so much of it as is to be taken up in works of necessity and mercy[466]) in the public and private exercises of God's worship:[467] and to that end, we are to prepare our hearts, and with such foresight, diligence, and moderation, to dispose and seasonably dispatch our worldly business, that we may be the more free and fit for the duties of that day.[468]

God's instruction to keep the Sabbath was intended for you. That's right: for you and for me. Therefore, it is important for us to observe it as well as to understand its purpose. We are to partake in both the public and private worship of our Lord. This again emphasizes the importance of the *gathering of believers* to encourage each other onto good works throughout the other six days.

One question we should have for ourselves is, *Does my church equip and encourage the body of believers into faithful service, or is the church focused on sacraments, incense, and tradition?* Is your attendance just fulfilling an obligation, or are you edifying and being edified by others? The Sabbath is one day set apart to focus on worship.

---

[466] Mt 12:1-13
[467] Isa 58:13; Lk 4:16; Ac 20:7; 1Co 16:1,2; Ps 92:(title); Isa 66:23; Lev 23:3
[468] Ex 20:8; Lk 23:54,56; Ex 16:22,25,26,29; Ne 13:19–WLC Q117b

MAY 23

THE SABBATH DAY: GOVERNED

It is the responsibility of the leaders of households and of public faculties to ensure the observance of the Sabbath.

The charge of keeping the Sabbath is more specially directed to governors of families and other superiors because they are bound not only to keep it themselves but to see that it is observed by all those that are under their charge and because they are prone oft times to hinder them by employments of their own.[469]

God knows that once man is in motion to generate sustenance, he will take every opportunity to increase his harvest. People are weak in naturally following God. They must have godly leaders to follow. Children will not observe household rules without their parents. We tend to stray away without sound guidance.

I wonder what would happen if a given Super Store corporately observed the Sabbath, closing their doors on Sunday with a sign posted, "See you in Church." We might hope it would be rewarded by its actions, but that should not be its goal. The only purpose should be for rest and worship. It would still be an encouraging example.

As the head of my household, attending church has never been optional for my family. I furthermore did not give room for complaining. Today, as our children are in their late teens, they have adopted the routine of Sabbath observance. I pray for their continued obedience.

---

[469] Ex 20:10; Josh. 24:15; Ne 13:15,17; Jer 17:20,21,22; Ex 23:12–WLC Q118

MAY 24

SINS AGAINST THE SABBATH

The condition of one's heart is the key to faithful observance and true worship.

The sins forbidden in the fourth commandment are all omissions of the duties required,[470] all careless, negligent, and unprofitable performing of them, and being weary of them;[471] all profaning the day by idleness, and doing that which is in itself sinful;[472] and by all needless works, words, and thoughts, about our worldly employments and recreations.[473]

The account of Eutychus falling out of a third-story window to his death is attributed here to the judgment of his carelessness during Paul's extended sermon. One might question the validity of my conclusion. Yet I submit to you that it is the only possible conclusion, based on context. He fell to his death due to his careless observance of keeping the Sabbath. How? By falling asleep during a message that ran until midnight? Was his death justified? I will leave it for you to wrestle with. By the way, he was raised back to life.

The point is that we are not to be disobedient, in any regard, to keeping the Sabbath, including not having a focused heart during worship. Where is your mind on Sundays? Pray to keep spiritually focused.

---

[470] Eze 22:26
[471] Ac 20:7,9; Eze 33:30-32; Am 8:5; Mal 1:13
[472] Eze 23:38
[473] Jer 17:24,27; Isa 58:13–WLC Q119

MAY 25

PURPOSE OF THE SABBATH

A question for our introspection. Are we going to resist a day of rest, designed for the purpose of rest and worship of God, on the excuse that he is not worthy of even one day in seven to receive it?

The reasons annexed to the fourth commandment, the more to enforce it, are taken from the equity of it, God allowing us six days of seven for our own affairs and reserving but one for himself, in these words, "Six days shalt thou labor and do all thy work."[474] *From God's challenging a special propriety in that day, the seventh day is the sabbath of the Lord thy God.*[475]

God is the Lord of the Sabbath. By definition, if he is Lord, he must have objects subservient to Him. Furthermore as Lord, he is above all and is served by his whole creation. Have we considered that God has created us for worship? We are to worship him in every aspect of our lives, specifically setting aside one day dedicated to his worship alone.

Could it really be that we are so selfish, that we would rather work for ourselves an extra day, rather than rest from our labors and worship the King? Isn't it amazing how deceitful we are to ourselves? God has reserved one day for himself. Everything intended for us in keeping the Sabbath is for our good and the glory of the Father. Do not short yourself on your rest that you might offer proper praise.

---

[474] Ex 20:9
[475] Ex 20:10–WLC Q120a

MAY 26

THE SABBATH ORDAINED

The Sabbath is to be observed by man and will be enforced by God. Man might not keep the Sabbath for a season, but he shall not escape judgment for his disobedience forever. We are shown:

From the example of God, who in six days made heaven and earth, the sea, and all that in them is, and rested the seventh day and from that blessing which God put upon that day, not only in sanctifying it to be a day for his service, but in ordaining it to be a means of blessing to use in our sanctifying it. Wherefore the Lord blessed the Sabbath day and hallowed it.[476]

God gives his decree of the Sabbath, ordering it to be observed. There is no double standard between God and man. God has shown us by his example in the Creation. God did not rest on the seventh day because he was exhausted from his work. Rather, God established the pattern for the Sabbath day, which he ordained.

What does it mean, the Lord "hallowed" the Sabbath? For something to be holy means that it was set apart. The Lord is holy because he is separate from all evil. The Sabbath is a day dedicated to the sole worship of the Lord without unnecessary labors. We rest from our work and we are to worship. Worship includes all things honoring to God: reading of the Word, believing that Word, singing praise, teaching, tithes and offerings, discipleship, evangelism, celebrations of God's goodness and His holidays and the like. Enjoy his day of rest.

---

[476] Ex 20:11–WLC Q120b

MAY 27

REMEMBER THE SABBATH DAY (PRT 1)

The word "remember" is set in the beginning of the fourth commandment,[477] partly, because of the great benefit of remembering it, we being thereby helped in our preparation to keep it.[478]

We will take the next few days to discuss this topic of "remembering the Sabbath." I would first off like to make an observation of this Commandment written by the very finger of God. It could be taken, when God says to "remember the Sabbath day, to keep it holy," that he wants his people to keep this Commandment in mind from this day forward. And this is a true statement. But the very word *remember* speaks directly to a previous event.

I believe that the context of this Fourth Commandment is God telling his people to remember the establishment of the original Sabbath day. This is referred to in the body of the commandment itself, "For in six days the Lord made heaven and earth, the sea, and all that in them is, and rested the seventh day: wherefore the Lord blessed the Sabbath-day, and hallowed it." We see here that the Sabbath was not originated on Mt. Sinai, but at the completion of God's creation and would have been established in the garden of Eden.

Therefore, the remembrance of the Sabbath is our reflection foremost on the pattern that God demonstrated for us than as a reminder to prepare ourselves spiritually for this weekly event.

---

[477] Ex 20:8
[478] Ex 16:23; Lk 23:54,56 with Mk 15:42; Ne 13:19–WLC Q121a

MAY 28

REMEMBER THE SABBATH (PART 2)

Remembering the Sabbath day means we are mindful to keep it:

And in keeping it, better to keep all the rest of the commandments[479] and to continue a thankful remembrance of the two great benefits of creation and redemption, which contain a short abridgment of religion.[480]

> It is good to give thanks to the Lord, And to sing praises to Your name, O' Most High; To declare Your loving-kindness in the morning, And Your faithfulness every night.
>
> Psalm 92:1-2

Keeping the Sabbath is all about genuine worship. Remembering to keep the Sabbath begins with the proper preparation. Do you recall experiencing a Sunday service where you are just not able to concentrate or feel your spirit is absent? This could be because we have failed in preparation for God's Sabbath. We remembered to go to church, but we forgot our purposeful intention.

Saturday or Sunday is not the significance. We celebrate on Sunday in continuance of what early Christians established. The resurrection of Christ on Sunday became the day of our redemption. We honor God's Sabbath day by taking one day in the week and setting it apart unto the worship of God and for our resting from labor. It is our responsibility to remember to keep the Sabbath day. Prepare yourself to worship Christ, the Lord of the Sabbath.

---

[479] Ps 92:(title) compared with Ps 92:13,14; Eze 20:12,19,20
[480] Ge 2:2,3; Ps 118:22,24; Ac 4:10,11; Rev 1:10–WLC Q121b

MAY 29

REMEMBER THE SABBATH (PART 3)

We further are commanded to "remember" the Sabbath day:

Partly because we are very ready to forget it,[481] for that there is less light of nature for it,[482] and yet it restrains our natural liberty in things at other times lawful;[483] that it cometh but once in seven days, and many worldly businesses come between.

We mentioned, during the introduction of this fourth commandment, that less than a generation ago, commerce was closed on Sundays in honor of the Sabbath. Today, you would be hard-pressed to find many people who think there is any difference between Sunday or any other day of the week. The Scripture points out that we easily forget the sacred and easily tend toward secular.

Take a look at our reference to Nehemiah. The Israelites had recently been delivered from the Egyptians, been fed manna from heaven, received water that God provided from a rock, and were on a journey to the Promised Land. The next comment is that they were proud and refused to obey God, neither were they mindful of these awesome and miraculous wonders they had experienced.

When we read a biblical account like that, we are bewildered at their arrogance. Yet we too tend to be led by our natural tendencies. This is why we must remember to "remember," lest we forget.

---

[481] Eze 22:26
[482] Ne 9:14-17
[483] Ex 34:21–WLC Q121c

MAY 30

REMEMBER THE SABBATH (PART 4)

Carrying out the thought from yesterday that the Sabbath comes once in seven days and worldly businesses come between:

And too often take off our minds from thinking of it, either to prepare for it, or to sanctify it[484] *and that Satan with his instruments much labor to blot out the glory, and even the memory of it, to bring in all irreligion and impiety.*[485]

Yesterday, we reviewed that, over time, we tend to forget the honoring of the Sabbath. There is a progression in our failure; we let our minds forget the importance of the Day, then we forget to prepare our spirit for worship, and we ultimately forget that God has set this day apart unto his glory. If we do not live our spiritual lives with purposed intention, we will grow complacent and dishonor our God.

Enter Satan. Behind the scenes, constantly directing his demons, Satan works hard through subtle deceptions to take our eyes off the prize. Many of the distractions are not sinful in themselves, but they distract from our sanctified time dedicated to rest and worship. Satan can also distract us from our pure religion and brings false aspects of our worship. How? Foremost by introducing false interpretations of God's doctrine, like those pastors who teach hell does not exist or that homosexuality is acceptable. Once truth is compromised within a church, why keep a little rule like the Sabbath?

---

[484] Dt 5:14,15; Am 8:5
[485] La 1:7; Jer 17:21,22,23; Ne 13:15-23–WLC Q121d

MAY 31

GOLDEN RULES

We have completed the four commandments that entail man's duty to God. We now will begin the last six commandments.

The sum of the six commandments that contain our duty to man is to love our neighbor as ourselves[486] and to do to others what we would have them to do to us.[487]

Jesus summed up the commandments: *to love God and love each other.* If we are living according to these ideals, we will keep the entirety of the Law. The concept is simple. The execution, not so much. The principle for the remaining six commandments is this: if we are loving our neighbors, we will not sin against them, likewise if we are transgressing these laws, we cannot possibly be loving him.

I will reveal my hand now. The most intriguing to me of these six commandments is the tenth. So stick with me through this next month because you will want to have a good understanding as we enter in to our duties to our neighbors, family, friends, and strangers.

Once again, I encourage your diligence in working through the nuances of these commandments. It is not without consequence if we transgress a law that we did not understand. God does not wink at ignorance, but holds us accountable to know the Word he reveals.

Father, I pray that you will keep our minds sharp as we focus on the details of your last six commandments. Your every word has value.

---

[486] Mt 22:39
[487] Mt 7:12

June 1

The Fifth Commandment

The fifth commandment is:

Honor thy father and thy mother: that thy days may be long upon the land which the Lord thy God giveth thee.[488]

We now begin the Lord's commandments that relate to our duty to man. It is fitting that we begin with our responsibility to our parents. What greater people do we have in our lives than the ones who loved us unconditionally and raised us to the best of their abilities? The love that our parents show us is the best example we have of the love of God for his children. (I understand that not all of us have been raised in a healthy environment, but the example is given with respect to the purposed, God-honoring family.)

It is likely that the review of this commandment and the responsibilities surrounding it will generate some guilt and shame as we realize how far we have fallen short in its keeping. However, this review is not intended to beat us up over our failings, but to show the importance of giving due honor. Some repentance may be in order, and so shall we honor God in his conviction of our hearts.

Lord, we ask you to prepare our hearts for these next days as we want your Word to change us. As your servants, we open our lives to have you to change us freely as you will. That we may be transformed by the renewing of our minds, that we may prove what is good, your perfect will.

---

[488] Ex 20:12–WLC Q123

June 2

Father and Mother

This generation has seen all but the extinction of due respect to our elders.

By father and mother, in the fifth commandment, are meant, not only natural parents,[489] but all superiors in age, and gifts,[490] and especially such as, by God's ordinance, are over us in place of authority, whether in family, church, or commonwealth.[491]

As we have handed over the education and discipline of our children to the schools and daycare centers, we have released an all-important biblical instruction of *training up a child in the way they should go* into the secular world of psychobabble. In this, we fail.

The responsibility begins in the home. Parents or guardians are to provide instruction to their children in the fundamentals of this command. As children mature, they grow in responsibility. Proper honoring of our parents is good and acceptable before God. The lack of this discipline is sin, yet we most easily trample upon it.

As we continue through this fifth commandment, we will realize that it is the heart of the remaining commandments of our duties to man and ultimately our honoring of God. That I may not offend you, Lord, guide me in honoring your command.

---

[489] Pr 23:22,25; Eph 6:1,2
[490] 1Ti 5:1,2; Ge 4:20-22; Ge 45:8
[491] 2Ki 5:13; 2Ki 2:12; 2Ki 13:14; Gal 4:19; Isa 49:23–WLC Q124

June 3

Honoring Our Superiors

The animosity between parent and child can easily transfer to the disrespect of other authority figures. The Fifth Commandment includes our superiors.

Superiors are styled Father and Mother, both to teach them in all duties toward their inferiors, like natural parents, to express love and tenderness to them, according to their several relations[492] and to work inferiors to a greater willingness and cheerfulness in performing their duties to their superiors as to their parents.[493]

As we gain responsibilities in adolescence, we may realize that we will not succeed if we dishonor teachers or our employers. It is then likely that we will display honor to our superiors out of necessity. Yet in this, we continue to break this command. This is because we have yet to recognize our heart condition. We lack love and tenderness to our parents. We lack cheerfulness in the workplace.

We are beginning to see the breadth of this commandment. Perhaps like me, you are seeing some attitudes in your life that need to be addressed, even if they may not be apparent to others. God continues to burn off the dross in the lives of the ones whom he loves.

Lord, thank you for refining my heart and my life. I long for you and am thirsty for truth. Give me a heart of compassion for my father, my mother, and for my superiors. Let me honor you by honoring them.

---

[492] Eph 6:4; 2Co 12:14; 1Th 2:7,8,11; Nu 11:11,12
[493] 1Co 4:14,15,16; 2Ki 5:13–WLC Q125

JUNE 4

THE BIG PICTURE

We can demonstrate our fear of God by honoring our parents, those in authority, and in submitting ourselves to our peers.

The general scope of the fifth commandment is the performance of those duties that we mutually owe in our several relations, as inferiors, superiors, or equals.[494]

The scope continues to deepen as we see now that we are to honor all people. Just as we began agreeing that our superiors as well as our parents must be honored, now it includes everyone else. The command does not take away the proper hierarchy of authority; not that a parent must submit unto the child. The principal that Jesus gave to us, *to love others as we love ourselves*, is shown in the general attitude of this commandment.

The biblical command could not be any more clear than the apostle Peter's summary to "honor all men. Love the brotherhood. Honor the king." We will explore the depth of our relationships with these groups in the coming days. The scope of this command is broad, but the Scriptures provide refined details.

The idea is to put others ahead of ourselves without ulterior motive. The worldly will show respect to others, but only as it advances their selfish cause. God looks into the heart. If pride is our motivation, we have failed this command. In humble obedience, we succeed.

---

[494] Eph 5:21; 1Pe 2:17; Ro 12:10–WLC Q126

June 5

Honoring Our Superiors (Part 1)

We live in a world where authority figures have set rules that infiltrate our everyday life. Whether at work, at play, or in government, we deal with bosses, referees, and law enforcers.

The honor that inferiors owe to their superiors is all due reverence in heart, word, and behavior; prayer and thanksgiving for them;[495] *imitation of their virtues and graces;*[496] *willing obedience to their lawful commands and counsels,*[497] *due submission to their corrections.*[498]

Malachi 1:6 says that we honor or dishonor God by the way in which we treat others. Our heart toward others may be showing resentment to God. Malachi's words foreshadow Jesus' condemnation of the goats at Judgment.

This command qualifies all those who fit a figure of authority. You might be thinking, *But you have no idea how demeaning my boss treats me!* You might be right that I don't understand, but God certainly does. God further understands exactly what attitude you have, even when it is internalized. This realization should give cause to caution your temper.

Lord, I repent of times I have offended you while despising another. Please help me see your face when I interact with others.

---

[495] Mal 1:6; Lev 19:3; Pr 31:28; 1Pe 3:6; Lev 19:32; 1Ki 2:19; 1Ti 2:1,2
[496] Heb 13:7; Php 3:17
[497] Eph 6:1,2,5,6,7; 1Pe 2:13,14; Ro 13:1-5; Heb 13:17; Pr 4:3,4; Pr 23:22; Ex 18:19,24
[498] Heb 12:9; 1Pe 2:18,19,20–WLC Q127a

June 6

Honoring Our Superiors (Part 2)

Our duties to the Fifth Commandment continue in the manner in which we demonstrate the honor of our superiors.

The honor that continues in our fidelity to[499] defense[500] and maintenance of their persons and authority according to their several ranks and the nature of their places,[501] bearing with their infirmities and covering them in love[502] so they may be an honor to them and to their government.[503]

This section covers the how of our responsibilities to this commandment. We are to be faithful to these persons in respect to the office they hold. In other words, we are to honor them irrespective of their personalities. We know that God is no respecter of persons. We follow his lead by respecting the position rather than the personality.

This commandment is not a call to passivity. We are to be active in loving them toward being honorable themselves. Pray for them. Let your light shine before them that they may see your good works and glorify the Father who is in heaven.

Our attitude should seek to match that of Christ's. Think about all he bears on our behalf and yet remains in continuous prayer for us.

---

[499] Tit 2:9,10
[500] 1Sa 26:15,16; 2Sa 18:3; Esther 6:2
[501] Mt 22:21; Ro 13:6,7; 1Ti 5:17,18; Gal 6:6; Ge 45:11; Ge 47:12
[502] 1Pe 2:18; Pr 23:22; Ge 9:23
[503] Ps 127:3-5; Pr 31:23—WLC Q127b

June 7

Dishonoring Others Is Sin

The failure of our duties to the Fifth Commandment is sin. As believers, we are to be avoiding the snares that tempt us to fail.

The sins of inferiors against their superiors are all neglect of the duties required toward them; envying at, contempt of, and rebellion against, their persons and places,[504] in their lawful counsels, commands, and corrections;[505] cursing, mocking, and all such refractory and scandalous carriage as proves a shame and dishonor to them and their government.[506]

This command does not stand against taking appropriate measures to change a negative relationship. Neither does it call bad superiors good. We may, in a democratic process, vote a representative out of their position. A league might fire a referee who makes biased calls. Our main directive is to be honorable for the sake of honoring God.

You might be saying, "The heart of this commandment is to honor my parents, and I can't very well fire them or vote them off the island." That's right, you can't. But here it comes back to honoring them with a godly love. Do you demonstrate patience and unconditional love? Are you praying for those who persecute you? Are you avoiding talking behind backs? Is your focus Jesus Christ? These are the ways to avoid such sin. These are heart issues.

---

[504] Mt 15:4-6; Nu 11:28,29; 1Sa 8:7; Isa 3:5; 2Sa 15:1-12; Ex 21:15; 1Sa 10:27
[505] 1Sa 2:25; Dt 21:18-21
[506] Pr 30:11,17; Pr 19:26—WLC Q128

JUNE 8
TURNING THE TABLES (PART 1)

Previously, we have been addressing our duties as subordinates. Today, we begin with man's duty as a superior.

It is required of superiors according to that power they receive from God and that relation wherein they stand, to love, pray for, and bless their inferiors,[507] to instruct, counsel, and admonish them; countenancing, commending,[508] and rewarding such as do well.[509]

When Jesus, on two separate occasions, turned over the tables of the moneychangers and beat them out of the temple with his makeshift whip, he was neither dishonoring his authority nor sinning in any way. There are acceptable times for righteousness to be displayed in expressed action. Being dutiful to honor others does not mean rolling over and playing dead. In fact, the opposite is true.

It is the responsibility of superiors to stand firm in the defense of righteousness. Leaders are, by definition, to lead. The instruction, however, is to lead in a godly manner. Through one's exhibited godly life, many shall fear and trust the Lord.

Lord, may my life be glorifying to you. May I live in a manner that testifies of your goodness, your justice, and your mercy. May I perform my duties in times of leadership as you would approve.

---

[507] Col 3:19; Tit 2:4; 1Sa 12:23; Job 1:5; 1Ki 8:55,56; Heb 7:7; Ge 49:28
[508] Dt 6:6,7; Eph 6:4; 1Pe 3:7; 1Pe 2:14; Ro 13:3
[509] Esth. 6:3–WLC Q129a

June 9

Turning the Tables (Part 2)

Our duties to the Fifth Commandment, as it pertains to our position as a superior to others, continue in our actions of:

Discountenancing, reproving, and chastising such as do ill;[510] protecting, and providing for them all things necessary for soul and body;[511] and by grave, wise, holy, and exemplary carriage, to procure glory to God, honor to themselves, and so to preserve that authority which God hath put upon them.[512]

Certainly, it would be impossible to give full attention to every need that crosses our paths. However, that does not exempt us from not using our spiritual gifts at all. We all stand to face Christ the Judge who condemns goats who ignore their responsibilities to others.

In case you think that I may be pushing this too far, it is the exact analogy that Jesus expressed. He addressed those whose actions did not match their profession with the words, "Depart from me, I never knew you." These will ask, "Lord, when did we see you and not honor you?" Then, the Lord will answer, saying, "Truly I say unto you, inasmuch as you did not honor the least of these, you did not honor me."

Our positions of leadership deserve our most humble and godly effort. Giving lip service to our faith is not enough.

Lord, we long to hear you say, "Well done!"

---

[510] Ro 13:3,4; Pr 29:15; 1Pe 2:14
[511] Job 29:12-17; Isa 1:10,17; Eph 6:4; 1Ti 5:8
[512] 1Ti 4:12; Tit 2:3-5; 1Ki 3:28; Tit 2:15—WLC 129b

JUNE 10

SINFUL NEGLECT (PART 1)

Leadership duties to the subordinate relationships we encounter are certainly important. However, it is also important that we not misrepresent these duties or abuse our authority.

The sins of superiors are, besides the neglect of the duties required of them, an inordinate seeking of themselves, their own glory, ease, profit, or pleasure;[513] *commanding things unlawful or not in the power of inferiors to perform;*[514] *counseling, encouraging, or favoring them in that which is evil.*[515]

As always, where pride leads, sin crouches at the door. The abuse of power is an easy snare in which to become entangled. Because there is a sense of power when we lead, we can associate this with respect. Therefore, the more one abuses authority, the more worth they might experience. Like a narcotic, increased abuse is necessary to obtain the next level of perceived power. A vicious cycle, indeed.

But we are not here to discuss the psychology of this sin, just the fact that the improper implementation of our authority breaks God's command. The shadow of our sin can corrupt others. Our trespass increases if we direct our subordinates to act likewise or in another unrighteous manner. Ask God to reveal any area in your life where you may be failing in righteous leading.

---

[513] Eze 34:2-4 (2) Php 2:21 (3) Jn 5:44; Jn 7:18; Isa 56:10,11; Dt 17:17
[514] Da 3:4-6; Ac 4:17,18; Ex 5:10-18; Mt 23:2,4
[515] Mt 14:8 compared with Mk 6:24; 2Sa 13:28; 1Sa 3:13—WLC Q130a

JUNE 11

SINFUL NEGLECT (PART 2)

We can overstep our authority with others by dictating rather than leading in a righteous manner. However, the sin exponentially increases when evil is the intended action or result of the instruction we give to our inferiors, by:

Dissuading, discouraging, or discountenancing them in that which is good;[516] correcting them unduly; careless exposing or leaving them to wrong, temptation, and danger;[517] provoking them to wrath;[518] or any way dishonoring themselves or lessening their authority by an unjust, indiscreet, rigorous, or remiss behavior.[519]

The warnings listed are for all who would do anything short of being an honorable leader. Failures like directing inferiors to sin or omitting the correcting of their own sinful actions.

With Satan at the helm, as the god of this world (system), evil leadership is everywhere. Unrighteous leaders have abused their power since the earliest historical accounts. Many leaders walk as wolves in sheep's clothing, only appearing to lead righteously. Whether one misleads a nation or just an individual, the sin of abusing our role as superiors is rebuked and judged by God.

May the Holy Spirit make us sensitive to this commandment.

---

[516] Jn 7:46-49; Col 3:21; Ex 5:17
[517] 1Pe 2:18-20; Heb 12:10; Dt 25:3; Ge 38:11,26; Ac 18:17
[518] Eph 6:4
[519] Ge 9:21; 1Ki 12:13-16; 1Ki 1:6; 1Sa 2:29-31–WLC Q130b

JUNE 12

EQUALITY

We have covered our duties to both our superiors and our inferiors. Today, we look at our responsibilities to our equals.

The duties of equals are to regard the dignity and worth of each other in giving honor to go one before another[520] and to rejoice in each other's gifts and advancement as their own.[521]

There are no surprises encountered here. Those of us, who have the mind of Christ, strive to build each other up in the Lord. If each person, of equal position, regards the other as more important than themselves, we will live out this command properly.

Children demonstrate our fleshy attitudes. Consider the child with a new toy. They want the whole world to know they have it, but they do not want anyone else to play with it. They argue about who gets to go down the slide first, receive the first ice cream cone, or be the first up to bat. Some adults behave as poorly. They want you to know how many Bible verses they memorized, when they're fasting, how long they raked the leaves at outreach event.

The mark of mature Christ followers is the one who builds up others in the faith. We are to encourage each other, and in this manner, we grow together and demonstrate the love of Christ to the world around us. Use your time rejoicing in the gifts of others. Build your community of believers to shine in the midst of a perverse and dark generation.

---

[520] 1Pe 2:17; Ro 12:10
[521] Ro 12:15,16; Php 2:3,4–WLC Q131

JUNE 13

MALFUNCTIONING VALUE

It is very easy to see the faults in others. However, recognizing our own shortcomings in how we treat people is a difficult task.

The sins of equals are, besides the neglect of the duties required,[522] the undervaluing of the worth, envying the gifts, grieving at the advancement of prosperity one of another,[523] and usurping pre-eminence one over another.[524]

The cold hard truth is that we just do not give energy to those whom we should most demonstrate our love. While at home, my guard goes down, my patience is short, and my attitude is not tempered. This is neglect any way you slice it. Neglect of my family, yes, but primarily neglect of my responsibilities to myself. The apostle Paul says that we must beat down our bodies daily and not let our flesh rule over us. It is up to us to walk in the Spirit. Why walk? Because it is a step-by-step process.

If we keep in step with the Spirit and pray always, we will be aware of those around us and our responsibility to them. We might see their needs or experience their gifts. We will repress jealousy, resentment, and destroy pride.

Lord, keep me aware that I am always representing you. Help me to encourage others. Help me to keep my eyes on the prize.

---

[522] Ro 13:8
[523] 2Ti 3:3; Ac 7:9; Gal 5:26; Nu 12:2; Esth. 6:12,13
[524] 3 Jn 9; Lk 22:24—WLC Q132

JUNE 14

THAT YOUR DAYS MAY BE LONG

The fifth is the first commandment with a promise attached to those who keep it. This shows us that God rewards obedience of honoring our parents. It further highlights the importance he places on our relationships.

The reason annexed to the fifth commandment, in these words, "That thy days may be long upon the land which the Lord thy God gives thee," [525] is an express promise of long life and prosperity, as far as it shall serve for God's glory and their own good, to all such as keep this commandment. [526]

God is covenantal. The relationships we have, beginning with our parents, should reflect the relationship that God has entered with his people. The blessings of a *long life and prosperity* to those who honor their earthly relationships is God's way of demonstrating his pleasure with our obedience. It also shows God's high value for our relationships.

It is no surprise then that maintaining relationships require a lot of work. Personality conflicts, power struggles, and pride can easily enter in to disrupt or destroy a godly relationship. We are to be accountable to our relationships and to diligently ensure the honoring of one another. One benefit we may receive is a long, prosperous life. But our primary goal is to glorify God through our actions. We are servants to a loving Creator who rewards obedience.

---

[525] Ex 20:12
[526] Dt 5:16; 1Ki 8:25; Eph 6:2,3–WLC 133

JUNE 15

THE SIXTH COMMANDMENT

As much as we learned about the depth of honoring our father and mother, it may seem unnecessary for the need to explore the next.

The sixth commandment is, Thou shalt not kill.[527]

This should be obvious, right? We all understand that it is morally wrong to murder someone. So what need have we to dig further into this? The answer is that we might know the heart of God. God's Law shows us his universal standards and what man's heart should reflect. We further will learn that this command does not only pertain to physical killing in cold blood, but also prohibits the evil thoughts and intentions against someone who has angered us.

Jesus introduced a twist to define murder; however, it is really a revelation of God's heart. God never changes, so it is not as if Jesus amends the commandment. He only shows its true depth. We shall explore this in closer detail in upcoming days.

For today, meditate on God's four-word statement, *Thou shalt not kill.* Consider how important life is to God. God is the source of all life, and even further, he has given man something special that no other creatures possess: a conscience, which he stamped into us when he created man *in his image*. Man does not run on instinct alone as other creatures, but under moral principles that God manifests to everyone. God gives life; man must not take it away.

---

[527] Ex 20:13–WLC Q134

JUNE 16

DEFENDING LIFE (PART 1)

All life is created and sustained by Almighty God. Only man has been stamped with his image, receiving an eternal soul by his very breath. We carefully handle human life accordingly.

The duties required in the sixth commandment are all careful studies and lawful endeavors to preserve the life of ourselves and others[528] by resisting all thoughts and purposes, subduing all passions,[529] and avoiding all occasions, temptations,[530] and practices, which tend to the unjust taking away the life of any.[531]

The opening comments above are all about the conscious consideration of how we handle the life of one another. Fallen and depraved because of sin, man's heart is desperately wicked and would murder in an instant if not restrained. A two-year-old would kill over candy if he had the strength to do so. We discipline children, and as they mature, they learn the consequences of uncivilized behavior.

Because of the sanctity of life, we must take every thought captive in regard to humanity. We must resist every thought of unjustly harming another. No other place is this more sacred than in the protection of life within the womb. In this regard, sinful man has thrown his conscience into the pit. Rest assured, every soul will be counted.

Lord, we repent of the selfish evil within our hearts.

---

[528] Eph 5:28,29; 1Ki 18:4
[529] Jer 26:15,16; Ac 23:12,16,17,21,27; Eph 4:26,27
[530] 2Sa 2:22; Dt 22:8; Mt 4:6,7; Pr 1:10,11,15,16
[531] 1Sa 24:12; 1Sa 26:9-11; Ge 37:21,22–WLC Q135a

JUNE 17

DEFENDING LIFE (PART 2)

Penetrating much deeper than the outright taking of life, the sixth commandment further requires:

Just defense against violence,[532] *patient bearing of the hand of God, quietness of mind, cheerfulness of spirit;*[533] *a sober use of meat, drink, physic (medication), sleep, labor, and recreations;*[534] *by charitable thoughts, love, compassion, meekness, gentleness, kindness.*[535]

Certainly, life is to be protected at every cost. However, the high regard for human life extends to the person's well-being. If our life is worth saving, it is also worth preserving and nurturing. Nowhere is this better demonstrated than in the mother's love and care for her children. We honor the sixth commandment when we display compassion for our fellow man, in both his life and his health.

The world has been in constant turmoil. Nations rage for control at the hands of evil men. It is not difficult for us to see that our own nation has taken many lives and destroyed many territories for their own gain. One day, we all will stand accountable, not only for not protecting life above all else, but for our indifference to the suffering around us. For those of us who have the Holy Spirit, we should all the more display his fruits in our compassion of human life.

---

[532] Ps 82:4; Pr 24:11,12; 1Sa 14:45

[533] Jas 5:7-11; Heb 12:9; 1Th 4:11; 1Pe 3:3,4; Ps 37:8-11; Pr 17:22

[534] Pr 25:16,27; 1Ti 5:23; Isa 38:21; Ps 127:2; Ecc 5:12; 2Th 3:10,12; Pr 16:26; Ecc 3:4,11

[535] 1Sa 19:4,5; 1Sa 22:13,14; Ro 13:10; Lk 10:33,34; Col 3:12,13–WLC Q135b

JUNE 18

DEFENDING LIFE (PART 3)

Our final duties to the Sixth Commandment are:

Peaceable, mild, and courteous speeches and behavior;[536] *forbearance, readiness to be reconciled, patient bearing and forgiving of injuries, and requiting good for evil;*[537] *comforting and assisting the distressed, and protecting and defending the innocent.*[538]

Jesus was clear to show us the depth of our depravity. We might argue that we have not murdered anyone. Jesus tells us to examine the attitude of our hearts. For if we are angry with someone without cause, we are in danger of the judgment. In the kingdom of God, it is all about the condition of one's heart.

The Sermon on the Mount begins with several phrases known as the Beatitudes. The word "beatitude" is derived from the Latin adjective *beatus,* which means happy, fortunate, or blissful. These set the stage for the godly attitudes that Jesus describes in the rest of his sermon. What many tend to miss, however, are Jesus' warnings against unrighteous attitudes and behaviors.

We can see now the extent to which our accountability reaches in this commandment. True happiness resides in individuals who honor God in their full being: heart, mind, and strength. Finally, Jesus exclaims our responsibility is to "be perfect, as God is perfect."

---

[536] Jas 3:17; 1Pe 3:8-11; Pr 15:1; Judges 8:1-3
[537] Mt 5:24; Eph 4:2,32; Ro 12:17,20,21
[538] 1Th 5:14; Job 31:19,20; Mt 25:35,36; Pr 31:8,9–WLC Q135c

JUNE 19

FORBIDDEN DEATH (PART 1)

There are justified reasons for taking the life of a man. God is a righteous God and he establishes the laws of justice. However, it is not acceptable for the individuals or governments to judge outside of God's law.

The sins forbidden in the sixth commandment are all taking away the life of ourselves or of others,[539] except in case of public justice, lawful war, or necessary defense[540] (and) the neglecting or withdrawing the lawful and necessary means of preservation of life.[541]

This generation has seen a turn from the preservation of life to the demanding of our rights to take it away. From pregnancy being turned over to the "choice" of the mother rather than the "right to life" of the baby inside. Onward to the assisted suicide debate where people claim to be fighting on terms of compassion over suffering. These are topics without a gray area in God's law.

There is nothing that happens outside of God's knowledge and to his ultimate glory. Furthermore, nothing takes place in the life of a believer, that works against their ultimate good. This is not to say that evil is good, for that is blasphemy, but only that evil has no dominion over God's purposes. There is no better place to be than in the center of God's will. Therefore, we are wise to not insert our will, regardless of our intentions, over what God prohibits.

---

[539] Ac 16:28; Ge 9:6
[540] Nu 35:31,33; Jer 48:10; Dt 20 throughout; Ex 22:2,3
[541] Mt 25:42,43; Jas 2:15,16; Ecc 6:1,2–WLC Q136a

JUNE 20

FORBIDDEN DEATH (PART 2)

Unwarranted death also includes those actions that in any way harm our life or other's. The forbidden sins of the Sixth Commandment continue with:

Sinful anger, hatred, envy, desire of revenge;[542] all excessive passions, distracting cares;[543] immoderate use of meat, drink, labor, and recreations.[544]

These actions, which fall in the middle of this section's warnings, seem petty when compared to murder. However, it is important to realize just how clear God's Word truly is when it comes to issues of the heart. The epistle of James clearly shows us that sin begins with our own desires and that it is here where we must stop it before we are entangled by our own lusts.

Is it strange that God includes our handling of food in the same category as murder? Look at your children: would you let them consume candy and pop all day? Of course not, because we know that without proper nutrition, their health will degrade. Therefore, any degree of neglect to the high value of life is sin.

Our objective, as believers, is to live a life that is holy and pleasing to God. If we allow the Holy Spirit to lead, he will prompt us to do what is right and also convict us when we do not.

---

[542] Mt 5:22; 1Jn 3:15; Lev 19:17; Pr 14:30; Ro 12:19
[543] Eph 4:31; Mt 6:31,34
[544] Lk 21:34; Ro 13:13; Ecc 12:12; Ecc 2:22,23; Isa 5:12–WLC Q136b

JUNE 21

FORBIDDEN DEATH (PART 3)

As you read these next sinful actions included within the Sixth Commandment, feel free to eliminate any which never applied to you.

Provoking words, oppression, quarrelling, striking, wounding,[545] and whatsoever else tends to the destruction of the life of any.[546]

I know. I couldn't eliminate any either. We want to say that we are not destroyers of life, but we know that we have fallen short.

If there was a one hundred dollar bill sitting on table, people who know me would say about me, "He would never think about taking it." What they mean is that they know my character and that I would not take it. Because the truth is, I am thinking about taking it! In my selfish mind, that bill is much better in my pocket than there on the table. I just do not take it because my conscience warns me of sin.

Evil does reside within me; that is, in my flesh. That fact should not be ignored. However, as a born-again believer, the Holy Spirit testifies within me that I am a child of God, and therefore, I should give no foothold to my flesh. I have been crucified with Christ and have died to sin; therefore, how can I live in it any longer? To do so is to live contrary to who I now am. This battle against our flesh continues, but we know that we are more than conquerors through Jesus Christ.[547]

---

[545] Pr 15:1; Pr 12:18; Eze 18:18; Ex 1:14; Gal 5:15; Pr 23:29; Nu 35:16,17,18,21
[546] Ex 21:18 to end–WLC Q136c
[547] Gal 2:20, Rom 7 and 8

JUNE 22

THE CHASTE SERVANT

Today, we begin our look into the Seventh Commandment.

The seventh commandment is, Thou shalt not commit adultery.[548]

Keep in mind the varying degrees that God has intended for us to understand in his one-sentence commandments. God not only wants us to keep the main theme of his law, but also to be weary of our initial lusts that lead to their final demise.

In his earthly ministry, Jesus turned the Pharisees' view of the Law on its ear. People can grow very proud of their achievements in keeping the law, thinking they are God-pleasers. However, just as Jesus relates our anger to murder, he relates our sexual lust to the very act of adultery. Who can escape this? The answer is no one. Jesus is showing us the principle intention of the Law is not to make us righteous, but rather to show us our inability to keep it. The Law exposes man's depravity, driving the humble to their knees in recognition of their need for a Savior. However, the proud harden their hearts and glory in themselves alone.

Over the next couple of days, we will explore the related adultery topics, the tangential sins and the attitudes that endanger our sanctification. We are to live holy lives unto the Lord. Are we willing to entertain the slightly unclean as long as it's not noticeable to anyone else? Let's prepare our hearts as I know we will be challenged.

---

[548] Ex 20:14–WLC Q137

JUNE 23

CHASTITY (PART 1)

If we have learned anything about the Commandments so far, it is that they encompass our entire person and not just the outward disposition that we allow the world to witness.

The duties required in the seventh commandment are chastity in body, mind, affections, words, and behavior[549] and the preservation of it in ourselves and others.[550]

One primary difference between God and our legal system is that the law only cares about one's outward behavior, where God is looking at the thoughts and intentions of the heart. The justice system cannot see the inward parts, but God does. I find it strange that I can convince myself that God might miss seeing my sin if I keep it quiet and dark. I know I'm deceiving myself, but that is the daily battle we face.

The world knows nothing of chastity. The attitude is one of only pride, exposure, and pleasure. Now, we might display modesty in ourselves, but our flesh desires the exposure of others. How about reality television like *The Bachelor* or *The Bachelorette*? These shows only glorify lust over multiple relationships that all run aground in the end. There is no holiness or chastity in these relationships, so how could there be anything left to maintain monogamous satisfaction? The odds run against them. Are we justified in allowing ourselves to call this entertainment? I say we are guilty of adultery if we do.

---

[549] 1Th 4:4; Job. 31:1; 1Co 7:34; Col 4:6; 1Pe 2:3
[550] 1Co 7:2,35,36–WLC Q138a

June 24

Chastity (Part 2)

The portal that Satan uses to entice us is our eyes. We covet from our lust of the flesh, the lust of the eyes, and the pride of life.[551] The Lord, however, instructs us through the hearing of his Word. The Holy Spirit prompts us through our knowledge of God's Word to maintain:

Watchfulness over the eyes and all the senses;[552] *temperance, keeping of chaste company, modesty in apparel.*[553]

These traits do not register with the world. The sad part is that they barely mean much more in the visible church. What is once considered outrageous in one generation becomes the norm in the next. The only way to maintain the standard is to have an anchored reference.

Avoiding the pitfalls of adultery is much more than ending up in a motel with someone other than your spouse. It begins with shielding our eyes at the moment of attraction. It continues with avoiding flirtatious conversation or wearing clothing that invites such an opportunity. We must be watchful for every snare of enemy.

Lord, once again we see the subtleties of the weakness of our flesh. Forgive our lack of consideration into just how quickly we can offend your holiness and our purity. Strengthen our resistance to this world and our reliance upon your Spirit to live as you have called us.

---

[551] 1Jn 2:16
[552] Job. 31:1
[553] Ac 24:24,25; Pr 2:16-20; 1Ti 2:9–WLC Q138b

JUNE 25

CHASTITY (PART 3)

Our new sensitivity since yesterday's study may have left us thinking that all sexual desire is wrong. Not at all. God has designed us with the desire for, not only procreation, but as the highest expression of love within a marriage. Therefore, our faithful duties continue in:

Marriage by those that have not the gift of continence;[554] conjugal love, and cohabitation; diligent labor in our callings;[555] shunning all occasions of uncleanness, and resisting temptations thereunto.[556]

The biblical mandate within the covenant of marriage is not to abstain from sexual pleasures, but to satisfy each other's needs and desires. The marriage is completed with the honoring between the spouses for their roles in the household.

God's law forbids intimate relations outside of marriage. One may not seek satisfaction before marriage or elsewhere after marriage. These types of acts are all adulterous. Furthermore, it is well published that the most sexually fulfilled people are those who honor God's plan within marriage.

It's never too late to honor God with one's life. Just as Jesus told the woman caught in adultery, "I do not condemn you. Go now and sin no more." As it is with any sin—repent and believe.

---

[554] 1Co 7:2,9
[555] Pr 5:19,20; 1Pe 3:7; Pr 31:11,27,28
[556] Pr 5:8; Ge 39:8-10–WLC Q138c

JUNE 26

NOTHING IMPURE (PART 1)

Our duties to honoring the Seventh Commandment are one of the best ways we can honor God. Because the manner in which we demonstrate our relationships on earth show the true value we place on our eternal relationship with the Father. Today, we begin our extensive look into the prohibited areas of this commandment.

The sins forbidden in the seventh commandment, besides the neglect of the duties required,[557] *are adultery, fornication, rape, incest, sodomy, and all unnatural lusts,*[558] *all unclean imaginations, thoughts, purposes, and affections.*[559]

It may seem unnecessary to cover these prohibitions in such detail. However, because the Bible provides such a thorough and comprehensive list of examples, we are saved from any ambiguity into such matters. We will do well to maintain the understanding that what our imaginations entertain is no less sinful than the actual actions. God looks on the heart.

God may be patient, but he is not slack in the judgment of fornication. We are not to pursue self-satisfaction, but work unto the glory of the Lord. For *those who practice such things will not inherit the kingdom of God.* If this does not send a shutter down your spine, then you do not have any comprehension of God's righteousness nor the cost of redemption.

---

[557] Pr 5:7
[558] Heb 13:4; Gal 5:19; 2Sa 13:14; 1Co 5:1; Ro 1:24,27; Lev 20:15,16
[559] Mt 5:28; Mt 15:19; Col 3:5–WLC Q139a

JUNE 27

NOTHING IMPURE (PART 2)

We can be our own worst judge. We tend to justify our actions or pretend that it is not that big of a deal. However, when it comes to corrupting the pure life that God intends for us, we must route out:

All corrupt or filthy communications, or listening thereunto; wanton looks, impudent or light behavior, immodest apparel;[560] prohibiting of lawful[561] and dispensing with unlawful marriages; allowing, tolerating, keeping of stews, and resorting to them.[562]

In reference to the opposite sex, I have heard some married people say, "I can look at the menu all I want." There is no room in God's purity for the entertaining of such sin. How can we be guarding our hearts when we are filling our eyes with temptation?

On the other side of the equation are those, particularly women, who do not dress conservatively. If your dress is revealing or provocative, you are not only breaking this commandment, but you are, more importantly, allowing an opportunity for the stumbling of those who look upon you. Certainly, even conservative apparel does not stop a man from his own lust, but we are to strive for purity on display.

Reflect on your modesty. How are you affecting others?

---

[560] Eph 5:3,4; Pr 7:5,21,22; Isa 3:16; 2Pe 2:14; Pr 7:10,13
[561] 1Ti 4:3; Lev 18:1-21; Mal 2:11,12
[562] 1Ki 15:12; 2Ki 23:7; Dt 23:17,18; Lev 19:29; Jer 5:7; Pr 7:24-27–WLC Q139b

JUNE 28

NOTHING IMPURE (PART 3)

Perhaps you have considered those who live in polygamy and wondered about the many accounts in the Old Testament? Has God changed his standard, or are we the ones who have abandoned it? God is unchanging and he never approved of:

Entangling vows of single life, undue delay of marriage;[563] having more wives or husbands than one at the same time;[564] unjust divorce, or desertion.[565]

God has set the highest standard for those who live the single life, who dedicate themselves wholly unto the Lord. The marriage he has also blessed when lived under the terms of monogamy. Marriage is designed to be maintained until parting by death. This is because marriage is a covenant relationship that is joined together, literally combined to make one unit, by God. Thus, divorce is the breaking of a God-sealed covenant, usurping his authority and blessing over the marriage.

Polygamy cannot be blessed of God because there is no covenant outside of "two becoming one." Furthermore, if we examine the biblical accounts of polygamy, we will see God's judgment follows unfaithfulness. God's standard remains unchanged. The marriage covenant is so important because it foreshadows the relationship that Church will have with Christ, our bridegroom.

---

[563] Mt 19:10,11; 1Co 7:7-9; Ge 38:26
[564] Mal 2:14,15; Mt 19:5
[565] Mal 2:16; Mt 5:32; 1Co 7:12,13–WLC Q139c

June 29

Nothing Impure (Part 4)

The following list displays the final actions that we will discuss that attach themselves to the category of adultery:

Idleness, gluttony, drunkenness, unchaste company,[566] *lascivious songs, books, pictures, dancing, stage plays,*[567] *and all other provocations to or acts of uncleanness, either in ourselves or others.*[568]

Now, before you begin exclaiming that this list is just too inclusive, you should be careful to follow the biblical footnotes. Activities like singing and dancing are not innately evil. It is the attachment of these actions with the motive of sexual enticement that turns them wicked. It is therefore a touchy subject because we don't always know where to draw the line in the sand, i.e., where does the innocence end?

It is in times like these when we need to be sensitive to the prompting of the Holy Spirit who will lead us in all righteousness. When it comes to food, drink, and leisure time, is the manner of our partaking done with clean hands and a pure heart? In times of excess, we are acting selfishly with the purposes that God has intended to be used for his glory. This study of the Seventh Commandment has revealed the level of importance that God places on our relationship with him, with others, and certainly with our spouses.

---

[566] Eze 16:49; Pr 23:30-33; Ge 39:10
[567] Eph 5:4; Eze 23:14-16; Isa 23:15-17; Isa 3:16; Mk 6:22; Ro 13:13; 1Pe 4:3
[568] 2Ki 9:30 with Jer 4:30 and Eze 23:40–WLC Q139d

JUNE 30

THE CHASTE HEART

We have completed our look into the Seventh Commandment. I thought it would be worth our while, to take a day, to let the breadth and depth of this command settle into our understanding. Each of us will pull something different out of this study, and I don't want to lead you into my world, but would rather the Spirit do his prompting.

The Psalmist shows us that gray areas do not exist in God's economy. Take a look at some of these phrases from Psalm 119, which describe the godly person:

Walks blameless in the law of the Lord (v.1), seeks God with the whole heart (v.2), does no iniquity (v.3), Word is hidden in the heart (v.11), that I may not sin against God (v.11), open my eyes that I may see wondrous things from your Law (v.18), your servant meditates on your statutes (v.23), remove me from the way of lying (v.29), I have chosen the way of truth (v.30).

There is no room for dabbling in sin. One cannot set the mark at a point below God's standard and call it good enough. The Psalmist speaks of an all out effort to walk godly without offense to the law. Further, he knows that failures will come and that mercy is still required to hold off the judgment. We remain in this struggle until he takes us home.

Our battle begins at our first point of weakness. The physical act of adultery may not ever be approached, but how about the fringe elements: our speech, our dress, our disposition? Are they honoring to God and to his perfect standard? Be holy for God is holy.

July 1

The Eighth Commandment

Up until now, we have been quite challenged with the commandments we have studied. It may not seem that there is much to learn beyond the face value of the final three commandments. However, I am certain that God will show us differently. Let's go!

The eighth commandment is, Thou shalt not steal.[569]

The command is simple enough, and there is no need for further definition. However, this is one of the most widely broken laws of every generation. The amount of litigation that relates to this command is staggering. From embezzlement to unauthorized information sharing, from common theft to insider trading and Ponzi schemes, these are the crimes that fill our media every day.

We know how it feels and what it means to be stolen from. It is something we have all experienced from both sides. The thief always justifies their reasons, thinking that their gain is more important than the harm to the victim. If I cheat on a test, there is no victim. If I report less income, the government is overtaxing me anyway. If I take some pens home from the office, it is only a few bucks. If the cashier rings the wrong price, that is not my problem.

We are not thieves because we steal. We steal because we are thieves. Our depravity runs deep, and although we might restrain ourselves, those who steal typically make their choices on risk versus reward rather than honoring God. In this study, we will dig into our responsibilities in honoring God beyond the physical act of theft.

---

[569] Ex 20:15

JULY 2

DUTIES OF THE EIGHTH (PART 1)

Starting off with the basics, we see that:

The duties required in the eighth commandment are truth, faithfulness, and justice in contracts and commerce between man and man,[570] rendering to everyone his due,[571] restitution of goods unlawfully detained from the right owners thereof.[572]

God's Word is the standard of truth. The foundation of the whole Law is truth. It follows that truth and honesty regulate the eighth commandment. Faithfulness is man's duty to an existing truth. Desertion of faithfulness is disobedience to our calling.

One party can steal a possession directly from another or they can breach a contract, leaving the other party without recompense. Either way, theft is the result. The justice system has gone through great extent to protect property, currency, trademarks, and patents. Our legal system is fashioned after God's righteous commands.

Publicly, man's duty is to the law that we can justly govern within a community. Perhaps we have been careful to be a fair business person. We might never think of outright stealing from someone. However, we would be wise to not be too proud of ourselves just yet. If we have learned anything thus far, it is that God is always looking beyond the act and into the intentions of our hearts.

---

[570] Ps 15:2,4; Zec 7:4,10; Zec 8:16,17
[571] Ro 13:7
[572] Lev 6:2–5 with Lk 19:8–WLC Q141a

JULY 3

DUTIES OF THE EIGHTH (PART 2)

Our duties to the eighth commandment move beyond respecting contracts and the possessions of others. We also have the responsibility of:

Giving and lending freely, according to our abilities, and the necessities of others;[573] moderation of our judgments, wills, and affections concerning worldly goods;[574] a provident care and study to get,[575] keep, use, and dispose these things, which are necessary and convenient for the sustentation of our nature and suitable to our condition.[576]

Has your pride been demolished? We are considered thieves when we are selfish. Malachi 3:8 says that we steal from God when we short him in our tithes and offerings. The New Testament says that our compassion for others is a demonstration of our love of God. True compassion is heartfelt sympathy followed by love in action.

Moving introspectively deeper, our view of possessions can be a hindrance. If we take pride in ownership or our accomplishments, we forget that God owns it all and we are merely stewards. Therefore, anytime we handle things in an ungodly manner, we are stealing by falling short of his intended purpose to the eighth commandment. Ask God to show the areas where you may be stealing from him and others.

---

[573] Lk 6:30,38; 1Jn 3:17; Eph 4:28; Gal 6:10
[574] 1Ti 6:6,7,9; Gal 6:14
[575] 1Ti 5:8
[576] Pr 27:23 to end; Ecc 2:24; Ecc 3:12; 1Ti 6:17,18; Isa 38:1; Mt 11:8—WLC Q141b

JULY 4

DUTIES OF THE EIGHTH (PART 3)

Our duties continue beyond possessions, but also to the law that protects them. We obediently are responsible to:

A lawful calling and diligence in it;[577] *frugality,*[578] *avoiding unnecessary lawsuits, and surety-ship, or other like engagements;*[579] *and an endeavor, by all just and lawful means, to procure, preserve, and further the wealth and outward estate of others, as well as our own.*[580]

That's right; we are to be proactive in procuring and preserving wealth. It is not a godly attitude to say, "God will provide," and do absolutely nothing. The Bible is crystal clear: if an able man doesn't work, then he doesn't eat. Furthermore, we are to be assisting others in obtaining sustenance of their own.

Godliness in living out the eighth commandment includes our responsibility to protecting justice. We are to stand up for the law. We are to give testimony when needed. We are to not use the law unnecessarily. In other words, we participate in the justice system, but never for personal gain above what is justly due. Those who sue others unjustly will, one day, face the Final and Righteous Judge. There they shall stand without excuse for abusing the very law that was intending to protect them. Do justly, love mercy, and walk humbly.

---

[577] 1Co 7:20; Ge 2:15; Ge 3:19; Eph 4:28; Pr 10:4
[578] Jn 6:12; Pr 21:20
[579] 1Co 6:1-9; Pr 6:1-6; Pr 11:15
[580] Lev 25:35; Dt 22:1-4; Ex 23:4,5; Ge 47:14,20; Ph 2:4; Mt 22:39—WLC Q141c

JULY 5

FORBIDDEN THEFT (PART 1)

Over the past couple of days, we have discussed our proactive responsibilities to the eighth commandment. Today, we begin our look into the areas we must avoid.

The sins forbidden in the eighth commandment, besides the neglect of the duties required,[581] are theft, robbery, manstealing (extortion), and receiving any thing that is stolen.[582]

These first definitions of stealing are obvious. However, this does not make them easy to keep. Our flesh is so incredibly selfish that it will lure us into fulfilling it in whatever way we will allow. We must keep in step with the Spirit at all times to avoid these pitfalls.

Our number one blind spot is self-justification. If we grab five bucks from our parents' wallet, we could say, "Oh...they would just give it to me anyway." How many subtle possibilities could there be to break this command? We should know, beyond doubt, that God's rules do not bend. Where value is taken without permission, God is betrayed.

As a reminder, God's standard is perfection. Even as good as we try to be, we must always be on watch for our sticky-fingered flesh. Godliness requires clean hands and a pure heart. Wow! This is tough already, and we have not even entered the less tangible areas.

---

[581] Jas 2:15,16; 1Jn 3:17
[582] Eph 4:28; Ps 62:10; 1Ti 1:10; Pr 29:24; Ps 1:18–WLC Q142a

JULY 6

FORBIDDEN THEFT (PART 2)

We are about encounter some increasingly difficult concepts of thievery. There is no distinction of the culprit being a person or a corporation, we are entirely responsible to uphold this law and individually we shall answer to God. We may not involve ourselves in:

Fraudulent dealing, false weights and measures, removing landmarks, injustice and unfaithfulness in contracts between man and man, or in matters of trust;[583] *oppression, extortion, usury,*[584] *bribery, vexatious lawsuits, unjust enclosures, and depopulations.*[585]

There are God-given freedoms, like those outlined in the US Constitution and the Bill of Rights, which are slowly yet strategically being dissolved. Every lobbyist, politician, and president who makes or supports policies that takes away from the people whom they are to represent are frauds and thieves. By their vote, they betray God.

What if a particular politician is mostly good, even a self-confessed praying man of God? Any person is only as good as the evil he justifies. If they waver at any point along the way, without repentance, then this is the true character of that person.

Of course, this isn't about them. It is about us. What theft are we justifying? What sins do we wink at? What injustice do we allow? Have we cast lots for his garments?

---

[583] 1Th 4:6; Pr 11:1; Pr 20:10; Dt 19:14; Pr 23:10; Am 8:5; Ps 37:21; Lk 16:10-12

[584] Eze 22:29; Lev 25:17; Mt 23:25; Eze 22:12; Ps 15:5

[585] Job 15:34; 1Co 6:6-8; Pr 3:29,30; Isa 5:8; Mic 2:2–WLC Q142b

JULY 7

FORBIDDEN THEFT (PART 3)

We are learning a plethora of ways one can be a thief. One can also break the eighth commandment by:

Engrossing commodities to enhance the price; unlawful callings, and all other unjust or sinful ways of taking or withholding from our neighbor what belongs to him, or of enriching ourselves;[586] covetousness; inordinate prizing and affecting worldly goods;[587] distrustful and distracting cares and studies in getting, keeping, and using them.[588]

Careful now. We have our first look at an intangible violation: covetousness. We will discuss this topic deeper in our look at the tenth commandment. However, it is worth noting that God does include this heart matter as well as our physical violations under this heading. The manner in which we handle our possessions and our envy of others are on equal terms in the eyes of God.

We must carefully handle the difficulty of planning and working toward our wealth with resistance to feed our lust for more and more. A steady diet of God's Word is our guide to a proper attitude of health, wealth, and happiness. The simple rule for a godly life is if our actions are more glorifying to God or to ourselves.

Lord, awake my sensitivity to a godly life. Grant me strength to deny my selfish desires and the capacity to recognize the material blessings you daily provide.

---

[586] Pr 11:26; Ac 19:19,24,25; Job 20:19; Jas 5:4; Pr 21:6
[587] Lk 12:15; 1Ti 6:5; Col 3:2; Pr 23:5; Ps 62:10
[588] Mt 6:25,31,34; Ecc 5:12–WLC Q142c

JULY 8

FORBIDDEN THEFT (PART 4)

The final violations of the eighth commandment are:

Envying at the prosperity of others;[589] as likewise idleness, prodigality, wasteful gaming; and all other ways whereby we do unduly prejudice our own outward estate,[590] and defrauding ourselves of the due use and comfort of that estate which God hath given us.[591]

There really is no reward for abandoning our current lifestyle just as a means of appearing humble. No. God provides to his servants as he sees fit. Our material blessings are not a curse to be abandoned. Rather, we are to be good stewards of our wealth for his glory. Recall that it was Jesus who gave us the example of God rewarding the faithful steward with increased wealth.

How about gambling? This is a violation that has a qualified gray area in that we are not to be wasteful with our possessions. Where is the line separating entertainment and wastefulness? It may be different for each of us, but we must handle it carefully from God's perspective. After all, we would not want to be breaking God's commands just for the entertainment value.

Thus completes our examination of the eighth commandment. We are not to steal in any way, nor do we want to defraud ourselves in the eyes of God. We demonstrate love's purity through obedience.

---

[589] Ps 73:3; Ps 37:1,7
[590] 2Th 3:11; Pr 18:9; Pr 21:17,21; Pr 28:19
[591] Ecc 4:8; Ecc 6:2; 1Ti 5:8–WLC Q142d

July 9

The Ninth Commandment

We have worked our way down to our final two duties that God gave to Moses. In our exploration of God's Law, we have been both blessed by God's righteousness and convicted by our own shortcomings. Rather than giving up in despair, we allow our desperation to cause us to lean fully on the benevolent strength of Christ.

The ninth commandment is, Thou shalt not bear false witness against thy neighbor.[592]

Relationships stand on integrity. The degree of depth in a particular relationship is therefore based on activity, duration, and faithfulness. Even a small breach of trust, early in a relationship, could bring an immediate demise.

Of course, when we deal with God' Law, his command extends much deeper than this one rule. The depth of the law reaches into the fabric of every aspect of a person's life. First, it is relevant to all associated areas of a particular law as it relates to God's righteousness. Secondly, it is binding to the heart of man, where evil is conceived, and tries to motivate us to feed our selfish flesh.

Heavenly Father, as we enter in to the ninth commandment, we ask you to open our ears to your Word and soften our hearts, which have been hardened by the guiles of this world. Our purpose is to serve and glorify you with our lives. We lay ourselves bare before you now.

---

[592] Ex 20:16 -WLC Q143

July 10

Preserving Truth

When our Lord was praying to the heavenly Father, in John 17, he spoke to the heart of truth. Jesus proclaims that eternal life only comes by knowing the One True God. He further states that God sanctifies us by his truth—his word of truth. It is therefore our duty to base our entire being on his word, which is the only truth.

The duties required in the ninth commandment are the preserving and promoting of truth between man and man and the good name of our neighbor as well as our own; appearing and standing for the truth;[593] *and from the heart, sincerely, freely, clearly, and fully,*[594] *speaking the truth, and only the truth, in matters of judgment and justice, and in all other things whatsoever.*[595]

Certainly, our duty to God is to live in an honest manner. This responsibility is carried into our relationships. It is manifestly impossible to please God spiritually while pilfering others. Our stand on truth must be consistent personally, privately, publically, as well as to God's entire revealed Word. It is not just confessing the truth, it is speaking and living out the truth in all things.

Lord, I repent for times when I twist, embellish, or sugarcoat my position to others. My spirit agrees with your Spirit that any aspect outside of truth breaks your command and is sin. Please open my heart and mind to respond appropriately to your Spirit's effective leading.

---

[593] Jas 2:15,16; 1Jn 3:17; Eph 4:28; Ps 62:10
[594] 1Ti 1:10; Pr 29:24; Ps 1:18; 1Th 4:6; Pr 11:1; Pr 20:10; Dt 19:14; Pr 23:10
[595] Am 8:5; Ps 37:21; Lk 16:10-12–WLC 144a

JULY 11

LOVING TRUTH

We have understood the definition of *truth* since our childhood. We must grow in the tangible areas of truth to understand its far-reaching responsibility. Our duties continue in:

A charitable esteem of our neighbors; loving, desiring, and rejoicing in their good name;[596] sorrowing for and covering of their infirmities;[597] freely acknowledging of their gifts and graces, defending their innocence.[598]

The ninth commandment is dedicated to how we handle our relationships with others. Today's section shows us how we manifest truth in the godly action of loving our neighbors. In a day and age when the media is looking for juicy bits of character flaws to exploit, are we joining the slander with our own gossip column? Or are we encouraging our friends and neighbors with grace and tenderness?

It may seem a bit contrary to speak of covering our neighbors' infirmities when the whole commandment is based on truth. However, this is not about sweeping their sins under a rug, but about acknowledging and confirming with them the grace of God and their pursuit of holiness.

Search me, O Lord! Help me not to offend thee, but to glorify you as I defend truth and love my neighbors in your righteous way.

---

[596] Heb 6:9; 1Co 13:7; Ro 1:8; 2 Jn 4; 3 Jn 3,4
[597] 2Co 2:4; 2Co 12:21; Pr 17:9; 1Pe 4:8
[598] 1Co 1:4,5,7; 2Ti 1:4,5; 1Sa 22:14–WLC Q144b

July 12

Defending Truth

I do not consider myself to be the envious type. Yet why is it that my first reaction to someone's success is disdain? It is because I was not presently godly minded. Our heart's demeanor is to be:

A ready receiving of a good report and unwillingness to admit of an evil report concerning them; discouraging tale-bearers, flatterers, and slanderers;[599] *love and care of our own good name and defending it when need requires; keeping of lawful promises;*[600] *studying and practicing of whatsoever things are true, honest, lovely, and of good report.*[601]

Make a practice out of defending others when they are being discussed negatively. First, consider the "dirt" as unlikely. Second, consider alternate intentions of that person; were they actually trying to be derogatory if it were true? Finally, consider what could it possibly benefit that person by talking negatively about them. This command is not saying we should not address negative behavior, but that it should be constructive and not in a slanderous fashion.

If someone defames you, it is not only acceptable to defend your own good name, but proper to do so. We can follow Paul's example of this. He admits his own sinfulness, yet defends his character as a converted believer by the grace of God. According to Micah, we are to do justly, love mercy, and walk humbly with our God.

---

599 1Co 13:6,7; Ps 15:3; Pr 25:23; Pr 26:24,25; Ps 101:5
600 Pr 22:1; Jn 8:49; Ps 15:4
601 Php 4:8–WLC Q144c

July 13

Sins of the Ninth (Part 1)

Today, we move from our duties to God's ninth commandment to the areas in which we are to prohibited.

The sins forbidden in the ninth commandment are all prejudicing the truth and the good name of our neighbors, as well as our own, especially in public judicature;[602] *giving false evidence, suborning false witnesses, wittingly appearing, and pleading for an evil cause, out-facing and overbearing the truth;*[603] *passing unjust sentence.*[604]

This first section is perhaps the most direct definition of *not bearing false witness against thy neighbor.* We understand the concept of providing an honest testimony, especially in a court of law. We don't really picture ourselves fabricating lies on the witness stand. However, does it make any difference to God if we are put under oath or are just speaking privately?

In trying protect our own good name, we blame-shift. It all started in the Garden of Eden. Eve blamed the serpent for deceiving her. Adam blamed the women for giving him the fruit. Even further, Adam blamed God because it was God who provided Eve as his wife. On and on it goes. Today, we still ultimately blame God for our own sinfulness until we recognize our far-reaching depravity. We end the lies when we expose our frailty and lean fully into God's strength.

---

[602] 1Sa 17:28; 2Sa 16:3; 2Sa 1:9,10,15,16; Lev 19:15; Hab. 1:4
[603] Pr 19:5; Pr 6:16,19; Ac 6:13; Jer 9:3,5; Ac 24:2,5; Ps 12:3,4; Ps 52:1-4
[604] Pr 17:15; 1Ki 21:9-14–WLC Q145

July 14

Sins of the Ninth (Part 2)

When it comes to lying, the sins of omission are just as bad as the sins of commission. Other sins of bearing false witness include:

Calling evil good and good evil; rewarding the wicked according to the work of the righteous and the righteous according to the work of the wicked;[605] *forgery, concealing the truth, undue silence in a just cause,*[606] *and holding our peace when iniquity calls for either a reproof from ourselves, or complaint to others.*[607]

There are some who might think that minding their own business is always best. However, if this includes concealing the truth, then that person is guilty of false testimony. Likewise, if we are in a position to correct somebody else from the error of their ways and we do not, then we also dishonor them.

How can we expect to live in honor to the truth, while we do not expose error? This does not mean that we ignore compassion while we rebuke another. We can handle these situations privately, with grace, so they can realign with Spirit without embarrassment.

As for ourselves, if we are shown the error of our ways, then we should be quick to correct the matter, and if necessary, make a confession to those we offended. Honoring God is a life of sanctification wrought with repentance upon failure.

---

[605] Isa 5:23
[606] Ps 119:69; Lk 19:8; Lk 16:5,6,7; Lev 5:1; Dt 13:8; Ac 5:3,8,9; 2Ti 4:6
[607] 1Ki 1:6; Lev 19:17; Isa 59:4–WLC Q145b

July 15

Sins of the Ninth (Part 3)

How many ways are there to lie? Hundreds? As you go through this list below, take into account the nuances that distinguish them.

Speaking the truth unseasonably, or maliciously to a wrong end, or perverting it to a wrong meaning, or in doubtful and equivocal expressions, to the prejudice of truth or justice;[608] speaking untruth, lying, slandering, backbiting, detracting, tale-bearing,[609] whispering, scoffing, reviling,[610] rash, harsh, and partial censuring.[611]

If anyone has trouble understanding their own depravity, they only need compare themselves to this list. I certainly stand guilty of every last one. Our hearts can be desperately wicked. Before God gave us a new heart, we were so deceived that we did not even know that our lies demonstrates our hatred for God and his law.

At my uncle's funeral, one of his grandchildren gave a very memorable eulogy. My uncle had told him on more than one occasion, "Always tell the truth whatever the cost." He also would remind his family that in times of peril to "Pray to God and row toward shore." The lesson rings out: we are to trust the Lord with every aspect of our lives and at the same time, give every effort to live according to his standard. God gives us the ability, but we must apply the effort. Obedience is the only appropriate response as bond-slaves of Christ.

---

[608] Pr 29:11; 1Sa 22:9,10 & Ps 52:1-5; Ps 56:5; Jn 2:19 & Mt 26:60,61; Ge 3:5; Ge 26:7,9

[609] Isa 59:13; Lev 19:11; Col 3:9; Ps 50:20; Ps 15:3; Jas 4:11; Jer 38:4; Lev 19:16

[610] Ro 1:29,30; Ge 21:9 & Gal 4:29; 1Co 6:10

[611] Mt 7:1; Ac 28:4; Ge 38:24; Ro 2:1–WLC Q145c

JULY 16

SINS OF THE NINTH (PART 4)

We now move into some intricate areas of this commandment. Slyly deceptive and evermore obscure, yet lies just the same, including:

Misconstructing intentions, words, and actions;[612] flattering, vain-glorious boasting, thinking or speaking too highly or too meanly of ourselves or others;[613] denying the gifts and graces of God; aggravating smaller faults;[614] hiding, excusing, or extenuating of sins, when called to a free confession;[615] unnecessary discovering of infirmities; raising false rumors, receiving and countenancing evil reports, and stopping our ears against just defense.[616]

Sometimes, we lie to avoid embarrassment. However, sometimes, we are given a free pass to come clean without consequence, yet we still persist in the lie. It's all a pride issue. Whatever we can do to avoid, not just the discipline, but the embarrassment. We hide, just as Adam and Eve, yet we are exposed.

My heart and soul thirst for you. In a dry a barren land, where there is no water. The barren land is my drought of self-righteousness. Come and fill me with your Spirit. I come to your well, O Lord, knowing that when I drink, I shall never thirst again. You have washed over me. You have removed my iniquity. You are the living water.

---

[612] Ne 6:6-8; Ro 3:8; Ps 69:10; 1Sa 1:13-15; 2Sa 10:3
[613] Ps 12:2,3; 2Ti 3:2; Lk 18:9,11; Ro 12:16; 1Co 4:6; Ac 12:22; Ex 4:10-14
[614] Job 27:5,6; Job 4:6; Mt 7:3-5
[615] Pr 28:13; Pr 30:20; Ge 3:12,13; Jer 2:35; 2Ki 5:25; Ge 4:9
[616] Ge 9:22; Pr 25:9,10; Ex 23:1 Pr 29:12; Ac 7:56,57; Job 31:13,14–WLC Q145d

July 17

Sins of the Ninth (Part 5)

Our final day to study our endless attempts to fool others and defame God. We also bear false witness with:

Evil suspicion;[617] envying or grieving at the deserved credit of any, endeavoring or desiring to impair it, rejoicing in their disgrace and infamy;[618] scornful contempt, fond admiration; breach of lawful promises;[619] neglecting such things as are of good report, and practicing, or not avoiding ourselves, or not hindering what we can in others, such things as procure an ill name.[620]

The behaviors shown today display ourselves 180 degrees from the honorable and godly characteristics we ought to pursue. When we should be rejoicing with another's blessing, we are jealous. Other times, we rejoice at their problems, thankful they are not our own.

As we mature in Christ, we should discipline ourselves to adopt his heart for others. We should become servants because we now have a servant's heart. Just as Jesus washed the feet of his disciples (a task performed by the lowest of servants in a household), we should care for our neighbors in their time of need. It is fashionable to seek places of honor. The Pharisees loved their high places. Do you desire to be a Pharisee more than a slave of Christ?

---

[617] 1Co 13:5; 1Ti 6:4
[618] Nu 11:29; Mt 21:15; Ezr 4:12,13; Jer 48:27
[619] Ps 35:15,16,21; Mt 27:28,29; Jude 16; Ac 12:22; Ro 1:31; 2Ti 3:3
[620] 1Sa 2:24; 2Sa 13:12,13; Pr 5:8,9; Pr 6:33–WLC Q145e

JULY 18

AVOID THE GREEN MOVEMENT

Thou shalt not covet.

Thou shalt not covet thy neighbor's house, thou shalt not covet thy neighbor's wife, nor his man-servant, nor his maid-servant, nor his ox, nor his donkey, nor any thing that is thy neighbor's.[621]

The world believes the false notion that *the grass is greener on the other side of the fence.* If this statement seems outdated, we could replace the above possessions with: mansion, job, Mercedes, Harley, or John Deere tractor.

We are generally envious because we think that having what others have would in some way fulfill us. However, envy is one of the most potent causes of unhappiness, actually creating a void of a perceived need, making one feel empty. If envy persists, it can drive a person into depression or can make them physically ill. But enough of the psychology, look at the sin itself.

Covetousness is the one commandment, dealing with relationships between men, that takes place secretly within the heart. In other words, there was never legal prosecution against envy. That being said, how many crimes are committed with envy as their root? So we see that wickedness is first conceived in the heart before it is manifest in the flesh. Jesus exclaimed in Matthew 5:28, that the sins committed in the heart make us just as guilty as the act itself.

---

[621] Ex 20:17–WLC Q146

July 19

Pursue Contentment

We perhaps live in the most difficult era in regard to the ninth command. We are bombarded with endless advertisements. We are told that it is *stuff* that fulfills us. We believe it; just look at the credit mess that millions of people are in. We remain unfulfilled.

The duties required in the tenth commandment are such a full contentment with our own condition[622] *and such a charitable frame of the whole soul toward our neighbor, as that all our inward motions and affections touching him, tend unto, and further all that good which is his.*[623]

The pulse, especially in America, is *he who dies with the most toys, wins.* God knows that true happiness rests outside of one's possessions. Contentment is found in a Christ-centered life. We are responsible to control our inward emotions, which means as envious thoughts arrive, we filter them through the lens of a godly attitude and then we respond accordingly.

Avoiding envious thoughts is impossible. However, if we recognize them as the infiltration of the enemy, we can stop them in their tracks through the purity of the Spirit that reigns over our mortal bodies. It is a spiritual war. This is why we present ourselves to God as a living sacrifice.[624] Then we will walk in his good and perfect will.

---

[622] Heb 13:5; 1Ti 6:6
[623] Job 31:29; Ro 12:15; Ps 122:7-9; 1Ti 1:5; Esth. 10:3; 1Co 13:4-7–WLC Q147
[624] Rom 12:1-2

July 20

Avoid Discontentment

Dear God, If I only had a better job and made more money, then I could do more for you. I could start tithing. I could give more to the poor. I could show others how you bless me.

The sins forbidden in the tenth commandment are discontentment with our own estate,[625] envying and grieving at the good of our neighbor,[626] together with all inordinate motions and affections to anything that is his.[627]

The are many ways to be unsatisfied. Usually, our discontentment begins when we see someone else with something we would like to have. However, if you ever visited a third world country, you know that joy is rooted in something other than possessions. A Christian's joy is in the Lord. Is this demonstrated in your life?

Our selfishness shows through the most insignificant things. When your slice of pie is smaller, when you have to sit in the backseat, when your friends can afford a dream vacation. On and on it goes. Jealousy rages like a machine, unless we take our eyes off objects and put them on the Provider of all good and perfect gifts. Until we realize that all things we covet will turn to dust, we are living only for the moment. Those who obey the will of God abide forever.[628]

---

625 1Ki 21:4; Esth. 5:13; 1Co 10:10
626 Gal 5:26; Jas 3:14,16; Ps 112:9,10; Ne 2:10
627 Ro 7:7,8; Ro 13:9; Col 3:5; Dt 5:21–WLC Q148
628 1Jo 2:17

July 21

Pride in Our Own Ability

Is any man able to perfectly keep the commandments of God?

No man is able, either of himself[629] *or by any grace received in this life, perfectly to keep the commandments of God;*[630] *but doth daily break them in thought, word, and deed.*[631]

There are some who think that such a thought as this is, not only wrong, but dangerous because it gives license to sin. However, this is neither saying we must always nor that we cannot ever resist sinning. There are times, when we are abiding in the Spirit, that we don't sin. However, although our souls have been saved from sin, our flesh remains unredeemed. This is the battle we face every day, all day.

The Scriptures provided are crystal clear that our flesh lusts against the Spirit. There will always remain tension between our flesh and the Spirit. One of God's reasons for this is to keep us dependent upon him at all times. Sometimes, we have a good day and begin to think, *I'm really doing a great job.* Bam! Pride has entered it.

If in our flesh remains no good thing, how could we think it possible to walk perfectly? And yet, we are called to beat down our flesh daily, to live a sanctified life in pursuit of holiness. It is a battle that rages throughout our lives. So where is the victory? It is never by our best efforts to be sin free. It is in Christ, by his grace alone.

---

[629] Jas 3:2; Jn 15:5; Ro 8:3
[630] Ecc 7:20; 1Jn 1:8,10; Gal 5:17; Ro 7:18,19
[631] Ge 6:5; Ge 8:21; Ro 3:9-19; Jas 3:2-13–WLC Q149

July 22

Good Sin Is Bad Sin?

Are all transgressions of the law of God equally weighted in the sight of God?

All transgressions of the law of God are not equally heinous, but some sins in themselves, and by reason of several aggravations, are more heinous in the sight of God than others.[632]

The first sin was an act of disobedience, a single bite of a piece of fruit. Hardly what we would consider a capital crime. But through this so-called tiny sin, death entered. We are taught, in this first act of disobedience, that any sin and all sin is deserving of death. This is because sin cannot stand in the presence of a holy God.

This being true does not necessitate all sin be equal in degree. We all recognize that theft is not equal with murder, nor is a lustful thought as wicked as the act of adultery itself. Yet, we are not saying that God winks at some sin. The slightest sin qualifies us to receive hell. Jesus would endure the cross for any transgression.

Today's lesson is to show us that God does view some sins as more heinous than others. However, I think we tend to take away the seriousness of all sin. If you think you are a pretty good person, trying to do good things and treat others fairly and are able to stand before God on Judgment Day, hoping he grades on a curve, you are deceiving yourself. Before God, our self-righteousness is as filthy rags.

---

[632] Jn 19:11; Eze 8:6,13,15; 1Jn 5:16; Ps 78:17,32,56—WLC Q150

July 23

The Offender

What are those aggravations that make some sins more heinous than others? First, sins receive their aggravations:

From the persons offending: if they be of riper age,[633] *greater experience or grace, eminent for profession, gifts, place,*[634] *office, guides to others, and whose example is likely to be followed by others.*[635]

The first basis of the weight of any given sin is the level of authority that person has in society. That is why we are appalled when a politician, teacher, or pastor is caught in a scandal. We expect these people to live a life above reproach, to be an example to society and our children. Their sin will not be tolerated in the same manner we might shrug off the average citizen.

The highest level of expectation for righteous living belongs to those who have the greatest experience of saving grace. The person who fully understands the pit from which they have been saved should be the most sensitive to offending their Savior.

When you screw up as an older child, your parents might say, "You should know better than to do that." God's expectations are in the same vein. We are to hide his Word in our hearts that we might not offend him. We might sin less, but we hate it so much more.

---

[633] Jer 2:8; Job. 32:7,9; Ecc 4:13
[634] 1Ki 11:4,9; 2Sa 12:14; 1Co 5:1; Jas 4:17; Lk 12:47,48; Jer 5:4,5
[635] 2Sa 12:7-9; Eze 8:11,12; Ro 2:17-24; Gal 2:11-14–WLC Q151a

JULY 24

THE OFFENDED (PART 1)

What are those aggravations that make some sins more heinous than others? Second, sins receive their aggravations:

From the parties offended:[636] *if immediately against God, his attributes, and worship;*[637] *against Christ and his grace; the Holy Spirit, his witness, and workings.*[638]

We will take the first half of this list today and the balance of it tomorrow. It is not redundant that we are describing the first offended party as the Godhead. Certainly, all sins, first and foremost, offend the holiness of God. How offensive is any sin in the eyes of God? The tiniest sin would have been enough to send Jesus to cross for redemption's sake.

Sin is the separating factor between God and man. The moment Adam and Eve disobeyed God, they became spiritually dead. It didn't matter if they were sorry. Regret has no atoning quality; rather, it is the flesh's response to getting caught in our sin. The believing heart, on the other hand, shows true repentance for the offense against God.

We will do well to understand the exceedingly sinfulness of sin.

Father, help my conscious mind to be on active alert at all times. Thank you for showing me that there is no white lie. There is no small sin in your presence. Thank you for your mercy, which is new every morning.

---

[636] Mt 21:38,39
[637] 1Sa 2:25; Ac 5:4; Ps 51:4; Ro 2:4; Mal 1:8,14–WLC Q151b
[638] Heb 2:2,3; Heb 12:25; Heb 10:29; Mt 12:31,32; Eph 4:30; Heb 6:4-6

JULY 25

THE OFFENDED (PART 2)

Continuing from yesterday, sins receive their aggravations:

From the parties offended: against superiors, men of eminency, and such as we stand especially related and engaged unto;[639] *against any of the saints, particularly weak brethren,*[640] *the souls of them, or any other, and the common good of all or many.*[641]

Our sins are considered more heinous according to the stature of the person being offended. It is not that stealing a bike from a homeless person is less of a crime than stealing one from our wealthy boss. In fact, the homeless person is much more affected by the ordeal. However, our boss has high expectations of our character, and therefore, we have offended the intrinsic value of the relationship.

We are not here to determine whom it is more acceptable to sin against. Our objective is to show that the weightiness of sin is distinct and significant. Murder is not equal to theft, and our parents feel much worse when we lie than our friends do.

A bit of an inversion to this factor is how our sin may affect different degrees of believers. If I cause my weaker brethren to stumble in their walk with Christ, it is a more offensive violation than it is to a mature Christian whose faith does not waiver.

Lord, once again we call upon you for strength so that we do not offend you or others.

---

[639] Jude 8; Nu 12:8,9; Isa 3:5; Pr 30:17; 2Co 12:15; Ps 55:12-15
[640] Zeph 2:8,10,11; Mt 18:6; 1Co 6:8; Rev 17:6; 1Co 8:11,12; Ro 14:13,15,21
[641] Eze 13:19; 1Co 8:12; Rev 18:12,13; Mt 23:15; 1Th 2:15,16; Josh. 22:20–
    WLC Q151c

JULY 26

THE OFFENSE (PART 1)

What are those aggravations that make some sins more heinous than others? Third, sins receive their aggravations:

From the nature and quality of the offense: if it be against the express letter of the law, break many commandments, contain in it many sins:[642] if not only conceived in the heart, but breaks forth in words and actions, scandalize others, and admit of no reparation:[643] if against means, mercies, judgments, light of nature,[644] conviction of consciousness, public or private admonition,[645] censures of the church, civil punishments.[646]

We have moved from the people affected by our sin into the degrees of sin itself. Sin is not evaluated in heaven on a scale of 1 to 10. This is not an Olympic event, but it is an evaluation of God's judgment. Our entire being is under the microscope at all times. We are called to live a holy life, separate from this world and in denial of our flesh. God's call to the believer is for ever-decreasing sin.

Since we cannot stop the infiltration of temptation, we must be improving our defensive strategies. The entertaining of a fleshy thought leads only to further demise. If our first reaction to temptation is resistance, we will turn our focus to Christ and honor him.

---

[642] Pr 6:30-33; Ezr 9:10-12; 1Ki 11:9,10; Col 3:5; 1Ti 6:10; Pr 5:8-12; Pr 6:32,33; Josh. 7:21

[643] Jas 1:14,15; Mt 5:22; Mic 2:1; Mt 18:7; Ro 2:23,24; Dt 22:22,28,29; Pr 6:32-35

[644] Mt 11:21-24; Jn 15:22; Isa 1:3; Dt 32:6; Am 4:8-11; Jer 5:3; Ro 1:26,27

[645] Ro 1:32; Da 5:22; Tit 3:10,11; Pr 29:1

[646] Tit 3:10; Mt 18:17; Pr 27:22; Pr 23:35–WLC Q151d

July 27

The Offense (Part 2)

Continuing from yesterday, sins receive their aggravations:

From the nature and quality of the offense: when our prayers, purposes, promises,[647] vows, covenants, and engagements to God or men:[648] if done deliberately, willfully, presumptuously, impudently, boastingly,[649] maliciously, frequently, obstinately, with delight, continuance,[650] or relapsing after repentance.[651]

As we evaluate the sin we face at every corner, we may feel desperation. This is exactly the point which God wants us. He wants us to realize our own complete inability and to see even the "little" sin as exceedingly sinful. Christian maturity gives us new glasses through which we see our world acutely aware of a righteous life.

It is common for believers to have their own thorn in the flesh. A sinful attitude or action that lingers on. It may be short-temperedness or foul language or even homosexual tendencies. We are not to justify our actions, saying, "This is just who I am." This what the world does: excusing their sin or even blaming God. As true believers, we can no longer live in sin. Our spirit cries out to the Father and we find strength in our weakness because of our reliance upon the strength of Christ. We give the glory to God when we depend on him.

---

[647] Ps 78:34-37; Jer 2:20; Jer 42:5,6,20,21
[648] Ecc 5:4-6; Pr 20:25; Lev 26:25; Pr 2:17; Eze 17:18,19
[649] Ps 36:4; Jer 6:16; Nu 15:30; Ex 21:14; Jer 3:3; Pr 7:13; Ps 52:1
[650] 3Jn 10; Nu 14:22; Zec 7:11,12; Pr 2:14; Isa 57:17
[651] Jer 34:8-11; 2Pe 2:20-22—WLC Q151e

JULY 28

THE CIRCUMSTANCES

What are those aggravations that make some sins more heinous than others? Fourth, sins receive their aggravations:

From circumstances of time and place:[652] if on the Lord's day, or other times of divine worship;[653] or immediately before or after these, or other helps to prevent or remedy such miscarriages:[654] if in public, or in the presence of others, who are thereby likely to be provoked or defiled.[655]

The above descriptions remind me of things my grandma might say. "No chewing gum in church" is one example. Although this may be a bit of legalism, the point is the honoring of God's sacred things. Sin that is manifest in these circumstances shows our disregard for the holy things of God. What God calls important, we must honor.

God has established many sacred days and laid them aside for his honor, our remembrance, and celebration of his goodness. To ignore their importance is to thumb our noses at God. Furthermore, our defilement at these times may negatively affect those around us.

Lord, thank you for showing me all of these way in which I might sin against you. I know the consequence of sin is death and that Jesus paid that price for me. Help me walk uprightly in that light.

[652] 2Ki 5:26; Jer 7:10; Isa 26:10
[653] Eze 23:37-39; Isa 58:3-5; Nu 25:6,7
[654] 1Co 11:20,21; Jer 7:8-10; Pr 7:14,15; Jn 13:27,30; Ezr 9:13,14
[655] 2Sa 16:22; 1Sa 2:22-24–WLC 151f

JULY 29

THE WAGES OF SIN

For the past couple of months, our devotional time has been dedicated to God's Law: the Ten Commandments. We have the duties of and the forbidden actions against these commands. We have also shown a plethora of possible sins associated with each. The remaining question is *why take so much time to evaluate our transgressions?*

Every sin, even the least, being against the sovereignty, goodness, and holiness of God and against his righteous law,[656] *deserves his wrath and curse,*[657] *both in this life and that which is to come;*[658] *and cannot be expiated but by the blood of Christ.*[659]

Here, we see the results of man's sin and its only remedy. Our sin is to be shunned; that is without a doubt. However, by its never-ending interference our lives, we are driven to despair. By the Law, we see God's righteousness and our depravity, wickedness, and hatred. To think, *I am generally good and will make it to heaven because God judges on a curve,* is the biggest and most common misnomer. All of a person's goodness is filth before a holy God, and our sin condemns us to judgment and eternal death. Oh! Our despair!

Many, with hardened hearts, will challenge this truth. They think that God will hear them out on Judgment Day. Yet, there will be only silence, a bowed knee in acknowledgement of their guilt, then hell.

---

[656] Jas 2:10,11; Ex 20:1,2; Hab. 1:13; 1Jn 3:4; Ro 7:12
[657] Eph 5:6; Gal 3:10
[658] La 3:39; Dt 28:15 to end; Mt 25:41
[659] Heb 9:22; 1Pe 1:18,19–WLC Q152

JULY 30

ESCAPING THE WRATH OF GOD

For those who carry their blind pride to the grave, the terror of God's wrath awaits. They have ignored what God requires of us that we may escape his judgment.

That we may escape the wrath and curse of God due to us by reason of the transgression of the law. He requires of us repentance toward God, and faith toward our Lord Jesus Christ,[660] and the diligent use of the outward means whereby Christ communicates to us the benefits of his mediation.[661]

Some, by hearing of the Word of God, knowing that they deserve God's wrath, and seeing Jesus' sacrifice on their behalf, repent and are saved through faith. Redemption is only by the blood of Christ.

The believer meets the requirements because God's grace was freely given unto him. Through regeneration by the Holy Spirit, man exercises faith toward Christ and repents of sin. There is no effort on man's part to attain salvation. The work was Christ's. He lived a sinless, perfect life. He paid the full price at the cross, satisfying God's requirement on behalf of all who believe.

We are to be certain of our calling. If you believe in Jesus, yet you question your salvation, verify his promises. For which believers' sins did Christ die? All of them for all time. Do you believe this? Do you hate your sin? You believe by his grace; therefore, live in his grace.

---

[660] Ac 20:21; Mt 3:7,8; Lk 13:3,5; Ac 16:30,31; Jn 3:16,18
[661] Pr 2:1-5; Pr 8:33-36—WLC Q153

July 31

The Believer's Life

Many people claim to be saved, even verbalizing their faith in Jesus. A mystery remains as to those whose truly believe. We see some waiver or even appear to abandon their faith. Although it is impossible to verify another's salvation, the corporate church practices its faith through outward means.

The outward and ordinary means whereby Christ communicates to his church the benefits of his mediation are all his ordinances, especially the word, sacraments, and prayer, all which are made effectual to the elect for their salvation.[662]

Over the next several days, we will take a deeper look into these disciplines of the Christ follower. We should note that it is by Christ and for his true believers alone that these practices are effectual. That is to say, those without saving faith may worship in like manner, but they receive no spiritual benefit. The prayer of the unrighteous avails nothing. It is meaningless.

These practices do not generate salvation, yet they are to be part of church life. Just as faith without works is dead, a believer should not live outside of the means in which Christ communicates his intercession.

God, prepare our hearts as we study the benefits of your mediation. Show us your purpose in these elements of our walk with you.

---

[662] Mt 28:19,20; Ac 2:42,46,47–WLC Q154

AUGUST 1

THE HOLY SCRIPTURES

How is the Word made effectual unto salvation?

The Spirit of God makes the reading, but especially the preaching of the word an effectual means of enlightening,[663] *convincing, and humbling sinners,*[664] *of driving them out of themselves, and drawing them unto Christ.*[665]

We are called to make a defense of the Scriptures, to be able to give a reason for that in whom we believe. In such a case, it is not we who are convincing another to believe, but he who testifies within us. The Bible, although infallible, logical, and true, does not convince everyone who hears. Our ears are closed and our eyes are blind until the Spirit of God, at his will, breaks through our stony hearts.

What explanation can be given about a person who stands against every word of God, suddenly recognizing their sin and seeing clearly the hope that is in Christ, giving testimony to the One who saved them? The miracle is the heart change. Jesus tells us that no man can see the kingdom of God unless he is born from above.

What good is it to tell someone that they need life when they don't know they are perishing?

Lord, let me proclaim your Word so you can perform your perfect work. It is only you, Lord, who can bring light out of darkness.

---

[663] Ne 8:8; Ac 26:18; Ps 19:8
[664] 1Co 14:24,25; 2Ch 34:18,19,26,27,28
[665] Ac 2:37,41; Ac 8:27-39–WLC Q155a

AUGUST 2

THE WORD MADE EFFECTIVE

The Spirit of God makes the reading, but especially the preaching of the word an effectual means:

Of conforming them to his image and subduing them to his will;[666] of strengthening them against temptations and corruptions;[667] of building them up in grace[668] and establishing their hearts in holiness and comfort through faith unto salvation.[669]

Many will resist the truth of this doctrine. Their primary misconception is that they can love God without his help. Failing to recognize their radical corruption, originally being haters of God, they think their wills are unaffected by the Fall. However, Jesus himself tells the us that we love him because he has first loved us.

Most presentations to receive Christ as Savior begin properly with a Gospel proclamation. However, they typically turn into a high-pressure sales pitch, complete with emotional arm-twisting to come forward and be saved. Faith is not a self-generated action. A person is regenerated by the transforming work of the Holy Spirit alone, through the hearing of the Word alone. Emotions may accompany the transformation, but they are not the cause.

Thank you, Lord, for opening my ears that I may hear.

---

[666] 2Co 3:18; 2Co 10:4-6; Ro 6:17
[667] Mt 4:4,7,10; Eph 6:16,17; Ps 19:11; 1Co 10:11
[668] Ac 20:32; 2Ti 3:15-17
[669] Ro 16:25; 1Th 3:2,10,11,13; Ro 15:4; Ro 10:13-17; Ro 1:16–WLC Q155b

AUGUST 3

READING OF THE WORD

Is the Word of God to be read by all?

Although all are not to be permitted to read the word publicly to the congregation,[670] yet all sorts of people are bound to read it apart by themselves, and with their families:[671] to which end, the holy scriptures are to be translated out of the original into vulgar languages.[672]

The handling of the Word of God in public is a sensitive topic. Regardless of what your position may be in this regard, one thing with which we must agree is that the hearing of the Scriptures is effective for those who are inwardly called of God.

The Scriptures are not to be withheld from common folk, but are to be read and understood by all who desire. The Roman Catholic church discouraged personal study and shielded people from reading by keeping the text in Latin, the language of scholars. However, the Reformation of the sixteenth century and the invention of the printing press quickly changed the tide, allowing for many nations to read the Scriptures in their native tongue.

It is a shame that most households have several Bibles just lying around, unread and gathering dust. Meanwhile, there are others who traverse many miles to hear the treasure of the Word read aloud.

---

[670] Dt 31:9,11,12,13; Ne 8:2,3; Ne 9:3-5
[671] Dt 17:19; Rev 1:3; Jn 5:39; Isa 34:16; Dt 6:6-9; Ge 18:17,19; Ps 78:5-7
[672] 1Co 14:6,9,11,12,15,16,24,27,28–WLC Q156

AUGUST 4

HANDLING OF THE WORD (PART 1)

The Scriptures allow the godly to explore to any depth they wish. A cursory reading allows for one to get the gist, but a true student will look into the context, the doctrine, the very words themselves to learn as much as possible about their saving God.

The Holy Scriptures are to be read with a high and reverent esteem of them;[673] with a firm persuasion that they are the very word of God, and that he only can enable us to understand them.[674]

If there is one thing that will shake the unbelieving, scholarly world, it is when they realize they cannot simply understand the Bible other than intellectually. Beyond regurgitating scripture references, facts, and figures, the Word is powerless to them. The power of the Word and its deeper understanding is only manifest by the Holy Spirit. For the believer, the Spirit increasingly reveals truth and maturity grows, precept upon precept. God hides these things from the so-called wise and has revealed them to babes.

The Bible, being our only source of special revelation, confirms our belief in the true God who proves he exists through the created world. More specifically still is the glory of redemption that is received through the hearing of the Word by the power of the Holy Spirit. If you claim to be a believer, your life should exemplify Christ and you should desire increased knowledge through the study of his Word.

---

[673] Ps 19:10; Ne 8:3-10; Ex 24:7; 2Ch 34:27; Isa 66:2
[674] 2Pe 1:19-21; Lk 24:45; 2Co 3:13-16—WLC Q157a

AUGUST 5

HANDLING OF THE WORD (PART 2)

Understanding the meaning of the Scriptures is only the first half of our equation. We must apply them to our life:

With desire to know, believe, and obey the will of God revealed in them; with diligence and attention to the matter and scope of them;[675] *with meditation, application, self-denial,*[676] *and prayer.*[677]

The eyes of the worldly have been blinded to the truth of God's Word. However, for the believer, we desire to know more and to be transformed into the image of the Author and Finisher of our faith. We have been redeemed by Christ, and now we conform our lives to him. We no longer keep on sinning. *How can we, who have died to sin, live in it any longer?* We pursue holiness and walk in the light.

The godly life does not happen automatically. Although the power is through Christ, the obedience is ours. It begins with desire. If we have little desire, perhaps we are not obedient to know him. Jesus will not sit on a shelf as a token of our so-called salvation. Jesus and the Word are interchangeable. If your Bible is gathering dust, you have unplugged from God. With this, everything suffers, evidenced by a fruitless walk and shallow prayer life.

God, awake me from my slumber that I may desire thee.

---

[675] Dt 17:10,20; Ac 17:11; Ac 8:30,34; Lk 10:26-28
[676] Ps 1:2; Ps 119:97; 2Ch 34:21; Pr 3:5; Dt 33:3
[677] Pr 2:1-6; Ps 119:18; Ne 7:6,8–WLC Q157b

AUGUST 6

PREACH THE WORD

Every believer has a testimony of the hope that is within them, but not every believer is gifted to be a preacher.

The word of God is to be preached only by such as are sufficiently gifted[678] *and also duly approved and called to that office.*[679]

The Scriptures are quite clear as to the diversity of the gifts within the body of Christ. The Word of God is to be studied by all, but only preached by those who are gifted in this manner. If just anyone was allowed to stand and exposit the Scriptures, we would have to endure poor speakers and shallow interpretations.

God is not a God of chaos, but of order; not of ambiguity, but of sound doctrine. The teaching man of God is able to discern biblical truth and clearly relay it to his students. It is the students' responsibility to receive the teaching with readiness, but then go to the Scripture and prove whether these things are so. The teacher does have the responsibility to teach sound doctrine, but the student does not blindly believe everything. We are each accountable to verify what we hear.

Lord, today you have confirmed the importance of allowing preachers to preach and the others to utilize their gifts as allocated. Help us to be content with our spiritual gifts and to use them for your glory. Do not allow envy creep in and make us ineffective in the service to which you have called us.

---

[678] 1Ti 3:2,6; Eph 4:8-11; Hos 4:6; Mal 2:7; 2Co 3:6–WLC Q158
[679] Jer 14:15; Ro 10:15; Heb 5:4; 1Co 12:28,29; 1Ti 3:10; 1Ti 4:14; 1Ti 5:22

AUGUST 7

THE PREACHER (PART 1)

Yesterday, we determined that only some are called to preach. How is the word of God to be preached by those with this gift?

They that are called to labor in the ministry of the word are to preach sound doctrine diligently, in season and out of season;[680] plainly, not in the enticing words of man's wisdom, but in demonstration of the Spirit, and of power;[681] faithfully, making known the whole counsel of God;[682]

Although this topic is about those who preach, it is important for all to understand. For if we are not proclaiming the Gospel, we are listening to those that do. We have the responsibility to sit under a preacher who provides sound doctrine, leading in the paths of God. If we do not sit with a discerning ear, we fail ourselves and those around us who may be assuming our endorsement.

There is no perfect preacher, but that does not mean that no man is qualified. The preacher points to the Word of God as his only source of truth. His teaching must be comprehensible in explaining the harmony of the Bible, allowing the deep things of God to be held in tension. He should also be able to provide answers to questions, demonstrating his comprehension of that particular doctrine.

Lord, thank you for faithful ministers of the Word.

---

[680] Tit 2:1,8; Ac 18:25; 2Ti 4:2
[681] 1Co 14:19; 1Co 2:4
[682] Jer 23:28; 1Co 4:1,2; Ac 20:27–WLC Q159a

AUGUST 8

THE PREACHER (PART 2)

They that are called to be ministers are to preach:

Wisely, applying themselves to the necessities and capacities of the hearers;[683] *zealously, with fervent love to God and the souls of his people;*[684] *sincerely, aiming at his glory, and their conversion,*[685] *edification, and salvation.*[686]

These descriptions accompany the godly preacher who instructs with sound doctrine. These are filtering tests to any who teach the word. A preacher giving biblical truths without zeal for the Gospel he proclaims demonstrates the Word as ineffective. And yet, zeal without truth is far worse. Godly passion accompanies authentic love for doctrine.

To what end is the preaching of the gospel? That all would hear the Word and those who are called of God would be converted, become disciples, and learn all the things of God. There is one primary external purpose for the believers, to make disciples. There is one primary internal purpose, to live a sanctified life, i.e., a life set apart unto God and his worship.

Lord, your ways are right and worthy to be followed. Let our ears hear your words from those who preach. Let our discernment come from you, that we may know thy truth.

---

[683] Col 1:28; 2Ti 2:15; 1Co 3:2; Heb 5:12-14; Lk 12:42
[684] Ac 18:25; 2Co 5:13,14; Php 1:15,16; Col 4:12; 2Co 12:15
[685] 2Co 2:17; 2Co 4:2; 1Th 2:4-6; Jn 7:18; 1Co 9:19-22
[686] 2Co 12:19; Eph 4:12; 1Ti 4:16-18–WLC Q159b

AUGUST 9

RECEIVE THE WORD OF TRUTH

What is our responsibility when we listen to Bible teaching?

It is required of those that hear the word preached, that they attend upon it with diligence, preparation, and prayer; examine what they hear by the scriptures;[687] receive the truth with faith, love, meekness, and readiness of mind, as the word of God;[688] meditate, and confer of it;[689] hide it in their hearts, and bring forth the fruit of it in their lives.[690]

There are basically three methods to receive the preached Word. First is to blindly believe what is preached. Second is to be closed to your hearing. Third are those who listen to the Word alertly with a desire to learn, then go to their Bible and verify that the teaching is consistent with Scripture.

One thing that we must take into consideration when hearing God's Word is the fact that no preacher is infallible. But that does not mean that they err on all counts. God enables truth to be effectively filtered to the listener. The Spirit also allows our existing knowledge of truth to test against the teaching that we are receiving. Finally, the Bible itself corrects any contradictions we may have heard. With a prayerful heart, we are to test all things against other Scriptures, with the knowledge that the Spirit will lead us into all righteousness.

[687] Pr 8:34; 1Pe 2:1,2; Lk 8:18; Ps 119:18; Eph 6:18,19; Ac 17:11
[688] Heb 4:2; 2Th 2:10; Jas 1:21; Ac 17:11; 1Th 2:13
[689] Lk 9:44; Heb 2:1; Lk 24:14; Dt 6:6,7
[690] Pr 2:1; Ps 119:11; Lk 8:15; Jas 1:25–WLC Q160

AUGUST 10

SACRAMENTS

How do the sacraments become effectual means of salvation?

The sacraments become effectual means of salvation, not by any power in themselves, or any virtue derived from the piety or intention of him by whom they are administered, but only by the working of the Holy Ghost, and the blessing of Christ, by whom they are instituted.[691]

In baptism and in the Lord's Supper, we are obedient to the Sacraments that have been instituted to those who believe. In this doctrine, we must carefully handle the term *effective means of salvation*. It does not mean that the power of salvation rests in man's participation of these sacraments. Salvation remains solely by the grace of God, through faith of the regenerate. Yet the manifestation of belief abides in obedience to these sacraments that are commanded.

Our participation in the sacraments is not a work unto salvation, it is participation in the blessings which accompany it. The Lord Jesus, when he was baptized, did not do so because he needed repentance. Yet Jesus gave his reason *to fulfill all righteousness*. Likewise, Jesus commands that believers be baptized and participate in the Lord's Supper and we are to obey this call.

Lord, as we dig into the sacraments to which you have commanded, we ask that you open our eyes to these blessings.

---

[691] 1Pe 3:21; Ac 8:13,23; 1Co 3:6,7; 1Co 12:13–WLC Q161

AUGUST 11

WHAT IS A SACRAMENT?

A sacrament is an holy ordinance instituted by Christ in his church,[692] to signify, seal, and exhibit unto those that are within the covenant of grace,[693] the benefits of his mediation, to strengthen and increase their faith, and all other graces; to oblige them to obedience;[694] to testify and cherish their love and communion one with another; and to distinguish them from those that are without.[695]

There is nothing that the Lord would ever have us do that would not be for the benefit of those who love him. His graciousness is never ending and the sacraments to which he has commanded us are not for vain ritual nor a routine to display our own high place.

Believers are strengthened in our faith. We see results in another's life and recognize what Christ has done for them. We participate ourselves and show the outward sign of the assurance to our salvation. What amazing grace has been poured out for us that we may continually remember what Jesus accomplished on that cross for us and recognize that we are raised with him.

We partake in these holy ordinances because we are called to obedience to our Master. We were once slaves to sin and its darkness; now we have been purchased by Christ and we walk in his light. Recognizing Jesus' lordship, we are obligated to his sacraments.

---

[692] Ge 17:7,10; Ex 12; Mt 28:19; Mt 26:26-28
[693] Ro 4:11; 1Co 11:24,25; Ro 15:8; Ex 12:48
[694] Ac 2:38; 1Co 10:16; Ro 4:11; Gal 3:27; Ro 6:3,4; 1Co 10:21
[695] Eph 4:2-5; 1Co 12:13; Eph 2:11,12; Ge 34:14–WLC Q162

AUGUST 12

THE TWOFOLD SACRAMENT?

It is critical that we understand the areas that are relevant to the believer's participation in the sacraments.

The parts of a sacrament are two: the one an outward and sensible sign, used according to Christ's own appointment; the other an inward and spiritual grace thereby signified.[696]

The Old Testament believers were not made God's people because they were circumcised, but by their act of faith they performed the sign of the covenant that God provided. Similarly today, our baptism is the outward sign of what has already taken place internally.

The second part of the sacraments is inward. The inward reality is previous to the outward sign. The Holy Spirit regenerates the condemned depravity, then the new believer can walk out his renewed life. So the Sacraments are inward spiritually and outward signified.

Two parts are consistent with the makeup of man. We are both physical and spiritual beings. God does not touch the spirit of man and leave him to live in corruption. The spiritual rebirth of man will always manifest itself outwardly. The apostle Paul clarifies this, "How shall we, that are dead to sin, live in it any longer?" (Romans 6:2). He goes on to show how our physical baptism represents the spiritual reality already taking place. This is why anyone who claims to be born again, yet their outward life perpetuates in sin, cannot be truly saved.

---

[696] Mt 3:11; 1Pe 3:21; Ro 2:28,29–WLC Q163

AUGUST 13

TWO SACRAMENTS

I was raised in the Catholic Church that formally has seven sacraments—Baptism, Confirmation, Holy Communion, Confession, Marriage, Holy Orders, and the Anointing of the Sick. However:

Under the New Testament, Christ hath instituted in his church only two sacraments, baptism and the Lord's Supper.[697]

I am not trying to point out the differences between Christian faiths, but only as a means of clarification for those of us who are familiar with the Catholic practices, I felt it important to distinguish the sacraments that are directly instituted by Jesus Christ. The other sacraments listed, although being in some manner integral in a believer's life, are not described as an effective means in salvation.

Again, as a matter of review, these Christ-instituted *sacraments signify, seal, and exhibit those within the covenant of grace.* The Lord has blessed us with every spiritual blessing. He has graciously administered salvation unto us; by his blood, he purchased us. We symbolically enter the grave and are raised with him through baptism. Furthermore, he has called us to remember his sacrifice through the celebration of the Lord's Supper. Both of these we will cover in greater detail in the days ahead.

Lord, you have paid the ultimate price to redeem your elect. Your grace is overpowering. Your mercy is overwhelming.

---

[697] Mt 28:19; 1Co 11:20,23; Mt 26:26-28–WLC Q164

AUGUST 14

BAPTISM

Many people will argue that baptism is not necessary for one to be saved. However, they are missing baptism's bigger picture.

Baptism is a sacrament of the New Testament, wherein Christ hath ordained the washing with water in the name of the Father, and of the Son, and of the Holy Ghost to be a sign and seal of in-grafting into himself, of remission of sins by his blood, and regeneration by his Spirit;[698] of adoption and resurrection unto everlasting life;[699] and whereby the parties baptized are solemnly admitted into the visible church, and enter into an open and professed engagement to be wholly and only the Lord's.[700]

Those who minimize baptism's importance have neither considered its significance nor the Savior who instituted it. As salvation itself, baptism is a gift to the believer. Freely instituted by Christ to his church to come freely to salvation and be washed clean from sin and death. We come up out of the water, symbolizing our resurrection with Christ unto life everlasting.

Those who are raised with Christ will not experience the second death. The second death comes to unbelievers at the Judgment of Christ. He will cast them into the eternal lake of hell's fire, because of their rejection of God. How great a salvation, for we deserve nothing less, yet Christ has set his grace upon us whom he made righteous.

---

[698] Mt 28:19; Gal 3:27; Mk 1:4; Rev 1:5; Tit 3:5; Eph 5:26
[699] Gal 3:26,27; 1Co 15:29; Ro 6:5
[700] 1Co 12:13; Ro 6:4–WLC Q165

AUGUST 15

WHO RECEIVES BAPTISM?

There are varying thoughts as to the baptism of infants. Some do, some do not, and some churches leave it up to the parents to decide. However, as to the baptism of the cognizant, the answer is clear.

Baptism is not to be administered to any that are out of the visible church and so strangers from the covenant of promise, till they profess their faith in Christ and obedience to him,[701] but infants descended from parents, either both or but one of them professing faith in Christ, and obedience to him, are, in that respect, within the covenant, and to be baptized.[702]

All who confess Jesus as Lord are to be baptized. For children, they must be able to voice their understanding of Jesus' work on the cross for their forgiveness of sins. Some people point to the age of twelve, which is when children of the Old Covenant were formally recognized to make a mature decision.

Returning to the baptism of infants, there are good arguments both ways. For those opposed to infant baptism, the basic points are that an infant cannot voice a testimony of faith and that there are no direct references to a single count of infant baptism in Scripture. Those for infant baptism point to circumcision under the Old Testament. Infants were circumcised under this sign. Therefore, baptism is the parallel sign under the New Covenant.

---

[701] Ac 8:36,37; Ac 2:38
[702] Ge 17:7,9 compared with Gal 3:9,14 and Col 2:11,12 and Ac 2:38,39 and Ro 4:11,12; 1Co 7:14; Mt 28:19; Lk 18:15,16; Ro 11:16–WLC Q166

AUGUST 16

BAPTISM REVISITED (PART 1)

Some churches perform baptism immediately upon a person's confession of Christ, while others hold special services dedicated to those who would better understand this act of obedience. For those, previously baptized as infants, they can use this opportunity as their decisive public testimony.

The needful but much neglected duty of improving our baptism is to be performed by us all our life long, especially in the time of temptation and when we are present at the administration of it to others;[703] by serious and thankful consideration of the nature of it, and of the ends for which Christ instituted it, the privileges and benefits conferred and sealed thereby, and our solemn vow made therein;[704]

Baptism is not a "do it, then forget it" act. It is something that remains part of our lifelong walk with Christ. When we are in the midst of temptation, we consider the fact that we can no longer live in sin and that our being raised with Christ has delivered us from the death which sin originally brought. Each baptism we witness recalls our own.

In the next couple of days, we will discuss some things which are pertinent to remember of our own baptism and the accomplishment of Christ on our behalf.

Lord, forgive me for times that I have forgotten my own baptism. Refresh my soul to consider its cost and benefits.

---

[703] Col 2:11,12; Ro 6:4,6,11
[704] Ro 6:3-5–WLC Q167a

AUGUST 17

BAPTISM REVISITED (PART 2)

We remember and improve our baptism:

By being humbled for our sinful defilement, our falling short of, and walking contrary to the grace of baptism, and our engagements;[705] *by growing up to assurance of pardon of sin, and of all other blessings sealed to us in that sacrament;*[706] *by drawing strength from the death and resurrection of Christ, into whom we are baptized, for the mortifying of sin, and quickening of grace.*[707]

If one thing is certain for the Christian, it is that we never escape the knowledge of our sin. Although as we mature in Christ, we typically sin less often and less grievously, we hate even the little sin which remains more and more. Our flesh remains and we fall short. However, Christ has completed the work, and by our baptism, we remember the forgiveness we received and the eternal life we possess.

Through Jesus Christ, we have assurance of salvation. We trust his Word that has guaranteed our justification. We no longer consider the power of sin, but know that sin itself was put to death at the cross. Jesus took our failure to the Law, which was against us and we could not keep, and nailed it to the cross. We know that we have life because Jesus was raised from the dead. Through the remembrance of our baptism, we also have assurance that we were raise with him.

---

[705] 1Co 1:11-13; Ro 6:2,3
[706] Ro 4:11,12; 1Pe 3:21
[707] Ro 6:3-5–WLC Q167b

AUGUST 18

BAPTISM REVISITED (PART 3)

By the recalling the association we have with Christ through our baptism, we draw strength in our new life through baptism:

And by endeavoring to live by faith, to have our conversation in holiness and righteousness, as those that have therein given up their names to Christ;[708] and to walk in brotherly love, as being baptized by the same Spirit into one body.[709]

The Christian life is not difficult, it is impossible. Just as we could not achieve righteousness on our own, do we think we could now sustain our own salvation? By no means. We live only because Christ lives in us. Therefore, by the knowledge of what has already taken place for us, we now live a life set apart unto the Lord and his righteousness.

Our identity is now in Christ and our citizenship is now in heaven. We live as strangers in a strange land among strange people. Our duty, as we are temporarily left in this present age, is to share the Gospel. Those who would be disciples, we teach. Then, as adopted children of God, we walk together as brothers and sisters with Christ.

Lord, thank you for the lessons we have learned during this review of our baptism. Help us to remember our baptism that we might not sin against thee and live in light that we are raised with Christ. Grant us assurance in our salvation that we may live boldly.

---

[708] Gal 3:26,27; Ro 6:22; Ac 2:38
[709] 1Co 12:13,25,26,27–WLC Q167c

AUGUST 19

THE LORD'S SUPPER

The second sacrament that Jesus appointed is the Lord's Supper. Its purpose is far reaching, just as is our baptism.

The Lord's Supper is a sacrament of the New Testament wherein, by giving and receiving bread and wine according to the appointment of Jesus Christ, his death is showed forth and they that worthily communicate feed upon his body and blood to their spiritual nourishment and growth in grace, have their union and communion with him confirmed;[710] testify and renew their thankfulness, and engagement to God, and their mutual love and fellowship each with other, as members of the same mystical body.[711]

Jesus' words, "Do this in remembrance of me," call believers to observe and practice the receiving of the elements to which he identified his body and blood. The elements neither exist nor are transformed into the literal body and blood of Christ, yet are only symbolic of what was sacrificed on behalf of the elect.

We will spend the next several days discussing the elements, what they communicate to us, the manner in which believers are to receive them, and our spiritual attitude after we partake.

Lord, you offered your body to be crushed under the weight of the wood and all that it represented. You shed your blood and by it forgave the sins of those you call. Through your Supper, we remember.

---

[710] Lk 22:20; Mt 26:26-28; 1Co 11:23-26; 1Co 10:16
[711] 1Co 11:24; 1Co 10:14-16,21; 1Co 10:17–WLC Q168

AUGUST 20

REMEMBERING CALVARY

Christ hath appointed the ministers of his word, in the administration of this sacrament of the Lord's supper, to set apart the bread and wine from common use, by the word of institution, thanksgiving, and prayer; to take and break the bread, and to give both the bread and the wine to the communicants: who are, by the same appointment, to take and eat the bread, and to drink the wine, in thankful remembrance that the body of Christ was broken and given, and his blood, shed for them.[712]

In the Lord's Supper, we celebrate Christ's death. This does not sound right, celebrating death. However, when we realize that this is the culmination of God's eternal plan, that Jesus is the *Lamb slain from the foundation of the world,*[713] it is only right that we celebrate. God's plan never fails or falters, but has worked perfectly according to his ultimate timing and purpose.

The Lord's Supper is for our benefit to regularly remember this perfect work. We may think that God could have accomplished the redemption of his elect by other means. However, this is not so. Jesus confirmed this for us in his prayer in the garden. He asked the Father if there was any other way to let *this cup* pass by him. By the will of the Father and the obedience of the Son, we know that there was no other way. God set the price for sin, death. It was only by the shedding of innocent blood that sins could be forgiven. Remember!

---

[712] 1Co 11:23,24; Mt 26:26-28; Mk 14:22-24; Lk 22:19,20–WLC Q169
[713] Rev 13:8

AUGUST 21

FEEDING ON CHRIST (PART 1)

There has been confusion over the centuries as to what, exactly, is the physical form of the elements.

As the body and blood of Christ are not corporally or carnally present in, with, or under the bread and wine in the Lord's supper,[714] and yet are spiritually present to the faith of the receiver, no less truly and really than the elements themselves are to their outward senses.[715]

The Roman Catholic church believes that the elements of the bread and wine are literally transformed in the physical body and blood of Christ during the mass by what they term "transubstantiation." They, in error, believe that this is the continuation of the work at the cross.

That the work of Christ was complete in the single act at the Cross is best argued directly by the Scripture itself. Hebrews 10:10-14 states:

> By this will we have been sanctified through the offering of the body of Jesus Christ once for all. And every priest stands daily ministering and offering time after time the same sacrifices, which can never take away sins; but He, having offered one sacrifice for sins for all time, sat down at the right hand of God, waiting from that time onward until His enemies be made a footstool for His feet. For by one offering He has perfected for all time those who are sanctified.

That Christ died once and for all is imperatively clear.

---

[714] Ac 3:21
[715] Mt 26:26,28–WLC Q170a

AUGUST 22

FEEDING ON CHRIST (PART 2)

The body and blood of Christ, though not physically present, are spiritually present to the faith of the receiver:

So they that worthily communicate in the sacrament of the Lord's supper, do therein feed upon the body and blood of Christ, not after a corporal and carnal, but in a spiritual manner, yet truly and really,[716] *while by faith they receive and apply unto themselves Christ crucified, and all the benefits of his death.*[717]

That the bread and wine are only symbolic of the body and blood of Christ does not in any way make the Lord's Supper inferior to the false teaching of the Roman Catholic faith. Jesus said, "Do this in remembrance of me," not "Do this to continue my unfinished work."

Jesus' closing statement from the cross was *teleo* (in Greek). In John 19:30, the word in English states, "It is finished." It means *to bring to a close, to finish, to end*. It was used to mark business transactions as satisfied or *paid in full*. The cross satisfied God for all time. Believers' sins can never be punished again since that would violate his justice.

The celebration of the Lord's Supper is the remembrance of the perfect work that Jesus accomplished on our behalf. He paid the price, in full, which satisfied the Father's justice. Do not forget the body and blood, which purchased your redemption. Praise be to God!

---

[716] 1Co 11:24-29
[717] 1Co 10:16–WLC Q170b

AUGUST 23

COMING TO THE TABLE (PART 1)

When we go to a formal dinner, we prepare ourselves for the event. In a deeper essence, the same is true of the Lord's Supper.

They that receive the sacrament of the Lord's supper are, before they come, to prepare themselves thereunto, by examining themselves of their being in Christ, of their sins and wants;[718] of the truth and measure of their knowledge, faith, repentance.[719]

Preparation for an event of remembering? Perhaps, there is nothing more important. Preparation for the Lord's Supper is fully a spiritual act and in order for this sacrament to be effective, the believer has to prepare spiritually. Unlike the formal dinner event we mentioned earlier, where it is mostly physical: cleaned up, dressed up, and an empty stomach; the Lord's Supper is Scripture knowledge, prayer, meditation on the Word, and hunger only for spiritual truth.

The more Scripture we know and understand, the deeper our comprehension is of what Christ accomplished in his life, death, and resurrection. We are told to come to the cross in a penitent frame of mind, confessing our sin, and proclaiming thanks for the forgiveness granted to us through his shed blood. We meditate on the Scriptures that have permeated our soul, causing us an even deeper desire for more knowledge of the height, depth, length, and breadth of the love of Christ.[720] It is all available in the remembrance of his body and blood.

---

[718] 1Co 11:28; 2Co 13:5; 1Co 5:7 compared with Ex 12:15
[719] 1Co 11:29; 1Co 13:5; Mt 26:28; Zec 12:10; 1Co 11:31–WLC Q171a
[720] Ep 3:18

AUGUST 24

COMING TO THE TABLE (PART 2)

The balance of spiritual preparation for the Lord's Supper includes the extension from self examination to our

Love to God and the brethren, charity to all men, forgiving those that have done them wrong;[721] of their desires after Christ, and of their new obedience, and by renewing the exercise of these graces,[722] by serious meditation, and fervent prayer.[723]

As important as self-preparation is for the Lord's Supper, it does remain a Church community experience. This means that having peace within ourselves is not the end of the experience. The Lord tells his disciples, in no uncertain terms, that the world will know us by our love for one another. Specifically, our love, as it is manifest within the body of believers, is a witness to the true religion.

The call is not for unrealistic, perfect human behavior. It is a call to be quick to restore each other in brotherly love. Discipline will be necessary at times, but grace should never be left out. The intended purpose is to create motivation for prompt restoration back into the fold. All the while, prayer and meditation is necessary to keep a godly and biblical disposition.

Lord, forgive the times I have come to your table without proper preparation. Increase my desire to be a better disciple.

---

[721] 1Co 10:16,17; Ac 2:46,47; 1Co 5:8; 1Co 11:18,20; Mt 5:23,24
[722] Isa 55:1; Jn 7:37; 1Co 5:7,8; 1Co 11:25,26,28; Heb 10:21,22,24; Ps 26:6
[723] 1Co 11:24,25; 2Ch 30:18,19; Mt 26:26–TWLC Q171b

AUGUST 25

UNCERTAINTY IN COMMUNION

There are times when believers, especially those who recently have confessed Jesus as Lord, have doubts of their salvation.

One who doubteth of his being in Christ, or of his due preparation to the sacrament of the Lord's supper, may have true interest in Christ, though he be not yet assured thereof.[724]

The stipulation is that one must be in Christ in order to properly participate in the Lord's Supper. Therefore, one who is unsure may feel unworthy to partake in the communion. The fact is, in and of ourselves, we are not worthy. However, salvation is by grace alone, and for those who recognize their sinfulness and freely receive his forgiveness, they can trust that there are no further requirements.

Doubt is the natural response to fleshy thinking. Our flesh, which remains unredeemed, wrestles against our spirit. Once Satan loses a soul to Jesus, he switches tactics. He goes from telling you, "There is no God," to discouraging you, "You're disappointing God, and you'll never stay saved." These tactics can make us feel defeated, and we may become ineffective in our walk.

Until we are raised incorruptible, we do have this battle to fight. The good soldier comes to the fight prepared. We are to put on the whole armor of God,[725] which includes believing God's promises.

---

[724] Isa 50:10; 1Jn 5:13; Ps 88 throughout; Ps 77:1-12; Jonah 2:4,7–WLC Q172a
[725] Ep 6:10-18

AUGUST 26

TESTING OUR SINCERITY

Even in doubt, a person can still have true interest in Christ:

And in God's account hath it, if he be duly affected with the apprehension of the want of it,[726] and unfeignedly desires to be found in Christ,[727] and to depart from iniquity.[728]

Do you ever have doubts? You can ask yourself these questions. First: *Do I love God perfectly?* Answer: No. Second: *Do I love God as much as I should?* Answer: No. Because this means with *all my heart, all my soul, with all my mind, and with all my strength.* Yet this is our command. So the third question: *Do I love God at all?*

If we can say that we love God for who he is and for what he has done for us, then we know that we are his children. This is because of the fact that we can only love him because he has first loved us. Before we are converted, we hate God. We run away and hide from him. When we believe, we see our sin, we run to him for refuge.

The other half of running toward God is running away from sin. We repent, which literally means to change our mind, to turn our back on sin or the temptation. Jesus says, "If you love me, keep my commandments." As we mature in Christ, we show we love him more by sinning less. Because of his body and his blood, we are released from sin's chains and can come to his table without condemnation.

---

[726] Isa 54:7-10; Mt 5:3,4; Ps 31:22; Ps 73:13,22,23
[727] Php 3:8,9; Ps 10:17; Ps 42:1,2,5,11
[728] 2Ti 2:19; Isa 50:10; Ps 66:18-20–WLC Q172b

AUGUST 27

STANDING ON GOD'S PROMISES

What if you doubt the assurance of your faith, put yourself through a verification process, finding that you trust Jesus died on the cross and rose from the dead for your sins, yet remain in doubt?

In which case (because promises are made, and this sacrament is appointed, for the relief even of weak and doubting Christians[729]), he is to bewail his unbelief, and labor to have his doubts resolved;[730] and, so doing, he may and ought to come to the Lord's supper, that he may be further strengthened.[731]

Some people ask the Lord to forgive a sin that they have previously asked forgiveness. This could be repeated time and time again, yet they do not feel forgiven. To which I believe the answer is for them to again ask the Lord's forgiveness. Only this time, not for the old sin, but for their unbelief. That's right: their unbelief that Jesus did not do what he promised, which is to remove our sins as far as east is from west.

They may also have to learn to forgive themselves. When Jesus asked the woman caught in adultery, "Where are your accusers? Is there no one left to accuse you?" she answered him, "No one, sir." Then Jesus said, "Neither do I condemn you. Go and sin no more." We must trust his forgiveness, knowing we may come to the Lord's Supper.

---

[729] Isa 40:11,29,31; Mt 11:28; Mt 12:20; Mt 26:28
[730] Mk 9:24; Ac 2:37; Ac 16:30
[731] Ro 4:11; 1Co 11:28—WLC Q172c

AUGUST 28

CONFESSION OVERRULED

The occurrence of someone being kept from celebrating the Lord's Supper with the congregation is possible.

Such as are found to be ignorant or scandalous, notwithstanding their profession of the faith, and desire to come to the Lord's supper, may and ought to be kept from that sacrament, by the power which Christ hath left in his church,[732] until they receive instruction and manifest their reformation.[733]

Typically, if someone is kept from the communion table, they would have been informed prior to the celebration. This would keep from disrupting the service and the prayerful state of the other members. This action would not necessarily prohibit the offender from participating in the rest of the church service, where if they did attend, they would be encouraged to penitently seek the Lord.

Church discipline is not only acceptable; it is mandated by the Lord. One example of discipline's due process is shown to us in Matthew's Gospel, chapter 18. The intent is not to harm the offender's faith, but to restore him as gently as possible. However, if there is no repentance, then the offender is excommunicated as they have revealed their heart.

Lord, help us to be faithful to the disciplinary actions within the Church. We want your Supper to be highly regarded in our lives.

---

[732] 1Co 11:27-31 compared with Mt 7:6 and 1Co 5 and Jude 23 and 1Ti 5:22
[733] 2Co 2:7–WLC Q173

AUGUST 29

THIS IS MY BODY (PART 1)

We have moved from our preparation for the Lord's Supper to our disposition while receiving the elements.

It is required of them that receive the sacrament of the Lord's supper, that, during the time of the administration of it, with all holy reverence and attention they wait upon God in that ordinance.[734]

Having spiritually prepared ourselves for the Lord's Supper, we now maintain a sanctified attitude throughout the memorial. We worship a Holy God and the ground that we enter during communion is holy ground. Listen to the Psalmist express those who may enter:

> Who shall ascend into the hill of the Lord? Or, who shall stand in His holy place? He who has clean hands and pure heart; who has not lifted up his soul to an idol, nor sworn deceitfully. He shall receive the blessing from the LORD, and righteousness from the God of his salvation.
>
> Psalm 24:3-5

Therefore, this is our disposition during the Supper. We recognize God's holiness, and we approach in our most sanctified attitude. We do not pretend that there is anything holy within ourselves, but rely fully on Christ's covering to allow us to enter into his holiness. Holiness is not our perfection, but it is our purposeful separation from anything unclean in honor of God.

Lord, we come to your table with complete and holy reverence.

---

[734] Lev 10:3; WLC 12:28; Ps 5:7; 1Co 11:17,26,27–WLC Q174a

AUGUST 30

THIS IS MY BODY (PART 2)

When receiving the sacrament of the Lord's Supper, the participant is to reverently and

Diligently observe the sacramental elements and actions,[735] *heedfully discern the Lord's body, and affectionately meditate on his death and sufferings, and thereby stir up themselves to a vigorous exercise of their graces.*[736]

This is not to say that we build up our emotional state in an unnatural fashion. Rather, we are careful to ensure we have put ourselves in a godly attitude of affection for the event we are remembering, the death of our Lord. It is a heightened awareness of the Lord's passion along with the deep meaning of the communion elements.

Why focus on death? Shouldn't we be paying more attention to the resurrection of our Lord? There is a time and purpose for all things, and because Jesus has asked us to partake in communion in remembrance of what he has done for us, we obey. Another reason we focus on death is because we recall the wages of our sin. We owed the debt, but Jesus paid it out of his eternal love.

Although we will never fully comprehend the magnitude of his love on this side of heaven, each time we earnestly receive this sacrament, we do grow in knowledge. No greater love has a man than he lay down his life for his friends. Are you a friend of God?

---

[735] Ex 24:8 compared with Mt 26:28
[736] 1Co 11:29; Lk 22:19; 1Co 11:26; 1Co 10:3,4,5,11,14–WLC Q174b

AUGUST 31

THIS IS MY BODY (PART 3)

The result of one's proper spiritual state and mind-set as they partake in the Lord's Supper is the exercise of their graces:

In judging themselves, and sorrowing for sin;[737] in earnest hungering and thirsting after Christ, feeding on him by faith, receiving of his fullness, trusting in his merits, rejoicing in his love, giving thanks for his grace;[738] in renewing of their covenant with God, and love to all the saints.[739]

With Jesus as our model of perfection, we have a mirror in which to behold ourselves and expose our flesh that we might judge ourselves properly. We have no satisfaction in ourselves, but we are completed and fulfilled in Christ.

This is contrary to the world's thinking, where we are told that all the power resides within ourselves, and we just have to will it out, and we can perfect ourselves. The New Age movement is actually old-school, going back to Adam and Eve who, for a moment, thought they could do it better than God. For this reason, we remember Jesus through this sacrament so we do not, for any moment, think that since that we have forgiveness, we can proceed in this Christian life on our own. In terms of redundancy, we remember so we will not forget.

---

[737] 1Co 11:31; Zec 12:10
[738] Rev 22:17; Jn 6:35; Jn 1:16; Php 1:16; Ps 63:4,5; 2Ch 30:21; Ps 22:26
[739] Jer 1:5; Ps 1:5; Ac 2:42–WLC Q174c

September 1

Communion Reflections (Part 1)

The way in which a believer worships after communion is equally important to the preparation before and the attitude during it.

The duty of Christians, after they have received the sacrament of the Lord's supper, is seriously to consider how they have behaved themselves therein, and with what success;[740] if they find quickening and comfort, to bless God for it, beg the continuance of it,[741] watch against relapses, fulfill their vows, and encourage themselves to a frequent attendance on that ordinance.[742]

Reflecting upon the business we perform with God during the Lord's Supper is vital action to bring closure to the celebration. *Was my attitude congruent with the Spirit? Did I properly prepare my heart before hand? Did I confess with a penitent heart? Am I inspired to beat down my flesh with even more fervor?* If my answers are *yes*, then I continue to walk in step with the Spirit.

The Lord's Supper is a building point in the Christian faith. We grow in knowledge of the Lord's work on the cross, and we grow in holiness through the sanctifying work of the Holy Spirit. If we maintain our duties, we will not find this celebration just a matter of routine or tradition, but we will look forward to this sacred time with a growing passion.

Lord, thank you for the regular reminder of your love for me. Please burn off the dross in my life and refine me toward your purity.

---

[740] Ps 28:7; Ps 85:8; 1Co 11:17,30,31
[741] 2Ch 30:21,22,23,25,26; Ac 2:42; Ps 36:10; SS 3:4; 1Ch 29:18
[742] 1Co 10:3,4,5,12; Ps 50:14; 1Co 11:25,26; Ac 2:42,46—WLC Q175a

SEPTEMBER 2

COMMUNION REFLECTIONS (PART 2)

There may be occasions when we do emerge from the Lord's Supper having accomplished our duties to the event.

But if they find no present benefit, more exactly to review their preparation to, and carriage at, the sacrament;[743] in both which, if they can approve themselves to God and their own consciences, they are to wait for the fruit of it in due time:[744] but, if they see they have failed in either, they are to be humbled, and to attend upon it afterward with more care and diligence.[745]

Partaking in this communion is not a competition. There are no so-called "points" lost with God. Rather, it is a matter of our duty to be more careful with our disposition in subsequent events. To handle this sacrament carefully and with intent to achieve the proper spiritual growth the Lord intends. This is his sacrament, given to us in memory of his life being laid down for his Church.

We stress the importance of Communion time. We must enter humbly and with penitence. We must set our minds upon Christ. We must comprehend his sacrifice. We must consider his body and his blood. We must see him forsaken of God as he took our sin upon himself. We must see him bruised and we must not turn our eyes away. His single act, for our eternal forgiveness, deserves our full attention. We will come to the table more diligent and thankful next Communion.

---

[743] SS 5:1-6; Eccles. 5:1-6
[744] Ps 123:1,2; Ps 42:5,8; Ps 43:3-5
[745] 2Ch 30:18,19; Isa 1:16,18; 2Co 7:11; 1Ch 15:12-14—WLC Q175b

SEPTEMBER 3

TWO SACRAMENTS AGREE

Let's consider the two sacraments that the Lord commands. First, let's consider where the two sacraments agree.

The sacraments of baptism and the Lord's supper agree, in that the author of both is God;[746] the spiritual part of both is Christ and his benefits, both are seals of the same covenant,[747] are to be dispensed by ministers of the gospel, and by none other,[748] and to be continued in the church of Christ until his second coming.[749]

Jesus spoke these two sacraments into the disciplines of his Church. As slaves of the Master, we obey his command because he is our Lord. We partake in both because we have entered into the family of God. The Spirit testifies within us that we are the children of God, and we, through these sacraments, give testimony to the world.

These two sacraments shall be practiced on earth until Jesus returns. The church visibly grows as more are baptized and the church points to the Cross through Communion, in remembrance of the Lamb who took away the sins of the world.

Lord, that I have glorified you in partaking of these sacraments. Where I have failed to be sincere, awaken my spirit when I remember your sacrifice in the Lord's Supper.

---

[746] Mt 28:19; 1Co 11:23
[747] Ro 6:3,4; 1Co 10:16; Ro 4:11; Col 2:12; Mt 26:27,28
[748] Jn 1:38; Mt 28:19; 1Co 11:23; 1Co 4:1; Heb 5:4
[749] Mt 28:19,20; 1Co 11:26—WLC Q176

SEPTEMBER 4

TWO SACRAMENTS DIFFER

Yesterday, we wrote about the areas in which the two sacraments agree. We now shall consider their distinguishing traits.

The sacraments of baptism and the Lord's supper differ, in that baptism is to be administered but once, with water, to be a sign and seal of our regeneration and in-grafting into Christ, and that even to infants;[750] *whereas the Lord's supper is to be administered often, in the elements of bread and wine, to represent and exhibit Christ as spiritual nourishment to the soul, and to confirm our continuance and growth in him, and that only to such as are of years and ability to examine themselves.*[751]

We have already discussed the debate over infant baptism. In these two sacraments, one main difference is that the Lord's Supper is a repeated event. We are to regularly partake in Communion, as members of his Church, that we may never forget the great act of love he showed at Calvary. Through the Lord's Supper, we are nourished and continue spiritual growth in Christ all the days of our life.

At baptism, we show outwardly the event of our spiritual birth into God's family. Once we are in the family, we behave as family members. There is no need to repeat the act of coming into the family. However, for our growth, we partake in the Lord's Supper regularly. We confirm ourselves to be his brethren through this Communion.

---

[750] Mt 3:11; Tit 3:5; Gal 3:27; Ge 17:7,9; Ac 2:38,39; 1Co 7:14
[751] 1Co 11:23-26; 1Co 10:16; 1Co 11:28,29–WLC Q177

September 5

Communicating with God

What is prayer?

Prayer is an offering up of our desires unto God, in the name of Christ, by the help of his Spirit;[752] *with confession of our sins, and thankful acknowledgement of his mercies.*[753]

Today, the only method man has for receiving God's direct and specific revelation is through the Scriptures themselves. The Scriptures, as they were originally written, were inspired of God. The term *inspired* biblically means *God-breathed*. God only speaks contemporarily to us through the written Word. This truth, however, does not mean that prayer is only a one-way street from us to God.

While in part, prayer is making our supplications known to God, it begins with acknowledgment of God's attributes, the confession of our sins, and our praise and thanksgiving for his forgiveness. The Holy Spirit intercedes on the believers' behalf and also confirms God's promises back to us. We will cover this further in the days ahead.

One amazing thing about prayer is that we have a Holy God who allows us to come into his presence to make our requests known. This has only been available to us since the crucifixion when the veil in the temple was torn in half. This symbolically shows us that our high priest had gained our direct access into the Holy of Holies. We should now recognize the importance of the contents of our prayers.

---

[752] Ps 62:8; Jn 16:23; Ro 8:26
[753] Ps 32:5,6; Da 9:4; Php 4:6—WLC Q178

SEPTEMBER 6

THE OMNISCIENT GOD

To whom do we pray?

God only being able to search the hearts,[754] hear the requests, pardon the sins, and fulfill the desire of all;[755] and only to be believed in, and worshipped with religious worship;[756] prayer, which is a special part thereof, is to be made by all to Him alone, and to none other.[757]

This lesson is clear. Our prayers are to be lifted to God and God alone. There are many who pray to Mary and other dead saints. Some do this out of ignorance and some because they are taught and practice this in their false religion. However, a prayer lifted to any, other than God Almighty, is both sinful and ineffective.

Saints are simply all the believers in the true God. They are not superior nor without sin. Dead saints do not make intercession on behalf of the living church. This is exactly opposite of what the Scriptures teach, which is that God alone intercedes for the saints. The other forbidden aspect of praying to saints is that they are dead. Necromancy is strictly forbidden. There is but one, omniscient God.

We have direct access to the Most Holy God, who alone can hear and answer our prayers, why would we pray to any other?

Lord Jesus, you alone are the way, the truth, and the life!

---

[754] 1Ki 8:39; Ac 1:24; Ro 8:27
[755] Ps 65:2; Mic 7:18; Ps 145:18,19
[756] Ro 10:14; Mt 4:10
[757] 1Co 1:2; Ps 50:15;Ro 10:14–WLC Q179

SEPTEMBER 7

IN HIS NAME

We have one mediator to the Father: that is Jesus Christ.

To pray in the name of Christ is, in obedience to his command, and in confidence on his promises, to ask mercy for his sake;[758] not by bare mentioning of his name,[759] but by drawing our encouragement to pray, and our boldness, strength, and hope of acceptance in prayer, from Christ and his mediation.[760]

Praying in Jesus' name is not simply a tagline to our prayers. Not a heavenly period, letting God know we are done communicating with him. Verbalized or simply just understood, it is the believer's acknowledgement that we are only able to approach God through Christ, who laid his life down on our behalf.

On my own, I stand naked as a sinner before God. Yet when God looks upon those for whom Jesus died, he sees Christ's imputed righteousness. Without Christ, there is no communion with God. That is not to say there is no relationship—for there is; it the relationship of a sinner in the hands of a righteous God. A relationship, without the Mediator, exists only in condemnation.

Lord, on my own I tremble in fear before you. Yet with Christ my Savior, you make your face shine upon me. You give me comfort that there is no safer place than in the outstretched arms of Jesus.

---

[758] Jn 14:13,14; Jn 16:24; Da 9:17
[759] Mt 7:21
[760] Heb 4:14-16; 1Jn 5:13-15 -WLC Q180

SEPTEMBER 8

HIS NAME IS HIS PURPOSE

The angel Gabriel announced to the virgin Mary that she would have a son and name him Jesus, meaning *Savior*. Jesus came to save, and we are enabled to come near to God by his name.

The sinfulness of man, and his distance from God by reason thereof, being so great, as that we can have no access into his presence without a mediator;[761] and there being none in heaven or earth appointed to, or fit for, that glorious work but Christ alone,[762] we are to pray in no other name but his only.[763]

There are many who think that God acknowledges every prayer of every person. Today's study eliminates this false concept. God sets the rules on whom he hears, and we only can come to the Father through the Son. We no longer are estranged; we are adopted as children of God, sealed by the Holy Spirit, whom makes our relationship with God as intimate as the child who runs into his daddy's arms.

There is a statement of Jesus' love for his disciples in the Gospel of John. It says that Jesus *loved them to the end*. This is to say that he loves his own to the *uttermost*, unsurpassed love. We were completely separated from God by our sin, and now, by Jesus alone, we have been brought near. Close to God, in spite of our own sinfulness. He saves us, he enables us to see the kingdom of God, he gives us access to the Father. There is no other name! Jesus!

---

[761] Jn 14:6; Isa 59:2; Eph 3:12
[762] Jn 6:27; Heb 7:25-27; 1Ti 2:5
[763] Col 3:17; Heb 13:15–TWLC Q181

SEPTEMBER 9

THE HOLY SPIRIT

Yesterday, we mentioned the Holy Spirit's part in our adoption as children of God. The Holy Spirit is through whom God lives in us, changing our hearts, enabling us unto obedience and in prayer.

We not knowing what to pray for as we ought, the Spirit helps our infirmities, by enabling us to understand both for whom, and what, and how prayer is to be made; and by working and quickening in our hearts (although not in all persons, nor at all times, in the same measure) those apprehensions, affections, and graces which are requisite for the right performance of that duty.[764]

The Holy Spirit is, quite literally, God at work within us. If we are left to ourselves, we shall remain in the darkness of our own wicked hearts. In our unredeemed state, we are led by our own lusts, looking only to fulfill our fleshly pride. Left in this state, we are blind to God's righteousness, we are deaf to his Word, and we are spiritually dead.

Salvation is of the Lord. The Holy Spirit gives life to those upon whom God sets his grace. The redeemed are raised from spiritual death to life, their ears are opened to receive and believe the Gospel, and that same Spirit leads us in the paths of righteousness. We come into union with God, yet in our flesh, we do not know how to pray as we ought, so the Holy Spirit intercedes, helping our infirmities in prayer. All thanksgiving goes to God for calling us unto himself and adopting us by his Spirit and interceding for our prayers that we may know him.

---

[764] Ro 8:26,27; Ps 10:17; Zec 12:10–WLC Q182

September 10

Praying for Others

The Holy Spirit helps us in our prayers, but not only in behalf of ourselves. Our prayers are to include those around us.

We are to pray for the whole church of Christ upon earth; for magistrates, and ministers;[765] *for ourselves, our brethren, yea, our enemies;*[766] *and for all sorts of men living, or that shall live hereafter, but not for the dead, nor for those that are known to have sinned the sin unto death.*[767]

Our prayers are not to try and convince God of our desires for these things, but that God's perfect will be done. We do not know whom God is saving; it could be our worst enemy. I must remember that I was once an enemy of God, undeserving of his love. Therefore, I should treat others with the love of Christ, knowing that my enemy could soon be my brother.

Whose life might God possibly touch? This is for whom we should pray. For this reason, we do not pray for the dead. Their position was sealed with God at their last breath. We know that God is always just and none who belong to him, slip through his fingers.

We are also to pray for those in positions of authority in the church and those in public service. Government is ordained by God to uphold the social order. We pray for God to govern the affairs of men.

---

[765] Eph 6:18; Ps 28:19; 1Ti 2:1,2; Col 4:3
[766] Gen 32:11; Jas 5:16; Mt 5:44
[767] 1Ti 2:1,2; Jn 17:20; 2Sa 7:29; 2Sa 12:21-23; 1Jn 5:16–WLC Q183

September 11

Praying for Things

Praying for people and their particular spiritual or vocational position is the first half of the prayer equation. The second half is to pray for God to move, according to his will, for righteous results.

We are to pray for all things tending to the glory of God,[768] *the welfare of the church, our own or others good;*[769] *but not for anything that is unlawful.*[770]

Righteous prayers do not seek results that fit our selfish desires, but glorify God, his will, and his kingdom purposes. For a person to pray for a particular result in a sporting event is one example of shallowness in prayer. However, for an athlete to pray for their best effort and character to honor God regardless of the outcome shows maturity in a righteous prayer.

The same intentions can be demonstrated when praying for one's church. A prayer to become a mega-church versus a prayer that if we will just take care of the *depth* of our ministry, God will take care of its *breadth*. If we seek to entice the world to Christ through worldly methods, we will just end up with a worldly church. However, if we call the world to repentance through the plain teaching of his Word, we will see those come to faith and put off the world.

God, transform my prayer life to honor you in all things.

---

[768] Mt 6:9
[769] Ps 51:18; Ps 122:6; Mt 7:11; Ps 125:4
[770] 1Jn 5:14–WLC Q184

SEPTEMBER 12

HOW DO WE PRAY?

Many people pray; few pray rightly. This is not an arrogant statement. We have learned that there is one Mediator between God and man, the Lord Jesus Christ. This leaves us with the follow conclusions. The majority of the world's people pray to the wrong god, with the wrong intentions, and without effect. However, even for the Christian, we often miss the mark in our prayer life.

We are to pray with an awful apprehension of the majesty of God and deep sense of our own unworthiness, necessities, and sins;[771] with penitent, thankful, and enlarged hearts;[772] with understanding, faith, sincerity, fervency,[773] love, and perseverance, waiting upon him, with humble submission to his will.[774]

Righteous prayer begins with the biblical perspective to whom we are praying: a purely righteous, holy, and sovereign God. A God who must act righteously against sin. A God whose holiness would destroy any man who dare look upon him without a proper veil. A God who can bring good to pass from evil events.

Once we understand within our revealed knowledge who this God is, we then recognize our own unworthiness: the depth of our sinful flesh, the lust of our eyes, and the pride of life. Finally, through our salvation by Christ, we submit to his perfect will in our lives.

---

[771] Ecc 5:1; Ge 18:27; Ge 32:10; Lk 15:17-19; Lk 18:13,14
[772] Ps 51:17; Php 4:6; 1Sa 1:15; 1Sa 2:1
[773] 1Co 14:15; Mk 11:24; Jas 1:6; Ps 145:18; Ps 17:1; Jas 5:16
[774] 1Ti 2:8; Eph 6:18; Mic 7:7; Mt 26:39–WLC Q185

SEPTEMBER 13

DIRECTION IN PRAYER

We can learn how to pray by studying the godly prayers of the Old and New Testament saints. What shines forth is the heartfelt cry of the penitent, seeking direction and intervention from the Most Holy God. In their frail humanity, they leaned heavily into their Lord.

The whole word of God is of use to direct us in the duty of prayer,[775] *but the special rule of direction is that form of prayer which our Savior Christ taught his disciples, commonly called the Lord's Prayer.*[776]

We are going to spend the next several days breaking down the Lord's Prayer. What we see, as patterns of prayer, in the study of biblical saints is beautifully summed up in the prayer the Lord taught. What is commonly called the Lord's Prayer is really better referred as the Disciples' Prayer. Jesus gave this prayer as a pattern for all believers. (One can find a personal prayer of Jesus in John's Gospel, chapter 17.)

What we shall see in this study is the divine efficiency of this prayer to provide the pattern for our entire prayer life. Beginning with our Heavenly Father, continuing with six petitions to his sovereignty, and concluding with our reliance upon him, this prayer provides us with a fully comprehensible pattern to speak with our God.

Prepare your hearts to hear the wisdom the Lord gave us to walk with him in prayerful communion.

---

[775] 1Jn 5:14
[776] Mt 6:9-13–WLC Q186

SEPTEMBER 14

THE LORD'S PRAYER

Take a moment to recite the Lord's Prayer. Take each phrase into consideration. This prayer is nothing short of incredible. Only Jesus could construct such a short prayer with such depth and completeness.

The Lord's prayer is not only for direction, as a pattern, according to which we are to make other prayers, but may also be used as a prayer, so that it be done with understanding, faith, reverence, and other graces necessary to the right performance of the duty of prayer.[777]

Many people rattle off this prayer on a regular basis. However, I wonder how much thought they put into their words. Just before giving his disciples this prayer, Jesus warns that we should not prayer in vain repetition (which is how the pagans were praying: repeating a prayer in hopes that quantitative prayers would be persuasive).

Sincerity comes from the heart, not by the words alone. We can only worship God in spirit and in truth. If our spirit is not agreeing with his Spirit or if our prayers are shallow and selfish, there is no truth, and therefore, our prayers are absolutely worthless.

Prayer begins with God's sovereignty. It continues with reverence and thanksgiving. It is as natural as breathing for those who live gloriously in the perfect will of our Savior. Prepare for a journey into this masterful pattern of prayer that the Lord has given to us.

---

[777] Mt 6:9 compared with Lk 11:2–WLC Q187

SEPTEMBER 15

BREAKING IT DOWN

How many parts does the Lord's Prayer consist?

The Lord's Prayer consists of three parts: a preface, petitions, and a conclusion.[778]

This does not sound very theological. Why leave a statement of a simple fact on its own? Especially one that pertains to most events: "It has a beginning, a middle, and an end." Well, the reason is because there is a lot behind each section. It is our responsibility to have a solid understanding of the three parts and how they apply to us.

The biblical believer understands that the pattern of this prayer is foundational to their entire Christian life. We understand that we have no capacity in ourselves, but that we are fully dependent on the Holy Spirit to work within us. We also know our tendency is to rely upon ourselves, sometimes giving authority to the old flesh instead of letting God sit on the throne of our life.

The fact that we have three parts in Lord's Prayer helps us to understand our focus points throughout every conversation we have with God. This keeps us from a thoughtless prayer like this:

> Yo Big Fella, I need a new car. Set me up with a nice ride...please. Oh, and my back is aching; can you work some of Your magic on that, too? Thanks, Dude! Amen.

The scary thing is this is some people's view of God.

Lord, open my heart to hear how you would have me pray.

---

[778] The Westminster Larger Catechism–Question 188

September 16

The Preface

It all begins with whom we are addressing in our prayer.

The preface of the Lord's prayer (contained in these words, Our Father, which art in heaven[779]) teaches us, when we pray, to draw near to God with confidence of his fatherly goodness and our interest therein;[780] with reverence, and all other childlike dispositions, heavenly affections, and due apprehensions of his sovereign power, majesty, and gracious condescension:[781] as also, to pray with and for others.[782]

Our Father—this is an immediate recognition that our prayers are inclusively pertaining to the true children of God. Certainly, we can have individualistic prayer; however, the Lord's Prayer is the pattern for the types of things for which we should all pray. Only the children of God may rightly call him, *Our Father in heaven.* In review, true children are those adopted by God and sealed by the Holy Spirit.

With the spiritual paternal relationship established, we now have set the stage for the intimacy of that relationship and the promises we may rightly communicate. Knowing that there is no safer place than in the loving arms of our Father, that all things are directed to our ultimate good in this life, and that we have the promise of a heavenly reward is how we are prepared to continue in our prayers.

[779] Mt 6:9
[780] Lk 11:13; Ro 8:15
[781] Isa 64:9; Ps 123:1; La 3:41; Isa 63:15,16; Ne 1:4-6
[782] Ac 12:5–WLC Q189

SEPTEMBER 17

HOLY, HOLY, HOLY

And one cried to another and said: "*Holy, holy, holy* is the LORD of hosts; The whole earth is full of His glory!"

Isaiah 6:3

In the first petition (which is, Hallowed be thy name[783]) acknowledging the utter inability and indisposition that is in ourselves and all men to honor God aright,[784] we pray that God would by his grace enable and incline us and others to know, to acknowledge, and highly to esteem him, his titles, attributes, ordinances, word,[785] works, and whatsoever he is pleased to make himself known by.[786]

Holiness is the only characteristic of God that is emphasized in triplet. The Scriptures do not say that God is, *Love, love, love* or *Mercy, mercy, mercy*. God's holiness is his most distinguishing characteristic. To say "Hallowed be thy name" is to define all that comes with the name, all that he is known by.

The other immediate acknowledgement is that we ourselves, are not holy, but filled with radical corruption. There is nothing that we do to make ourselves right with God, it is something that he did for us. The acknowledgement of his grace bestowed upon us, through our faith and repentance, is our deepest recognition of this relationship. We come to our Father in heaven, only because he has enabled us to see our need for a Savior, making it possible to approach him in prayer.

---

[783] Mt 6:9

[784] 2Co 3:5; Ps 2:15

[785] Ps 67:2; Ps 83:18; Ps 86:10-15; 2Th 3:1; Ps 147:19,20; Ps 138:1-3; 2Co 2:14,15

[786] Ps 145 throughout; Ps 8 throughout–WLC Q190a

SEPTEMBER 18

HALLOWED BE THY NAME

Continuing in the recognition and acknowledgment of God's holiness as the first petition of our prayers, we highly esteem God:

And to glorify him in thought, word, and deed;[787] that he would prevent and remove atheism, ignorance, idolatry, profaneness, and whatsoever is dishonorable to him;[788] and, by his overruling providence, direct and dispose of all things to his own glory.[789]

Once we have been gifted with faith to see God and his holy character, we then can respond to live our lives fashioned in holiness. We do this through obedience to his Word and in our actions, with servant's heart, as Jesus demonstrated. We believe, yet we do not believe perfectly, and we need God to help our remaining unbelief. We are continually being perfected by God and we strive for such a life.

By God's holy name, the dross is burned out of our lives. Just as gold is made more pure with each pass through the fire, so is our life purified when exposed to the cleansing fire of God's holiness.

When the seraphim proclaimed the holiness of God, he sat upon his throne. For us to be transformed, God must be on the throne in our lives. There is no honorable relationship if we think we can still reign over ourselves. As purchased possessions from the slave market, we should recognize the lordship of Christ over us.

---

[787] Ps 103:1; Ps 19:14; Php 1:9,11
[788] Ps 67:1-4; Eph 1:17,18; Ps 97:7; Ps 74:18,22,23; 2Ki 19:15,16
[789] 2Ch 20:6,10,11,12; Ps 140:4,8—WLC Q190b

September 19

The Coming Kingdom (Part 1)

If believers are to pray for a coming kingdom, that must mean that we do not currently reside within God's kingdom.

In the second petition (which is, Thy kingdom come[790]), acknowledging ourselves and all mankind to be by nature under the dominion of sin and Satan,[791] we pray, that the kingdom of sin and Satan may be destroyed, the gospel propagated throughout the world, the Jews called,[792] the fullness of the Gentiles brought in.[793]

Both the Old and New Testaments exclaim that the earth and its fullness belong to the Lord. For God's good and sovereign purposes, he has turned the sinful earth over to Satan, whom the Scriptures call the god of this world. If this were not so, certainly Jesus would have rebuked Satan for making an invalid offer during the temptation in the desert (Luke 4:5-8).

Knowing that Satan has authority over earth's kingdoms should give us plenty of insight into the true backing of its many wicked leaders. Satan often comes as a wolf in sheep's clothing. Our final hope rests not in living in a free country, but in God's promised coming kingdom.

Meanwhile, we see God's longsuffering to save everyone who will ever respond to his call. Time will not be cut short for their sake.

---

[790] Mt 6:10
[791] Eph 2:2,3
[792] Ps 67:1,18; Rev 12:10,11; 2Th 3:1; Ro 10:1
[793] Jn 17:9,20; Ro 11:25,26; Ps 67 throughout—WLC Q191a

September 20

The Coming Kingdom (Part 2)

Included in praying for God's coming kingdom, we pray for:

The church furnished with all gospel-officers and ordinances, purged from corruption, countenanced and maintained by the civil magistrate:[794] *that the ordinances of Christ may be purely dispensed, and made effectual to the converting of those that are yet in their sins, and the confirming, comforting, and building up of those that are already converted.*[795]

This may be Satan's world, but Christ does reign in his redeemed people. Therefore, as an assembly of believers, we must allow Christ to rule over his Church. We work out the Master's orders to make disciples and teach them his every command. We also hold each other accountable to living a sanctified life to the glory of God.

Our godly duty also includes civil responsibilities. We might not belong to this world, but we are to live godly lives while here. We are directed to obey the righteous laws of our government. We may partake in public service so long that it is not contrary to God's law.

We also pursue the coming kingdom through evangelism and through edification of believers. Knowing that God has already won, we need not be discouraged with the deterioration of this world system. We have the promise of God's coming kingdom, and therefore, we encourage one another with this reminder: *Come, Lord Jesus!*

---

[794] Mt 9:38; 2Th 3:1; Mal 1:11; Zeph 3:9; 1Ti 2:1,2
[795] Ac 4:29,30; Eph 6:18-20; Ro 15:29,30,32; 2Th 1:11; 2Th 2:16,17–WLC Q191b

September 21

The Coming Kingdom (Part 3)

While we wait in joyful anticipation of God's kingdom, to what final regard should this petition be prayed?

That Christ would rule in our hearts here,[796] and hasten the time of his second coming, and our reigning with him forever:[797] and that he would be pleased so to exercise the kingdom of his power in all the world, as may best conduce to these ends.[798]

That God would save a wretch such as me is incredible enough. But for the coming kingdom to include reigning positions of authority for us is beyond comprehension. It seems like God may have overfulfilled our salvation. We do not know all that will be done according to his purpose and good pleasure of which we are the beneficiaries. When I consider the depth of his love, how dare I continue in sin?

During Satan's earthly rule, God has never for a moment taken his hands off the wheel. To this day, no creature has ever stepped beyond what God has purposefully allowed: no tower has fallen, no crime committed, no infant's death. Yet we all stand responsible for our sinful thoughts and actions. In the coming kingdom, the redeemed will only have pure intentions and perform them for his glory.

Lord, we pray for your coming kingdom on earth. That you would gather your people from all generations and bring peace.

---

[796] Eph 3:14-20
[797] Rev 22:20
[798] Isa 64:1,2; Rev 4:8-11- WLC Q191c

SEPTEMBER 22

GOD'S WILL ON EARTH (PART 1)

We spoke of the fact that everything happens according to God's perfect knowledge and the nothing has ever taken place that he has not permitted. What is God's will?

In the third petition (which is, Thy will be done in earth, as it is in heaven[799]) acknowledging that by nature, we and all men are not only utterly unable and unwilling to know and do the will of God,[800] but prone to rebel against his word, to repine and murmur against his providence, and wholly inclined to do the will of the flesh, and of the devil.[801]

The first thing we must understand is that there are three main distinctive types of God's will to be considered. The first is God's *decreed will*; this is tantamount to the sovereign will of God, his choice for your life. This *will* is never frustrated.

The second type is the *perceptive will* of God. This is where God sets righteous expectations, but it is possible for man to violate them. In this sense, man can and does go against the will of God. We acknowledge our depravity and our rebellion to his will.

The third is God's will of *disposition*. It defines what is pleasing to him. A day will come when God will be perfectly obeyed by his redeemed people. This is the time when God's kingdom comes to earth and sin no longer exists.

---

[799] Mt 6:10
[800] Ro 7:18; Job. 21:14; 1Co 2:14
[801] Ro 8:7; Ex 7:7; Nu 14:2; Eph 2:2–WLC Q192a

SEPTEMBER 23

GOD'S WILL ON EARTH (PART 2)

As God's children, we have his Spirit living within us, enabling us to please him as we walk in the Spirit.

We pray, that God would by his Spirit take away from ourselves and others all blindness, weakness, indisposedness, and perverseness of heart;[802] and by his grace make us able and willing to know, do, and submit to his will in all things, with the like humility, cheerfulness,[803] faithfulness, diligence, zeal, sincerity, and constancy,[804] as the angels do in heaven.[805]

We are called to a holy life, a life separate from sin and worldly ways. Although we will never completely escape sin in this life, we should see regular growth in our spiritual life; sinning less frequently and intensely and all the while hating *that* sin more than ever. It is God that enables us to submit to his will.

The more mature we grow in Christ, the more we realize our full dependency on him. The good news is we can depend on him! He will never fail us, leave us, or forsake us. God rewards those who diligently seek him and his truth. He blesses us with every spiritual blessing. Now we pray for his continued work in our lives to help transform us that we may live more in line with his perfect will. Lord, increase my faith and desire to walk in your light.

---

[802] Eph 1:17,18; Eph 3:16; Mt 26:40,4; Jer 31:18,19
[803] Ps 119:1,8,35,36; Ac 21:14; Mic 6:8; Ps 100:2; Job 1:21; 2Sa 15:25,26
[804] Isa 38:3; Ps 119:4; Ro 12:11; Ps 119:80; Ps 119:112
[805] Isa 6:2,3; Ps 103:20,21; Mt 18:10–WLC Q192b

September 24

Our Daily Bread (Part 1)

For those of us who have been raised in prosperous communities, we rarely give thought to where our next meal is coming from, let alone if we might not eat at all. When we understand that every good and perfect gift comes from above, we give humble thanks.

In the fourth petition (which is, Give us this day our daily bread[806]) acknowledging, that in Adam, and by our own sin, we have forfeited our right to all the outward blessings of this life, and deserve to be wholly deprived of them by God, and to have them cursed to us in the use of them.[807]

As in all of God's blessings, we do not understand the gift until we understand our need. It is not that we are entitled to daily nutrition. On the contrary, through our sin, we earn only depravity. Therefore, we can understand that our most basic necessities are blessings and acts of grace from our heavenly Father.

Furthermore, in our fallen state, not only do we not deserve blessings from God, but we actually deserve curses heaped against us. We deserve stones instead of bread and serpents instead of fish. But God is so gracious, he blesses us way above our daily survival needs.

Heavenly Father, thank you for helping me see more clearly the bounty of your goodness in spite of my rebellion and blindness. Forgive my self-sufficient attitude. Your grace is revealed in every blessing.

---

[806] Mt 6:11
[807] Ge 2:17; Ge 3:17; Ro 8:20,21,22; Jer 5:25; Dt 28:15 to end–WLC Q193a

September 25

Our Daily Bread (Part 2)

In our prayers, we acknowledge that by our sin we forfeit any blessings in this life, such as our daily bread.

And that neither they of themselves are able to sustain us, nor we to merit, or by our own industry to procure them;[808] *but prone to desire, get, and use them unlawfully:*[809] *we pray for ourselves and others, that both they and we, waiting upon the providence of God from day to day in the use of lawful means, may, of his free gift, and as to his fatherly wisdom shall seem best, enjoy a competent portion of them.*[810]

Without God, we are not merely left to fend for ourselves. The final answer is without God, we cannot fend at all. Understand that God is more than Creator, he is our sustainer. This means that without God's input, not a single planet stays in orbit, not one breath is taken, not a single cell divides. Likewise, even if we were able to till the soil, it is God alone who gives the increase. Are we getting it yet?

Therefore, in praying to God for our daily bread, we are acknowledging God's provision in all things. As our heavenly Father, he is our provider and protector. Every gift we enjoy in this life is of God. His goodness is displayed for all the world to experience, yet how many give thanks? Do you see God honored around you? More importantly, do you honor God when you are around others?

---

[808] Dt 8:3; Ge 32:10; Dt 8:17,18
[809] Jer 6:13; Mk 7:21,22; Hos 12:7; Jas 4:3
[810] Ge 43:12-14; Ge 28:20; Eph 4:28; 2Th 3:11,12; Php 4:6–WLC 193b

SEPTEMBER 26

OUR DAILY BREAD (PART 3)

When we pray for our daily provisions, we are not praying just for that day's provisions. We begin with today.

And have the same continued and blessed unto us in our holy and comfortable use of them,[811] and contentment in them;[812] and be kept from all things that are contrary to our temporal support and comfort.[813]

The scope of our prayer for daily bread is both wide and deep. Jesus, in this masterful prayer, has shown us, in one short phrase, the all-encompassing provision of the Father. Our understanding of this will make us grateful beyond anything we have ever expressed. We subconsciously take a breath and God works to provide oxygen through the lungs, to the blood, servicing every portion of our body through miles of veins and capillaries. How could we ever boast in ourselves?

When you look at God's blessings in this manner, it is easy to see how people can spend hours in prayer rather than thirty seconds it takes to recite the Lord's Prayer.

Lord, you are worthy of thoughtful consideration. Forgive the times I rush through a pray out of a sense of obligation. You desire all of me and the best of me. Guide my spirit to reflect your glory and appreciate your every blessing.

---

[811] 1Ti 4:3-5
[812] 1Ti 6:6-8
[813] Pr 30:8–WLC Q193c

SEPTEMBER 27

FORGIVE US OUR DEBTS (PART 1)

Many people pray, few seek forgiveness. They pray to their cosmic genie, make their requests or perhaps some kind of trade offer to their god and hope, without any assurance of an answer.

In the fifth petition (which is, Forgive us our debts, as we forgive our debtors[814]) acknowledging, that we and all others are guilty both of original and actual sin, and thereby become debtors to the justice of God; and that neither we, nor any other creature, can make the least satisfaction for that debt.[815]

Without forgiveness, there is no benevolent, two-way communication with God. Sin separates us from God. The first act of God in restoring the relationship after the sin of Adam was a blood sacrifice. Neither Adam nor any of us could do one act of restoration on our own. *Without the shedding of blood, there is no remission of sin.*

We are so corrupt that we think we can make it to heaven by being a *pretty good* person. Listen carefully, without Christ, God would only see your filth. Perfection is the standard and anything less fails instantly and eternally. So who can make to heaven? No one unless God intervenes in like manner as he did with Adam. Thus, the Gospel.

Those who hear the Word of Truth, understand their demise, and seek refuge in Christ's work alone find forgiveness. In this manner, only the redeemed few have been given the right to this petition.

---

[814] Mt 6:12
[815] Ro 3:9-22; Mt 18:24,25; Ps 130:3,4—WLC Q194a

SEPTEMBER 28

FORGIVE US OUR DEBTS (PART 2)

Once we trust the Gospel in which we heard, we are given the right, as adopted children of God, to run to the Father and receive forgiveness for our continued shortcomings in this life.

We pray for ourselves and others that God of his free grace would, through the obedience and satisfaction of Christ, apprehended and applied by faith, acquit us both from the guilt and punishment of sin,[816] accept us in his Beloved.[817]

The obedience of Jesus at the cross effectually paid for every sin that ever was, or ever would be, committed by those who are accepted in Christ. Because the cross is an eternal plan of God, those accepted include the Old Testaments saints, who by faith, believed in the promised Messiah yet to come.

We continue to pray to our God, acknowledging our sin and turning from it, knowing that it is forgiven but not without a high price. Do we see the immeasurable love of God that he would send his Son, who deserves nothing but the full inheritance of God's kingdom, to suffer and die on our behalf? Jesus, who took upon himself every burden and torment of the world's sin, deserving to be high and lifted up on a throne of glory, was high and lifted up on a cross of corruption.

This is the love of God: that he sent his own son to die that we might live through him. See your sin? See the cross? See forgiveness!

---

[816] Ro 3:24-26; Heb 9:22
[817] Eph 1:6,7–WLC Q194b

SEPTEMBER 29

FORGIVE US OUR DEBTS (PART 3)

Once we have realized our eternal forgiveness, we pray for God to;

Continue his favor and grace to us, pardon our daily failings, and fill us with peace and joy, in giving us daily more and more assurance of forgiveness;[818] which we are the rather emboldened to ask, and encouraged to expect, when we have this testimony in ourselves, that we from the heart forgive others their offences.[819]

Today's lesson is perhaps the most difficult to swallow, especially if one is just a babe in Christ. When we came to Christ, we could see our sin and the separation from God that accompanied it. We were grateful to be forgiven and accepted in Christ. But then, we are resistant and slow to forgive others who may have offended us.

We might justify our right to be angry or hold a grudge. After all, *God might forgive them, but why should we?* Or we might defiantly say, "Okay, I'll forgive them, but I'll never forget what they did." Oh, the depth of our pride!

If God has forgiven us, we are to reciprocate this love to the world around us. Our willingness to forgive others will grow as we mature in Christ, yet not without obedience and an honest inspection of our own forgiven state. The deep understanding of own forgiveness is manifest in our forgiveness of those who betray us. Is there anyone in your world whom you have yet to forgive?

---

[818] 2Pe 1:2; Hos 14:2; Jer 14:7; Ro 15:13; Ps 51:7-10,12
[819] Lk 11:4; Mt 6:14,15; Mt 18:35–WLC Q194c

SEPTEMBER 30

LEAD US NOT INTO TEMPTATION

Breaking these petitions into parts sometimes leaves us with an incomplete thought. The idea is to acquire a comprehension of the foundation of each petition and then explore its depth and solution through the power of God's intervention.

In the sixth petition (which is, And lead us not into temptation, but deliver us from evil[820]) acknowledging, that the most wise, righteous, and gracious God, for divers holy and just ends, may so order things, that we may be assaulted, foiled, and for a time led captive by temptations;[821] that Satan, the world, and the flesh, are ready powerfully to draw us aside, and ensnare us.[822]

The Scriptures are implicitly clear: *God does not tempt us.* However, God does allow us to be put to the test and face temptations. Why? I cannot answer this, except to say in our temptations, God has his purpose. We know that we learn reliance upon God, and that he also promises not test us beyond what we are capable. Further, if there was anything that was beyond our existing strength, he makes a way of escape that we may be able to endure it.

Temptations come at us from many directions. Satan can put temptations in our midst. We are also tempted by our own sinfulness: *the lust of the flesh, the lust of our eyes, and the pride of life.* Our ultimate petition is that God deliver us from the Evil One, Satan.

---

[820] Mt 6:13
[821] 2Ch 32:31
[822] 1Ch 21:1; Lk 21:34; Mk 4:19; Jas 1:14–WLC Q195a

OCTOBER 1

THE SIXTH PETITION

When we pray that the Lord *lead us not into temptation*, we acknowledge the evil desires of this world.

And that we, even after the pardon of our sins, by reason of our corruption, weakness, and want of watchfulness,[823] *are not only subject to be tempted, and forward to expose ourselves unto temptations,*[824] *but also of ourselves unable and unwilling to resist them, to recover out of them, and to improve them.*[825]

Being born again does not eliminate our flesh. We are given a new heart and the Holy Spirit takes residency within us, but our fallen humanity lingers. We remain subjects to the temptations of this world. In fact, we may continue to seek them if we are not following the lead of the Spirit. We are told that *the spirit is willing, but the flesh is weak.*

We might despair in our own corruption, crying, "Who will deliver us from this body of death?" The answer is, *Thanks be to God, through Jesus Christ, our Lord.*

We walk in this life in a concept commonly called *already, but not yet*. What does this mean? In short, it means that we have *already* been saved, but as long as we remain in this life, we have *not yet* realized perfection. In other words, we are already saved out of this world, we are being saved still, and we will be finally saved when Christ returns.

---

[823] Gal 5:17; Mt 26:41
[824] Mt 26:69-72; Gal 2:11-14; 2Ch 18:3 with 2Ch 19:2
[825] Ro 7:23,24; 1Ch 21:1-4; 2Ch 16:7-10–WLC Q195b

OCTOBER 2

DELIVER US FROM EVIL

We recognize that without God's intervention we would be lead captive through our temptations. By ourselves, we are unable to conquer our temptations and are:

Worthy to be left under the power of them.[826] *we pray, that God would so overrule the world and all in it, subdue the flesh, and restrain Satan,*[827] *order all things, bestow and bless all means of grace, and quicken us to watchfulness in the use of them, that we and all his people may by his providence be kept from being tempted to sin.*[828]

After we recognize our inability to earn God's favor, we must lean totally on his power to govern our temptations. The strongest temptation will come at the hands of Satan. Praying for God to *deliver us from the evil one* shows our need of deliverance. Satan is far superior to us in intelligence, scripture knowledge, and aware of our weaknesses. To try and go against Satan on our own is a lost battle. We need guidance, protection, and rescue.

So are we not responsible for our own behavior? Quite the contrary. Just as we are not able to save ourselves, but are fully responsible for our rejection of grace; likewise, we are without excuse when we succumb to temptation. The difference for those of us under grace is we have God's provision to escape temptation when it arises, with the promise it will never be overbearing to us.

---

[826] Ps 81:11,12
[827] Jn 17:15; Ps 51:10; Ps 119:133; 2Co 12:7,8
[828] 1Co 10:12,13; Heb 13:20,21; Mt 26:41; Ps 19:13–WLC Q195c

OCTOBER 3

ENABLED TO STAND

But we all, with unveiled face, beholding as in a mirror the glory of the Lord, are being transformed into that same image from glory to glory, just as by the Spirit of the Lord.

2 Corinthians 3:18

We pray that we may be kept from temptations.

Or if tempted, that by his Spirit we may be powerfully supported and enabled to stand in the hour of temptation:[829] *or when fallen, raised again and recovered out of it, and have a sanctified use and improvement thereof:*[830] *that our sanctification and salvation may be perfected, Satan trodden under our feet, and we fully freed from sin, temptation, and all evil, forever.*[831]

The concluding promise of God for his children is that if we are allowed to be tested, it will never be more than which God has prepared us. Furthermore, if it was beyond our spiritual maturity, God provides the way of escape that we would be able to bear it.

The promise does not eliminate our failures. We still fight against our flesh and, by our weakness, sometimes stumble into sin. It is at these moments we recognize our prideful failure in self-reliance and repent. We must be diligent to not take our eyes off the prize.

Lord, protect me from myself and from Satan's snares. Amen.

---

[829] Eph 3:14-17; 1Th 3:13; Jude 24
[830] Ps 51:12; 1Pe 5:8-10
[831] 2Co 13:7,9; Ro 16:20; Zec 3:2; Lk 22:31,32; Jn 17:15; 1Th 5:23—WLC Q195d

OCTOBER 4

THINE IS THE KINGDOM

The earth is the Lord's and the fullness thereof. All that is in this universe, seen and unseen, belong to God. This means that all things are subject to his sovereign will. There is both comfort and fear in the reality of that statement.

The conclusion of the Lord's prayer (which is, For thine is the kingdom, and the power, and the glory, forever. Amen.[832]) teaches us to enforce our petitions with arguments,[833] which are to be taken, not from any worthiness in ourselves, or in any other creature, but from God.[834]

The conclusion of the Lord's Prayer is the most reassuring statement for the child of God. Why? Because as children of God, we can acknowledge his fatherly love for us. Furthermore, we know that *all things work together for good, to those who love God, who are the called, according to his purpose.* And if all things are working for our good, then nothing is working ultimately against us.

This understanding is paramount, that we are in the center of God's will and to us belongs the inheritance of his kingdom. With the understanding of this truth, we find ourselves fully dependent on the One who redeemed us from the pit. We find no assurance in our own ability, nor in the powers of this world that lead only to destruction. The world is passing away, but we shall abide forever.

---

[832] Mt 6:13
[833] Ro 15:30
[834] Da 9:4,7,8,9,16,17,18,19–WLC Q196a

OCTOBER 5

POWER AND GLORY, FOREVER

The Lord created and sustains every aspect of his creation. We recognize that he alone is worthy to receive our petitions.

And with our prayers to join praises, ascribing to God alone eternal sovereignty, omnipotency, and glorious excellency; in regard whereof, as he is able and willing to help us,[835] so we by faith are emboldened to plead with him that he would, and quietly to rely upon him, that he will fulfill our requests.[836] And, to testify this our desire and assurance, we say, Amen.[837]

Ascribing to God these magnificent traits does not mean that we contribute to their veracity. Acknowledgement is our agreement with these traits. God is all of these things because his Word is true. We do not establish reality, we only testify to God when we agree with it.

God's Word cannot fail. God's people stand upon the rock of his truth. Jesus is the Word. He is the truth. He is the way. He is the life. We began our study of the Westminster Confession with the truth and inerrancy of the Holy Scriptures. We conclude with God in his rightful place, on his throne, as author and finisher of our faith.

Our doctrine comes from a Holy God, through his holy Scriptures. Our obedience is to grow in our knowledge of the Lord our God. We may rest in the promises we find within.

---

[835] Php 4:6; 1Ch 29:10-13; Eph 3:20,21; Lk 11:13
[836] 2Ch 20:6,11; 2Ch 14:11
[837] 1Co 14:16; Rev 22:20,21–WLC Q196b

OCTOBER 6

WESTMINSTER CONFESSIONS

Over the past nine months, we have completed our brief look at the Larger Catechism of the Westminster Confession of Faith. The Confession itself was completed in 1646 as a reformed look at thirty-three essential doctrines of the Christian faith. The catechism is a question/answer education of the teaching in a systematic way to initiate us into the fullness of Christian life.

During the remaining portion of the year, we will examine selected doctrines of the Westminster Confession itself. The assurance of our faith in Christ is increased by our diligence to search out these doctrines as they are manifest in the Bible. To believe anything simply because it fits our personal bias is prideful and foolish. God has never established truth on a relative basis. For anyone to say, "You have your truth and I have mine," as a means to create peace between differing opinions is a disrespect to God himself and truth altogether.

For those who might want to argue that they do not believe in the Bible, therefore they can *establish their own truth*, they might not understand that even outside of religion there cannot exist contrary positions that are both true. That is, God's laws of logic and reality cannot be broken. One principle of logic is the *law of non-contradiction*, which states the something cannot be both "A" and "non-A" at the same time and in the same relationship.

The principle of non-contradiction is universally true; in religion, in science, and in philosophy, 2 + 2 = 4, always. Jesus is either the only way to the Father or he is not. Without a doubt, he is!

OCTOBER 7

THE HOLY SCRIPTURES

Similar to our look through the Large Catechism, we will only be taking a sampling of the truths established in the Westminster Confession. You will do well to go beyond these brief devotions and search the Scriptures, for in them is harmony of these truths.

Although the light of nature and the works of creation and providence do so far manifest the goodness, wisdom, and power of God, as to leave men inexcusable, yet are they not sufficient to give that knowledge of God, and of his will, which is necessary unto salvation; therefore it pleased the Lord, at sundry times, and in divers manners, to reveal himself, and to declare his will unto his Church, wholly unto writing.[838]

We believe in thirty-nine Old Testament and twenty-seven New Testament books, which are given by inspiration of God, to be the rule of faith and life. We confirm these as the Holy Scriptures of God, and that, in their original form, are inerrant and infallible under the authority of God as he breathed them through his servants' pens.

When we encounter difficult passages, we are enlightened by other passages that speak clearly on the matter. Although some argue that the many years of translations have introduced gross changes and errors from the original script, it has been well established through thousands of archeological discoveries, there are only minor stylistic changes, with literally no changes to the meaning of the passages.

---

[838] The Westminster Confession of Faith (hereby WCF) Chapter 1-i,

OCTOBER 8

GOD

Why did we place our study of the Holy Scriptures prior to looking at God himself? Although God is previous (in order) to the Scriptures, it is the Scriptures that provide our revelation of God.

There is but one only living and true God who is for his own glory, most loving, gracious, merciful, long-suffering, abundant in goodness and truth, forgiving iniquity, transgression, and sin; the rewarder of them that diligently seek him; and withal most just and terrible in his judgments; hating all sin; and who will by no means clear the guilty.[839]

The most crucial element of believing in God is believing in the *true* God. Belief in elements that do not fit the God of the Holy Scriptures expose points of idolatry in us. We must refine our beliefs according to the revealing of the Word and not conform God to fit the worldview we like best.

The day is coming when each of us will stand, without excuse, before the throne of the most righteous Judge. Furthermore, we will stand mute without a defense for the lies we chose to believe.

But God is merciful, you say? True. But not without condition. He is merciful to those *who diligently seek him*. If we deny his authority over us, can we claim to be seeking him? Repent of any disbelief and seek the One, Holy, and True God.

---

[839] TWC Ch2-i

OCTOBER 9

THE HOLY TRINITY

The Trinity does mean that there are three Gods. Although the word *trinity* does not exist in the Scriptures, it is the word we choose to confirm the three distinct persons as they are revealed to us.

In the unity of the Godhead, there be three persons of one substance, power, and eternity: God the Father, God the Son, and God the Holy Ghost. The Father is of none, neither begotten nor proceeding; the Son is eternally begotten of the Father; the Holy Ghost eternally proceeding from the Father and the Son.[840]

Although we will certainly never fully comprehend the Trinity, we can see clear distinctions (without separation of God himself) as the Word presents them to us. For example, when we think of the Creation, we initially think of God the Father. But we also see the entire creation being attributed to the Son in passages like John 1:3, "All things were made by Him," and Col 1:16-17, "All things were created by Him and for him...and by Him all things consist."

Jesus told his disciples, "He who has seen Me, has seen the Father."[841] Jesus did not mean that he *was* the Father because later, he would pray to the Father and show his eternal place with the Father. It is beyond us to comprehend the eternal relationship within the Godhead, but we can believe every passage as God reveals. God is above us and God is near, both transcendent and eminent.

---

[840] TWC Ch2-iii
[841] John 14:9

OCTOBER 10

GOD'S ETERNAL DECREE (PART 1)

God did not create the universe, put it in motion, then sit back, and let chance run its course. He has continued to sustain the very laws of physics that he has put in place. He has been involved with every cell division of every living thing from all time.

God, from all eternity, did, by the most wise and holy counsel of His own will freely, and unchangeably ordain whatsoever comes to pass.[842]

It is ironic that this doctrinal statement might bring resistance from some, as this doctrine is not just a reformed thought. Neither is it purely a Christian doctrine, but it would be agreed with in nearly all monotheistic world religions. The statement is really a description of who God is, the manifestation of his rule over his universe.

God is sovereign and rules only within his decree. *Yet so, as thereby neither is God the author of sin,*[843] *nor is violence offered to the will of the creatures; nor is the liberty or contingency of second causes taken away, but rather established.*[844]

This doctrine gives us comfort. By it, we know that nothing or no one can thwart the eternal plan of God. We have no fear of anything happening that God has not ordained. For the believer, we rest in knowing that all things work together for our ultimate good.

---

[842] WCF Ch3-ia
[843] Jas 1:13,17; 1Jn 1:5
[844] Ac 2:23; Mt 17:12; Ac 4:27,28; Jn 19:11; Pr 16:33

OCTOBER 11

GOD'S ETERNAL DECREE (PART 2)

Some would say that God, being eternal, sees down the corridors of time and then makes his decree based upon what he knows will come to pass.

Although God knows whatsoever may or can come to pass upon all supposed conditions,[845] *yet hath he not decreed anything because he foresaw it as future, or as that which would come to pass upon such conditions.*[846]

To consider the alternative means that there must have been a point where God had to learn. To suggest this in any capacity is to deny a sovereign God. His knowledge is only based upon his holy and perfect and eternal decree.

God was not surprised when Lucifer fell, when Adam and Eve ate of the fruit, nor when Cain killed Abel. He is neither surprised when we sin. This should give us great comfort as God's children. Why? Because this means that we cannot disappoint God. One can only be disappointed when they expected a different result. This does not excuse our sinful behaviors, for we can still grieve the Holy Spirit. Strive to honor God in a holy life.

One child squirmed as he learned that God knows all: "You mean that God sees everything I do?" To which the parent replied, "Yes. God loves you so much that he can't take his eyes off you!"

---

[845] Ac 15:18; 1Sa 23:11,12; Mt 11:21,23
[846] Ro 9:11,13,16,18–WCF Ch3-ii

OCTOBER 12

GOD'S ETERNAL DECREE (PART 3)

People usually do pretty good with the eternal decree of God up until the point of God's election of particular men to salvation.

By the decree of God, for the manifestation of His glory, some men and angels[847] are predestinated unto everlasting life, and others foreordained to everlasting death.[848]

For today, we will look at God's predestination of man. The first thing that we will establish is our confirmation that *all have sinned and fall short of the glory of God.*[849] The second thing is to understand the just punishment of our sin: *the wages of sin is death.*[850] Finally, we acknowledge that there is nothing we can do to earn salvation, *not by works, lest anyone should boast.*[851]

With the agreement of our sin, its resulting death, and the inability to save ourselves, we are left only with the hope of a Sovereign God who sets his mercy upon his foreordained elect, saving them by his grace alone. Those who remain unredeemed receive justice. Therefore, some receive justice and some receive mercy. There are none who receive injustice.

Are you saved? Do you confirm salvation by grace alone?

---

[847] 1Ti 5:21; Mt 25:41
[848] Ro 9:22,23; Eph 1:5,6; Pr 16:4–TWC Ch3-iii
[849] Rom 3:23
[850] Rom 6:23
[851] Eph 2:8-9

OCTOBER 13

GOD'S ETERNAL DECREE (PART 4)

When we are honest with ourselves in dealing with the secret things of God, we will find peace in his eternal decrees. We are to search diligently, confirming the hope that lies within us.

The doctrine of this high mystery of predestination is to be handled with special prudence and care,[852] *that men, attending the will of God revealed in His Word, and yielding obedience thereunto, may, from the certainty of their effectual vocation, be assured of their eternal election.*[853] *So shall this doctrine afford matter of praise, reverence, and admiration of God,*[854] *and of humility, diligence, and abundant consolation, to all that sincerely obey the Gospel.*[855]

We wrestle with the apparent paradox of God's election and the willful choice of man to follow Christ. It is difficult because we witness some people who portray themselves as Christians for a season, but later forsake Christ altogether. We stand on God's Word for those who ultimately deny God; *they went out from us, but they were not of us; for if they had been of us, they would have continued with us.*[856]

We cannot determine, for certain, another's conversion. However, we are commanded to search out the authenticity of our own calling and election. Nothing shall separate us from his love.

---

[852] Ro 9:20; Ro 11:33; Dt 29:29
[853] 2Pe 1:10
[854] Eph 1:6; Ro 11:33
[855] Ro 11:5,6,20; 2Pe 1:10; Ro 8:33; Lk 10:20—WCF Ch3-viii
[856] 1Jo 2:19

OCTOBER 14

FREE WILL: NATURAL LIBERTY

The debate over the free will of man rages on. Is mankind autonomous or are we just puppets without any real choices? Inaccurate and incomplete thoughts from both of these viewpoints cloud the issue. We must look deeper into the God/man relationship.

God hath endued the will of man with that natural liberty, that it is neither forced, nor by any absolute necessity of nature determined, to good or evil.[857]

Many of us just breathed a sigh of relief. This statement shows that we are indeed free to make our own choices in life. Freedom includes our thoughts, choices, and our actions in response to those thoughts. The resultant of this liberty is the sole responsibility of our actions.

The Scriptures referenced show that man is able to, and does, act according to his own choices at every point throughout his life. A new question should have entered your mind, *If man acts according to his nature, then is his nature itself completely free from influence?* For this, we look beyond free will and into our nature.

Is every choice we make completely our own? The answer, we have determined is, *yes*. We live within the realm of our natural liberty. We also act individually, according to our nature. We have never made a choice against our own will. A person is never forced to sin. But all do.

Therefore, let us now ask, is man's nature itself free?

---

[857] Mt 17:12; Jas 1:14; Dt 30:19–WCF Ch9-i

OCTOBER 15

OUR FREE YET MUTABLE WILL

We look to the Scriptures for God's revealed truth. God created man in a sinless state. However, the Bible also shows us that man's nature changed when Adam was disobedient to the command of God.

Man, in his state of innocence, had freedom and power to will and to do that which was good and well-pleasing to God;[858] but yet, mutably, so that he might fall from it.[859]

Adam and Eve were created sinless, i.e., innocent from any wrong-doing against God's perfect holiness. Adam and Eve, being innocent, were also enabled with free, uninhibited will. However, the fact that God gave them a prohibition against eating from one tree shows us that they were also created with the ability to disobey.

If Adam and Eve did not have the opportunity to break God's command, it would have been only *then*, when we would have been able to say man did not have free will. The final fact that man, in his innocent state, did break God's command, shows us that the possibility to sin had to also exist.

The question that follows is, *What would have happened had Adam not eaten of the forbidden fruit?* Any answer we could speculate upon would be a moot point. The reality is that Adam did fail, as would any of us in that position. Since the fall, man's sinless nature was forever tainted and his will remains genetically tainted by this fall.

---

[858] Ecc 7:29; Ge 1:26.
[859] Ge 2:16,17; Ge 3:6–WCF Ch 9-ii

OCTOBER 16

PURITY LOST

What began in a state of innocence was lost, for all mankind, through the single act of disobedience by one man. The proverbial virus of inherited sin would be passed to all generations.

Man, by his fall into a state of sin, hath wholly lost all ability of will to any spiritual good accompanying salvation;[860] *so as, a natural man, being altogether averse from that good,*[861] *and dead in sin,*[862] *is not able, by his own strength, to convert himself, or to prepare himself thereunto.*[863]

The fall brought forth immediate spiritual death as well as decay unto physical death. Just as man can do nothing to prevent his final physical death, neither can he repair what was lost spiritually. In our fallen state, we are enemies of God and spiritually dead. We do not seek to do good, but evil. It is the potential consequences that deters us from all out wickedness.

A clear example of a person's true heart is shown in childhood. Nobody has to train a child to be naughty. A child will get into every sort of trouble and throw every imaginable tantrum in their natural state. It is only through a parent's training that a child learns to behave. Therefore, good behavior is learned; sin and wickedness are natural. Man, if left to himself, neither desires, nor is able, to be righteous.

---

[860] Ro 5:6; Ro 8:7; Jn 15:5
[861] Ro 3:10,12
[862] Eph 2:1,5; Col 2:13
[863] Jn 6:44,65; Eph 2:2,3,4,5; 1Co 2:14; Tit 3:3,4,5–WCF Ch9-iii

October 17

Freed from Bondage

As fallen, men are held captive by their sin. There is no righteousness in man that he desires the things of God. Man might seek good things, but only where he is satisfied.

When God converts a sinner and translates him into the state of grace, he frees him from his natural bondage under sin,[864] and by his grace alone, enables him freely to will and to do that which is spiritually good;[865] yet so as that, by reason of his remaining corruption, he doth not perfectly nor only will that which is good, but doth also will that which is evil.[866]

For the past few days, we have discussed the total depravity or the radical corruption of fallen man. The Scriptures make it crystal clear that man neither desires God, nor has the ability to redeem himself. This truth mandates that, in this state, man neither desires Christ, the cross, nor the salvation that lies within it.

Man is set free from his sinful bondage by the grace of God. Grace, by definition, cannot be earned. Grace is a gift bestowed freely from God upon those whom he has chosen to redeem. Once a man is freed by Christ's blood from his spiritual corruption, he then can, and freely will, believe. Although a redeemed man's corrupted flesh remains, he is now spiritually enabled to do that which is good and pleasing to God. The flesh and spirit remain at war during this life.

---

[864] Col 1:13; Jn 8:34,36
[865] Php 2:13; Ro 6:18,22
[866] Gal 5:17; Ro 7:15,18,19,21,23–WCF Ch9-iv

October 18

Our Final Freedom

If we are redeemed, we are spiritually able to do that which is pleasing and good in God's eyes. However, we will never do so perfectly because our flesh remains corrupt until our resurrection.

The will of man is made perfectly and immutably free to do good alone in the state of glory only.[867]

The apostle Paul explains the battle that rages between the will of our spirit and our flesh. He examines his own redeemed life in which he knows what good he ought to do, but he cannot perform it perfectly. He would be left in despair, but he secures his hope in the Savior, Jesus Christ. Knowing his inability, all thanks goes to God.

The day will come when we will see our Savior face-to-face. Our sinful flesh will be gone and we will finally see Jesus clearly through new eyes of righteousness. We will also receive new bodies that are free from corruption at the hour of our resurrection. This is the state of glory in which we will worship our God for all eternity.

Will there be a possibility of losing our state of glory? The answer lies in possibility of God to fail. Salvation rests in God alone and what he saves, he saves eternally. Listen to Paul's words in 1Timothy 4:17, "Then we...shall be caught up together with them in the clouds, to meet the Lord in the air: and so shall we ever be with the Lord."

Our secured hope is in seeing the glorious appearing of Christ.

---

[867] Eph 4:13; Heb 12:23; 1Jn 3:2; Jude 24–WCF Ch9-v

OCTOBER 19

HIS UNFAILING CALL

The Gospel is preached to all tongues, tribes, and nations. There are several responses to those who hear the saving message. Some hear and believe immediately, some hear but believe at a later time, some hear and appear to believe but later ultimately reject the free offer, and finally there are those who presently and finally reject God. The question is, *who are those that truly accept the gospel?*

All those whom God hath predestinated unto life, and those only, He is pleased, in His appointed and accepted time, effectually to call,[868] *by His Word and Spirit,*[869] *out of that state of sin and death in which they are by nature, to grace and salvation by Jesus Christ.*[870]

The first question we should ask is, *Isn't the call for all to repent and believe?* The answer must be first qualified and shown that there are two types of *calling*. The first is the general or *outward call* of the gospel. The outward call is that universal preaching of the gospel. The second type of call is the specific and effectual *inward call* that is the unfailing call of the Holy Spirit to those the Lord redeems.

The Lord expresses this more clearly when he states, *Many are called, but few are chosen.* The chosen, or elect of God, are those whom he effectually calls. What are we called to? The elect are called out of spiritual death by the power of God and unto eternal life. God's call to life raises us from spiritual death and never returns void.

---

[868] Ro 8:30; Ro 11:7; Eph 1:10,11
[869] 2Th 2:13,14; 2Co 3:3,6
[870] Ro 8:2; Eph 2:1-5; 2Ti 1:9,10–WCF Ch10-ia

OCTOBER 20

CREATE IN ME A CLEAN HEART

In unredeemed man lies a heart of stone. What can this man do to change his own heart? Nothing. This man can only live according to a heart that has no desire for God. We understand this by the manner of our prayers for spiritually lost loved ones. We pray for God to *open their eyes* and *give them ears to hear*. We know that without God's intervention, they cannot manifest their own change.

All those whom God hath predestinated unto life, and those only, he is pleased, enlightening their minds spiritually and savingly to understand the things of God;[871] *taking away their heart of stone, and giving unto them a heart of flesh.*[872]

Because of our hopeless self-sufficiency, we will want to cry, "Foul! That's not fair." But when we realize the only fair thing is for God to judge and condemn all sin, we will then see it is only by grace that any are saved. Our self-sufficiency earns us only death.

We have confirmed time and time again that we are dead in our sins. A dead man cannot drum up his own saving faith. The man who is raised from his spiritual grave, by the power of God alone, is enabled at that time to exercise his God-given faith. It is the Father of glory whom provides the spirit of wisdom. Where is wisdom in a dead man? It is absent, for there is no wisdom without the fear of God. Only when we receive the Spirit of God, are we enabled to follow.

---

[871] Ac 26:18; 1Co 2:10,12; Eph 1:17,18
[872] Eze 36:26–WCF Ch10-ib

OCTOBER 21

THE WILL OF MAN SET FREE

A man who is the son of Adam is held captive by sin. He thinks and acts based on his bondage, and in this state, he cannot please God nor pull himself into righteousness. It is only by God.

Renewing their wills and by his almighty power determining them to that which is good[873] *and effectually drawing them to Jesus Christ,*[874] *yet so as they come most freely, being made willing by his grace.*[875]

Why, when a sinful man is given the free offer to believe in Jesus and repent of his sins, can he not make this choice on his own? The answer is, because the natural man hates God and wants no part of him. But when God regenerates a man's heart, then he can and freely does come.

Some have argued that this doctrine drags some, against their will, into the kingdom. This is a false objection. Where before they could not determine that which is good, they now have been freed. They were blind, but now they see. They were dead, but now are spiritually alive and can see the kingdom.[876]

Lord, we lift your name with the utmost praise, for by your grace, you have opened our eyes and we have answered, "Yes, Lord."

---

[873] Eze 11:19; Php 2:13; Dt 30:6; Eze 37:27
[874] Eph 1:19; Jn 6:44,45
[875] SS 1:4; Ps 110:3; Jn 6:37; Ro 6:16,17,18–WCF Ch-10ic
[876] Jn 3:3

OCTOBER 22

BY GRACE ALONE

God's holiness demands that all forms of sin and disobedience receive justice. Yet sinful man remains, experiencing the pleasures of this life. The air in our lungs, the rain that falls to grow the fields, and all aspects of life that allow all men to continue to exist are mercies of God referred to as *common grace*. The grace of God that brings salvation to some men only is called *special grace*.

This effectual call is of God's free and special grace alone, not from anything at all foreseen in man;[877] who is altogether passive therein, until, being quickened and renewed by the Holy Spirit,[878] he is thereby enabled to answer this call, and to embrace the grace offered and conveyed in it.[879]

In the same manner that there is nothing man can do to earn the common graces of God, there is also nothing man can do to acquire the saving grace of God. Salvation is freely given by God to those whom he elected before the foundation of the world. At his own appointed time, God regenerates his elect. This act is known as spiritual rebirth and is the moment that man is made spiritually alive.

Just as a dead man cannot raise himself from the grave, a spiritually dead man cannot act upon spiritual matters. Once we are made alive by the power of God, we then instantaneously believe and answer the call. Give thanks to God of glory who raises you to life.

---

[877] 2Ti 1:9; Tit 3:4,5; Eph 2:4,5,8,9; Ro 9:11
[878] 1Co 2:14; Ro 8:7; Eph 2:5
[879] Jn 6:37; Eze 36:27; Jn 5:25–WCF Ch10-ii

OCTOBER 23

SALVATION AND ACCOUNTABILITY

We have previously confirmed the all persons are conceived, born, and live under sin. Furthermore, we know that salvation is by special grace alone and that there is nothing one can do to earn it.

Elect infants, dying in infancy, are regenerated and saved by Christ through the Spirit,[880] who worketh when, and where, and how he pleaseth.[881] So also are all other elect persons, who are incapable of being outwardly called by the ministry of the Word.[882]

This doctrine hits a tender spot for all of us. We protect the weak and the incapable. We nurture and sustain them until they are able to sustain themselves. If anything bad threatens them, we stand to protect and preserve them. Yet sin leaves all persons spiritually dead.

We again confirm that no man can do anything to save himself. We should also take a moment to comfort ourselves with the knowledge that God is perfect, upright, and that he never gives anybody injustice. We trust God's sovereignty in these matters.

Although Scripture is not plainly dogmatic about the salvation of the mentally incapable, we can lean on the testimony of God's Word. King David, whose young son had just died stated, speaking of the babe's salvation, "He cannot return to me, but I shall go to him." God is just and righteous.

---

[880] Lk 18:15,16; Ac 2:38,39; Jn 3:3,5; 1Jn 5:12; Ro 8:9
[881] Jn 3:8
[882] 1Jn 5:12; Ac 4:12–WCF Ch10-iii

OCTOBER 24

THE GENERAL CALL

The word is preached and a congregation hears the same gospel. Some accept and some reject the call to salvation. Why?

Others not elected, although they may be called by the ministry of the Word,[883] *and may have some common operations of the Spirit,*[884] *yet they never truly come unto Christ, and therefore cannot be saved.*[885]

We have continued to confirm that all men are fallen, spiritually dead, thoroughly depraved, and incapable of saving themselves. Therefore, if left to themselves, they have no ability to respond, redeemed to the gospel. Jesus said, "No man can come to Me, unless the Father who sent Me draws him" and, "Many are called, but few are chosen."[886]

When we say in our confession that an unregenerate man *cannot be saved*, we are not saying that God cannot save him, but that man is unable, without rebirth, to accept the saving call of the gospel. Within the visible church, it is impossible for us to see into another man's heart. It will only be manifest at the Day of Judgment that some never truly believed. In this truth, we must hold on to the fact the nobody receives injustice. Yet only those whom God saves receive his saving mercy.

---

[883] Mt 22:14
[884] Mt 7:22; Mt 13:20,21; Heb 6:4,5
[885] Jn 6:64,65,66; Jn 8:24—WCF Ch10-iva
[886] Jn 6:44; Mt 20:16, 22:14

OCTOBER 25

JUSTIFICATION (PART 1)

We finished yesterday's devotional with the confirmation that nobody receives injustice from God. So what is justification?

Those whom God effectually calleth He also freely justifieth;[887] *not by infusing righteousness into them, but by pardoning their sins, and by accounting and accepting their persons as righteous: not for anything wrought in them, or done by them, but for Christ's sake alone.*[888]

Outside of the man Jesus Christ, not one self-righteous person will enter heaven. However, every person that enters heaven will be deemed righteous. How is this possible? It is possible because Jesus paid the wages of sin for the elect. There is only One who is capable to pay the infinite cost of our sin, that is Jesus Christ the Righteous. God righteously accepts Christ's payment to satisfy his justice.

The analogy can be made by looking at our court system. Say I stand guilty for running a stop sign. The judge says the fine is a hundred dollars or thirty days in jail. If I cannot pay, I will go to jail. However, if an advocate steps in and pays the fine for me, the judge will smack his gavel and say, "Paid in full, you're free to go."

The advocate's payment does not make one righteous, but his payment is accounted as righteousness unto those he justifies. Justice is served and the elect receive mercy at the cost of Jesus' death.

---

[887] Ro 8:30; Ro 3:24–WCF Ch11-ia (see following note)
[888] The Westminster Confession Chapter 11, part "i", subset "a"

OCTOBER 26

JUSTIFICATION (PART 2)

Yesterday, we took our first look at our justification. Today, we continue further. God freely justifies not by making a person righteous;

Nor by imputing faith itself, the act of believing, or any other evangelical obedience, to them as their righteousness; but by imputing the obedience and satisfaction of Christ unto them,[889] *they receiving and resting on Him and His righteousness, by faith: which faith they have not of themselves; it is the gift of God.*[890]

This states that we are not given any attribute that turns us into a righteous person. However, we are enabled, through regeneration, to respond by faith and obedience to the gospel and receive Christ's righteousness as our own. Therefore, we can say that we are righteous only because of his righteousness.

We cannot bring anything to the party. You may say, "But don't I exercise faith to believe?" The answer is yes, you do, but that saving faith is itself a gift of God. We must remember that prior to regeneration we possess no ability or internal desire to believe. Our natural hearts are wicked and we are enemies of righteousness.

Can a person boast that they were smarter than another and that is why they believed while another rejects Christ? No, it was while we were yet sinners that Christ died for us.

---

[889] Ro 4:5-8; 2Co 5:19,21; Ro 3:22,24,25,27,28; Tit 3:5,7; Eph 1:7; Jer 23:6; 1Co 1:30,31; Ro 5:17,18,19
[890] Ac 10:44; Gal 2:16; Php 3:9; Ac 13:38,39; Eph 2:7,8–WCF Ch11-ib

OCTOBER 27

SAVING FAITH

What part of salvation may we take credit? Absolutely none. We have confirmed that both grace and faith are the gift of God. We are indeed saved by grace alone, through faith alone.

Faith, thus receiving and resting on Christ and His righteousness, is the alone instrument of justification;[891] yet is it not alone in the person justified, but is ever accompanied with all other saving graces, and is no dead faith, but worketh by love.[892]

A paintbrush is not what paints a portrait. It is the artist that performs the painting; the brush is only an instrument used by the artist. Furthermore, the paintbrush does not appear out of thin air, but it is also created by the painter to be used in his art. In a similar way, saving faith is a God-provided instrument that regenerate man uses to take hold of salvation. We do not, because we cannot, generate our own saving faith.

Although the Bible states that we cannot know the true heart of man, it also shows us that saving faith does not save a person unaccompanied. In other words, a regenerate man does not receive faith, believe unto salvation, then wait, and stagnate until his death. The truth is that a person who exercises true faith will always have that faith accompanied with godly actions of love and the pursuit of holiness.

Lord, thank you for the desire a holy life in spite of my flesh.

---

[891] Jn 1:12; Ro 3:28; Ro 5:1
[892] Jas 2:17,22,26; Gal 5:6–WCF Ch 11-ii

OCTOBER 28

JUSTICE SATISFIED

There was one righteous man who walked this earth. They wrongfully arrested him at night, dragged him through a kangaroo court with illegal prosecution, and although his innocence was always pronounced, they treated him like the world's most vile criminal.

Christ, by his obedience and death, did fully discharge the debt of all those that are thus justified, and did make a proper, real, and full satisfaction to his Father's justice in their behalf.[893]

The righteousness of Christ is transferred to every person who believes. Jesus received the most cruel punishment any man would ever receive. I do not have an answer to why the death of Christ was not enough in itself, but that such torture had to accompany it. One thing we can trust is that the heavenly Father must have demanded it for his satisfaction or it would not have happened.

> Who Himself bore our sins in His own body on the tree, that we, having died to sins, might live for righteousness—by whose stripes you were healed.
>
> 1 Peter 2:24

This lengthy and horrific execution was all performed upon the perfectly obedient Christ, so that the Father's justice would be satisfied. Furthermore, we receive his righteousness through this substitutionary death. When we begin to realize this was endured by Jesus, out of a pure act of love for those whom he redeems, we are left in awe of his love.

---

[893] Ro 5:8,9,10,19; 1Ti 2:5,6; Heb 10:10,14; Da 9:24,26; Isa 53:4,5,6,10,11,12– WCF Ch11-iiia

OCTOBER 29

NO OTHER WAY

It has been said that God, because he is God, could have gone about saving his people by any means he so chose. I disagree with this. God would not perform above what was necessary just for demonstration purposes. We actually can know that there was no other way to save his people.

Yet inasmuch as he was given by the Father for them, and his obedience and satisfaction accepted in their stead,[894] and both, freely, not for anything in them, their justification is only of free grace;[895] that both the exact justice and rich grace of God might be glorified in the justification of sinners.[896]

Some people say that Jesus' prayer in the garden, "Father, if it is Your will, take this cup away from Me; nevertheless not My will, but Yours, be done," is the obedient yet human side of Jesus asking that his death be bypassed that night. And although I agree that the human nature of Christ was likely in torment over what was to come, I think his question is recorded more for our benefit. It is by this question that we may know explicitly that there was *no other way.*

The price was set: death. The satisfaction was determined: the seed of the woman.[897] God receives the glory and we receive his grace.

---

[894] Ro 8:32; 2Co 5:21; Mt 3:17; Eph 5:2
[895] Ro 3:24; Eph 1:7
[896] Ro 3:26; Eph 2:7–WCF Ch11-iiib
[897] Ro 6:23; Ge 2:17, 3:15

October 30

Justification from Eternity

Yesterday, we discovered that the death of the Son of God was both mandatory and righteous. God's holiness demanded satisfaction and his Son's death was the only way to accomplish it. Yet this whole plan took place before time began.

God did, from all eternity, decree to justify all the elect;[898] and Christ did, in the fullness of time, die for their sins, and rise again for their justification:[899] nevertheless, they are not justified, until the Holy Spirit doth, in due time, actually apply Christ unto them.[900]

The Lord has the names of every person, who would ever believe, written in the Book of Life. These are the elect, whom God determined by his sovereign free will, to redeem as a gift to the Son.[901] However, although it may have been determined eternally by God, we are not actually saved until we are regenerated by the Holy Spirit.

I once was spiritually dead, blind, and deaf. It was not until grace saved me that I could see heaven, receive the gospel, and believe in eternal life. This shows us that God is able to perform that which he determines out of eternity. I could not do anything on my own. He begins this good work in us, and he completes it. Even now, our salvation is not fully realized. For we are yet to be perfected. Yet that day will come when we shall no longer have our sinful flesh to fight.

---

[898] Gal 3:8; 1Pe 1:2,19,20; Ro 8:30
[899] Gal 4:4; Ro 4:25
[900] Col 1:21,22; Gal 2:16; Tit 3:4-7–WCF Ch11-iv
[901] Re 17:8; Jn 17:2

OCTOBER 31

FORGIVEN AND THE FORGIVING

We can somewhat comprehend that God forgave our sins when we accepted Jesus' death on our behalf. However, it is more difficult to understand why the forgiveness continues when we so often fail.

God doth continue to forgive the sins of those that are justified;[902] and, although they can never fall from the state of justification,[903] yet they may, by their sins, fall under God's fatherly displeasure, and not have the light of his countenance restored unto them, until they humble themselves, confess their sins, beg pardon, and renew their faith and repentance.[904]

We do not want to play games with the salvation we have been given. The new man within us does not want to repeat the sins that our old man once did. We especially do not enjoy coming before the throne of God, knowing we failed him in the same way once again. Yet it is the very earnest of our hatred of sin and repentance that demonstrates we are indeed God's children.

We did not do anything to earn our salvation, and there is certainly nothing we can do to maintain it. If salvation was sustained by keeping God's Law, grace would cease to be grace. The weakness is on our side: God's redemption was once and for all time. We must keep our focus on Christ, for if we trust in ourselves, we will have no joy.

---

[902] Mt 6:12; 1Jn 1:7,9; 1Jn 2:1,2
[903] Lk 22:32; Jn 10:28; Heb 10:14–WCF Ch 11-v
[904] Ps 89:31,32,33; Ps 51:7-12; Ps 32:5; Mt 26:75; 1Co 11:30,32; Lk 1:20

NOVEMBER 1

ALWAYS BY FAITH

New Testament saints are saved by grace through faith. In the Old Testament, they were saved by the Law, correct? Not correct.

The justification of believers under the Old Testament was, in all these respects, one and the same with the justification of believers under the New Testament.[905]

Many people think that because the Jewish people lived under the Law of Moses, they were saved because they obeyed God's requirements. The ironic thing is that many believers today still think they will go to heaven because they generally keep the Law. They might believe they have received forgiveness through Jesus' death, but they just cannot let go of their own merit. The Bible clearly refutes this: "By the works of the law is no man justified."[906]

Abraham is the icon of salvation by faith. He sets the example for saints of all time when it is said that, "Abraham believed God, and it was accounted to him for righteousness."[907] We see that obedience is not what justifies a person, but works are only a demonstration of the faith that proceeds them. So how do we handle the fact that Jesus had not yet died for the sins of the world while the Old Testament saints were alive? The answer is that they looked forward according to faith and we look back according to ours. One Messiah saves those whose names are written, from all eternity, in the Book of Life.

---

[905] Gal 3:9,13,14; Ro 4:22,23,24; Heb 13:8–TWC Ch11-vi
[906] Ro 3:20; Ep 2:8-9
[907] Ge 15:6; Ro 4:3

November 2

Children of God

There is only one worthy Son, the man Jesus Christ. Attempts at self-works is not only worthless, but actually defiles God's holiness.

All those that are justified, God vouchsafes[908], in and for his only Son Jesus Christ, to make partakers of the grace of adoption:[909] by which they are taken into the number, and enjoy the liberties and privileges of the children of God.[910]

The fact that God saves our souls from the pit of hell is gracious enough. But the idea of being adopted into his family is beyond comprehension. And still further, we gain full inheritance to his riches.

My thoughts drift to the prodigal son. You know the story: a young man inconceivably asks for his inheritance before his father's death. The father acquiesces. After the son blows the lot, he finds himself starving and working the most defiling of jobs. He cowers back to his father to beg forgiveness. He intends to become a slave. However, the father runs and initiates the restoration with kisses of love.

The father of the prodigal positioned the undeserving son into the seat of highest honor. Similarly, God brings a remnant of vile sinners to repentance, ushers them into eternal life, adopts them, and honors them as joint heirs with Jesus. All the riches of glory that the Son deserves, we receive in like kind. Now that's some kind of adoption!

---

[908] vouchsafe—condescends to give or grant
[909] Eph 1:5; Gal 4:4,5
[910] Ro 8:17; Jn 1:12–WCF Ch12-ia

NOVEMBER 3

THE SPIRIT OF ADOPTION

When I experienced desperation as a child, I would run into the arms of my dad, knowing I would find refuge. Those the Lord justifies *have his name put upon them, receive the Spirit of adoption;[911] have access to the throne of grace with boldness;[912] are enabled to cry, Abba, Father.[913]*

There is no refuge like the arms of our heavenly Father. Through adoption, believers gain all of the benefits of the true Son. Our relationship with God has changed. Where we were once far off, God has now come near and the love he bestows upon us casts away all fear. Now, when we pray, we enter into direct communion with the Lord.

In a monarchy, commoners have no direct access to the king, unless you are summoned to him. If you took it upon yourself to go directly to him, you might likely be arrested. Well, our king has summoned us. The phrase *Abba* is an endearing term, much as in the way we say *Daddy*. It shows that the formalities have been covered, and now, it is all about a deep and loving relationship.

Let's be careful not to think that we now walk past the guards because of our own righteousness. We may enter because Christ the Righteous mediates for us. Not me, but Christ in me. He is our hope of glory. He has secured our place in the family of God.

---

[911] Jer 14:9; 2Co 6:18; Rev 3:12; Ro 8:15
[912] Eph 3:12; Ro 5:2
[913] Gal 4:6–WCF Ch12-ib

NOVEMBER 4

INHERITED PROMISES

What are the other benefits of being in the family of God? Through adoption, believers:

Are pitied, protected, provided for, and chastened by Him as by a Father;[914] *yet never cast off, but sealed to the day of redemption,*[915] *and inherit the promises, as heirs of everlasting salvation.*[916]

The Lord blesses us with every spiritual blessing. Our adoption is permanent. No one is ever cast out of the family that God has brought them into. By the same Spirit through which we have been adopted, we are also sealed until the day of redemption. When a person receives eternal life, that means everlasting inheritance.

The question that arises now is, *What manner of life ought we to now live?* The answer is that we are to live according the righteousness that we have been given. We are to strive, with all of our being, to live in manner worthy of the call. We have been given the Spirit, which gives us liberty to walk uprightly. This is our deliverance from the bondage of corruption. Our liberty, as Peter states, is not so that we can live maliciously, but as servants of God.

God, you have called us out of bondage, made us free from sin, and adopted us as your children. May we honor you at all times.

---

[914] Ps 103:13; Pr 14:26; Mt 6:30,32; 1Pe 5:7; Heb 12:6
[915] La 3:31; Eph 4:30
[916] Heb 6:12; 1Pe 1:3,4; Heb 1:14–WCF Ch12-ic

NOVEMBER 5

SANCTIFICATION

Having been delivered from the bondage of sin, we are called to a life of holiness. Sanctification is the process of growing in holiness.

They, who are once effectually called and regenerated, having a new heart and a new spirit created in them, are further sanctified really and personally, through the virtue of Christ's death and resurrection,[917] *by his Word and Spirit dwelling in them.*[918]

Although our obedience is an expression of our sanctification, it is not to our own credit that we separate ourselves from sin. Just as salvation is entirely the work of God, our sanctification is the resultant of the Spirit's work in us. Sanctification, as holiness, is the separation from sin. Sanctification is never completed in this life, but will be fully realized at the resurrection.

Practically speaking, sanctification is one's life conforming to the image of Christ. As we grow in knowledge, understanding, and obedience, our lives increasingly reflect Jesus. For some people, it is seen in the cleaning up of foul language. Others avoid drinking in excess as they understand that being intoxicated usurps being filled with the Holy Spirit. It is righteous life growth.

Sanctification is not achieved by works of righteousness, but by the transformation of one's mind. As a person truly believes, so does he act. The person who keeps Jesus' commands expresses true love.

---

[917] 1Co 6:11; Ac 20:32; Php 3:10; Ro 6:5,6
[918] Jn 17:17; Eph 5:26; 1Th 2:13–WCF Ch13-ia

November 6

Demand for Holiness

Some call themselves Christians, but live completely unsanctified lives. Their lip service is reprimanded by their actions. The Holy Spirit directs righteous actions in the believer in all areas.

The dominion of the whole body of sin is destroyed,[919] and the several lusts thereof are more and more weakened and mortified,[920] and they more and more quickened and strengthened in all saving graces,[921] to the practice of true holiness, without which no man shall see the Lord.[922]

A person who does not does not strive toward holiness is only demonstrating that the Holy Spirit is being repressed to work in their lives. Since holiness is required to see the Lord, it in the very least shows that this person is not passionately pursuing him.

Believers will, under the direction of the Holy Spirit, strive toward holiness in every area of their lives. It is not that quitting smoking in itself is an example of a sanctified life. A believer will yield under subjection of God's holiness. We react positively to the righteous life, looking for opportunities to honor our Lord.

In what ways does your life honor God? In what areas are you allowing the world to creep in? Seek righteousness and be rewarded.

---

[919] Ro 6:6,14
[920] Gal 5:24; Ro 8:13
[921] Col 1:11; Eph 3:16-19
[922] 2Co 7:1; Heb 12:14–WCF Ch13-ib

NOVEMBER 7

HOLINESS IN ALL OF ME

When man is saved, he is given spiritual life and a renewed heart with the ability to follow after God and his righteousness. The flesh, however, remains unredeemed until the Second Coming. That being said, we are required to bring our body in subjection to the Holy Spirit residing within us.

This sanctification is throughout in the whole man,[923] *yet imperfect in this life; there abides still some remnants of corruption in every part:*[924] *whence arises a continual and irreconcilable war; the flesh lusting against the Spirit, and the Spirit against the flesh.*[925]

We are at war. The war is spiritual and universal for every saved person. Although our spirit is aligned with the Holy Spirit, our flesh continues to long after the things of this world. We lust after the things we see, the things of this world, and our continual battle with pride. Pride, being the root of all sin, is why Lucifer fell and why we struggle against the Spirit.

Our flesh screams for fulfillment. It is persistent, cunning, and deceitful. However, our spirit agrees with Holy Spirit. We are given liberty to resist the temptations and we are enabled to pass every test. This is the challenge Christians face their entire lives. God promised not to allow us to be tempted above our ability. Our failings, although forgiven, are unacceptable and inexcusable. Stand firm on his promises.

---

[923] 1Th 5:23
[924] 1Jn 1:10; Ro 7:18,23; Php 3:12
[925] Gal 5:17; 1Pe 2:11–WCF Ch13-ii

NOVEMBER 8

PERSEVERING SANCTIFICATION

At times, we feel like we have lost the battle against sin. We fail and then we fail again. We wonder if we meant it the last time we repented. We press on, claiming that we will do better next time. Yet sometimes when we are feeling defeated, it feels like the devil will never take his foot off our throats. We are in war against sin.

In which war, although the remaining corruption, for a time, may much prevail,[926] *yet, through the continual supply of strength from the sanctifying Spirit of Christ, the regenerate part doth overcome;*[927] *and so, the saints grow in grace, perfecting holiness in the fear of God.*[928]

Feeling defeated is a normal yet sinful feeling. What do I mean? Simply this: that the feeling of defeat is the same as saying that sin has won. If this were true, then Jesus' claim as the Conqueror of sin is a lie. So by emotional defeat, we are saying that Christ is defeated. This would make us heretics. We must hold fast to the promises of God.

The Holy Spirit is the sanctifying power in our lives. We will go through growing pains, but we will never be defeated because the final war on sin has already been won. All Christians are going through a transformation toward the image of Christ. We grow from a low state of glory to a higher state of glory, and this is not of ourselves but by the Spirit of the Lord. Trust God's promise to work in you. The battle rages, but the war is won.

---

[926] Ro 8:23
[927] Ro 6:14; 1Jn 5:4; Eph 4:15,16
[928] 2Pe 3:18; 2Co 3:18; 2Co 7:1–WCF Ch13-iii

NOVEMBER 9

SAVING FAITH

One thing we typically learn, after being saved, is that our saving faith is not generated from within our own ability. We did not believe because we were smarter than someone else nor because we simply thought heaven was a better option than hell.

The grace of faith, whereby the elect are enabled to believe to the saving of their souls, is the work of the Spirit of Christ in their hearts,[929] and is ordinarily wrought by the ministry of the Word:[930] by which also, and by the administration of the sacraments, and prayer, it is increased and strengthened.[931]

There are many incredibly intelligent and intellectual people in this world who do not come to faith. There are even some people who have reported in their near-death experiences, of seeing, smelling, and hearing the potential torment of hell, yet they do not feel compelled to believe in the Gospel. They demand to live their own way.

Because man's heart is corrupt, wicked, and hates God, he neither can, nor will, turn his heart around. This is the state in which man would be left if God did not perform a heart transplant. The grace of faith is God's gift to those whom he enables to believe. So faith, though it is ours to exercise, is the work of the Holy Spirit. If you have a hard time grasping this, just ask yourself whom you thank for your salvation: yourself for believing or God for changing your heart?

---

[929] Heb 10:39; 2Co 4:13; Eph 1:17,18,19; Eph 2:8
[930] Ro 10:14,17
[931] 1Pe 2:2; Ac 20:32; Ro 4:11; Lk 17:5; Ro 1:16,17–WCF Ch14-i

NOVEMBER 10

FAITH AND HEARING GOD

A person cannot believe what he does not know. The hearing of the Word is only the information. Man can hear it, understand the content, and maybe even comprehend some significance to its meaning for man's relationship to his Creator. However, having faith unto salvation is beyond man's ability by knowledge alone.

By this faith, a Christian believes to be true whatsoever is revealed in the Word, for the authority of God himself speaking therein;[932] *and acts differently upon that which each particular passage thereof contains.*[933]

God graces saving faith to his elect. By the awakening of our spirit, the Holy Spirit enables us to receive the Word in a new light. It is by this saving faith that we believe unto salvation; by Christ's death, the forgiveness of sins; by his resurrection, our eternal life in him.

It has always baffled me that very smart people reject the free offer of grace. It is here that we must remember that the intelligence, of an accountable person, has no part in faith. This is because intelligence aside, we are dealing with spiritually dead people. A dead person cannot respond unless they are first raised to life.

Once a person is regenerated, they freely receive Gospel and are enabled to believe every Word that proceeds from the mouth of God. When we believe, we are motivated to act according to that belief.

---

[932] Jn 4:42; 1Th 2:13; Jn 5:10; Ac 24:14
[933] WCF (Westminster Confession of Faith) Ch14-iia

NOVEMBER 11

FAITH AND JUSTIFICATION

Yesterday, we spoke of the elects' ability to believe and act upon the truth of the Scripture. This includes:

Yielding obedience to the commands, trembling at the threatenings, and embracing the promises of God for this life and that which is to come.[934] *But the principal acts of saving faith are accepting, receiving, and resting upon Christ alone for justification, sanctification, and eternal life, by virtue of the covenant of grace.*[935]

There are too many positive results of saving faith to list. The primary aspect is that it is through faith that we are saved. All other graces leading to our obedience begin with the understanding that Jesus is Lord. We could not bring any payment to the wages of our sin. We could not stand as innocent before our Eternal Judge.

If we were to grow in sanctification every day for a hundred years, we would still be infinitely away from God's righteousness. It is only by our justification, through the work of Christ, that God does not cast us eternally into the outer darkness. Our sins are forgiven, and we are covered with his righteousness. All of this is generated before the foundation of world and without any choice of our own that God foresaw.

You have not chosen Me, but I have chosen you.

John 15:16

God sets his love upon whom he alone wills. We are his chosen people.

Many are called, but few are chosen.

Matthew 22:14

---

[934] Ro 16:26; Isa 66:2; Heb 11:13; 1Ti 4:8
[935] Jn 1:12; Ac 16:31; Gal 2:20; Ac 15:11–WCF Ch14-iib

NOVEMBER 12

FAITH ALWAYS PREVAILS

If saving faith was rooted in me, I would not be able to claim its perseverance. We can neither initiate nor sustain our own faith.

This faith is different in degrees, weak or strong;[936] may be often and many ways assailed and weakened, but gets the victory;[937] growing up in many to the attainment of a full assurance through Christ, who is both the author and finisher of our faith.[938]

So if this faith is from God, how can I claim its varying degrees of weakness? Perhaps the best explanation is to show that saving faith is perfectly effective, but not perfectly assuring. When we are graced with faith, we believe eternally. However, we only gain assurance of our faith through study, meditation, and prayer.

One possible deterrent for God not giving us immediate full assurance of faith is our problem with pride. If we did not have weakness, we might not rely of Christ's strength, but our own. Yet we know that it is in our weakness that we are made strong by him.

Faith itself gets the victory, not our self-willingness. We could not bring ourselves to spiritual life and we certainly cannot muster enough strength to carry our faith to the finish. Thank God that what he begins in us, he promises to complete until the Day of Jesus Christ. How is the assurance of your faith? Make your confidence sure.

---

[936] Heb 5:13,14; Ro 4:19,20; Mt 6:30; Mt 8:10
[937] Lk 22:31,32; Eph 6:16; 1Jn 5:4,5
[938] Heb 6:11,12; Heb 10:22; Col 2:2; Heb 12:2–WCF Ch14-iii

NOVEMBER 13

REPENT AND BELIEVE

If salvation is the gift of God, and grace, faith, and justification are also the gifts of this salvation, then the fruit of the obedient heart is also a gift of his grace. No one is saved without repentance.

Repentance unto life is an evangelical grace,[939] *the doctrine whereof is to be preached by every minister of the Gospel, as well as that of faith in Christ.*[940]

Repenting, in and of itself, does not produce salvation. But those who understand their sin in the light of the Gospel do earnestly repent. To repent is to change one's mind for the better. With a new heart that abhors sin, the believer turns from their wicked practices. It is in this manner that the believer is in the proper condition to accept forgiveness. A person who is not penitent seeks not after God.

An invitation for people to believe in Christ without a call to repentance is no Gospel presentation at all. A person will not come to Christ for salvation without knowing that they have something to be saved from. The idea that sin requires death and that Jesus took our punishment helps us understand that sin cannot be handled lightly. Those who love Christ cannot live with sin and will earnestly turn from it.

Lord, I ask you to reveal any sin in my life that I may turn from it. Help me to not let pride keep me from the blessings of repentance. May these next days awake my conscience of any harbored sin.

---

[939] Zec 12:10; Ac 11:18
[940] Lk 24:47; Mk 1:15; Ac 22:21–WCF Ch15-i

NOVEMBER 14

HATING SIN

We are not sinners because we sin; we sin because we are sinners. Salvation and our new heart gives us a new view of sin.

By it (repentance), a sinner, out of the sight and sense, not only of the danger, but also of the filthiness and odiousness of his sins, as contrary to the holy nature, and righteous law of God; and upon the apprehension of His mercy in Christ to such as are penitent, so grieves for and hates his sins, as to turn from them all unto God.[941]

Before the Holy Spirit renews our heart, we love our sin. We weigh only the consequences of getting caught against the benefits of sin's fulfillment. However, once we see our sin through godly eyes, our spirit goes to war against our flesh. We see the filth of our sin for what it truly is, rebellion against God.

The believer has a godly sorrow for sin. Our repentance is not just a clearing of our conscience, but a true turning away from thoughts and actions against God. The new man strives for a holy life, which is against the flesh that remains. We grow more careful not to sin against the holiness of God. We strive for a life that reflects Christ.

The flesh continues to rage against the Spirit. We lean fully on our Savior's strength, depending on the Spirit to keep us from the Evil One. God is faithful, not allowing us to be tempted beyond what we are able and we have no excuse for yielding to sin. Thanks be to God.

---

[941] Eze 18:30,31; Eze 36:31; Isa 30:22; Ps 51:4; Jer 31:18,19; Joel 2:12,13; Am 5:15; Ps 119:128; 2Co 7:11.–WCF Ch15-iia

November 15

Following after Christ

As believers, we can no longer walk satisfied in the ways of the world. We know that our sin is destructive, not only in our lives, but to those around us. The Spirit gives us a new motivation.

Purposing and endeavoring to walk with him in all the ways of his commandments.[942]

The believer is determined to keep God's righteous Law. Our failures make us grieve; however, we only grow more determined to live righteously. Our failures do not condemn us, but our remaining flesh will. This is not to excuse our sin nor our weakness. We are still fully responsible for our sin, and our desire for holiness grows on.

The world might deny any significant change in a believer's life. They hear us claim to be born again, but see our failures and chalk them up to a hypocritical life. Sometimes, this view is correct, especially when a believer pretends to be better than the sinner they truly are. However, a person is not hypocritical simply because they fail. A righteous person will call themselves out on their own sin, repent of it, and claim their reliance and forgiveness on the blood of Christ.

As believers, striving for a life of holiness, we must always point to Christ as the standard. We do not do anyone any good when we put ourselves in the high places. Let us show Christ as high and lifted up; first on the cross for the forgiveness of sins, then on his heavenly throne where he reigns forever and ever and ever.

---

[942] Ps 119:6,59,106; Lk 1:6; 2Ki 23:25–WCF Ch15-iib

NOVEMBER 16

NO PRIDE IN REPENTANCE

All men are commanded to repent of their sin. However, as in all things, there is nothing good that we can take credit for or apply as self-righteousness. Our repentance does not secure pardon, Christ does.

Although repentance be not to be rested in, as any satisfaction for sin, or any cause of the pardon thereof,[943] *which is the act of God's free grace in Christ;*[944] *yet it is of such necessity to all sinners, that none may expect pardon without it.*[945]

There is no saying, "I'll sin now and repent of it later." This trampling upon the blood of Christ is not from the heart of one who understands the love of God. We have no claim on forgiveness because of the act of our repentance. Forgiveness remains the free gift of grace. Our repentance is the result, not the cause of forgiveness.

We acknowledge that we are pardoned not because of our repentance, but by grace. However, we also recognize that without repentance, there is no forgiveness. This apparent paradox should not surprise us. We must keep in mind that God is always previous. We must believe to be saved, yet God saved us before the foundation of the world. We are called to holiness, yet not ours, but Christ's in us.

Every aspect of salvation is because of and through the work of God. We obey because we are enabled by the grace of God.

---

[943] Eze 36:31,32; Eze 16:61-63
[944] Hos 14:2,4; Ro 3:24; Eph 1:7
[945] Lk 13:3,5; Ac 17:30,31–WCF Ch15-iii

NOVEMBER 17

THE POWER OF SIN DESTROYED

A Pharisee, who tried his hardest to keep every aspect of God's Law, stood fully condemned by the very Law he took pride in keeping. However, the worst sinner who repents is forgiven.

As there is no sin so small but it deserves damnation;[946] *so there is no sin so great, that it can bring damnation upon those who truly repent.*[947]

The Bible speaks in extremes that the human mind cannot comprehend. How could the apparently good be bad and the apparently bad be good? Well, it cannot and it is not. That is a false question. We know that there is none who does good and that all are deserving of death.[948] Therefore, we know that if any man has eternal life, it is because Jesus Christ paid the price for his every sin.

Repentance is the display of a righteous man who acknowledges his evil ways and wicked thoughts and turns to God. He is also comforted by the knowledge of forgiveness that his repentance is sincere. The forgiven man seeks after God because he is made righteous and desires to glorify his Lord.

If we think that we have committed a sin beyond God's forgiveness, we deceive ourselves and need to repentant of that unbelief in and of itself. Shall we give sin power over God? May it never be!

---

[946] Ro 6:23; Ro 5:12; Mt 12:36
[947] Isa 55:7; Ro 8:1; Isa 1:16,18–WCF Ch15-iv
[948] Ps 14:3; Ro 6:23

NOVEMBER 18

PARTICULAR SIN

Martin Luther (1483-1547) would sometimes spend up to six hours repenting and confessing his every peccadillo, not privately but to his pastor. Now, while this seems over the top, it was his acknowledgment of the seriousness of sin. Contrast this with a person who rushes out a quick prayer, "Lord, forgive me of all my sin. Amen."

Men ought not to content themselves with a general repentance, but it is every man's duty to endeavor to repent of his particular sins particularly.[949]

Although it is not God's requirement to confess our sins for any specific length of time, a general repentance does not reveal earnest sorrow of one's sin. I think we all stand guilty of this from time to time. Perhaps, in our understanding of the completeness of Christ's forgiveness, we carelessly accept it. However, earnest repentance seeks not just forgiveness, but strength to not repeat the offense. We do not sorrow for a specific time, but for specific sin.

Believers, having the mind of Christ, see their sin as exceedingly sinful.[950] We mature toward sinning less often and less in degree, but we will feel worse about the sin that remains. This is the sanctifying work of the Spirit within us. We seek the Lord to refine us from all impurity. Our confession of particular sin is the evidence that we take God's holiness seriously. Earnestness reflects our values.

---

[949] Ps 19:13; Lk 19:8; 1Ti 1:13,15–WCF Ch15-v
[950] Ro 7:13

NOVEMBER 19

THE PARDON OF GOD

The man of God confesses his transgressions. The renewed spirit in man cries out and desires reconciliation.

As every man is bound to make private confession of his sins to God, praying for the pardon thereof[951] upon which, and the forsaking of them, he shall find mercy.[952]

Perhaps the most comforting aspect of our relationship with God is his promise to never forsake us. Though we sometimes fall hard into neglect of our call to a holy life, God knows the moment we realize our failings. The Spirit convicts us of sin and our obedience seeks forgiveness. We never deserve pardon. God's mercy is without limit, and our sincere repentance is never denied.

When Jesus confronted the woman caught in adultery, he knew she was guilty. First, Jesus convicted all her accusers of their own right to being stoned to death. Then, Jesus removed the penalty of her sin, telling her that he did not condemn her. He forgave her sin before she ever verbalized repentance. Finally, he sent her on her way, telling her to "Go and sin no more."

The point of repentance is the knowledge of sin and turning from it. Although it is not mentioned, the women's penitent heart is understood as she left forgiven and en route to not continue in sin. Our heart should match hers. Our pursuit of holiness shows our heart.

---

[951] Ps 51:4,5,7,9,14; Ps 32:5,6
[952] Pr 28:13; 1Jn 1:9–WCF Ch15-via

November 20

The Pardon of Men

The public life of a godly person will match the sincerity of their private life and relationship with God.

So he that scandalizes his brother, or the Church of Christ, ought to be willing, by a private or public confession and sorrow for his sin, to declare his repentance to those that are offended;[953] who are thereupon to be reconciled to him, and in love to receive him.[954]

There is no double standard. We cannot have an open relationship with God at the same time we live a hypocritical life with those around us. Right out of the gate, our hypocrisy would be seen as sin and therefore make repentance unattainable. For if we do not turn from our sin, then we have not repented at all.

Jesus explained how our relationships with people coincide with our worship of God. He said, "If you bring your gift to the altar and there remember that your brother has something against you, leave your gift there before the altar and go your way. First, be reconciled to your brother, and then come and offer your gift."[955]

Reconciliation is paramount in the life of believers. God is reconciling us to himself and we are to be reconciled one to another. The message is one of grace. God forgives and we seek forgiveness. The mark of our understanding of our forgiveness is how we forgive others.

---

[953] Jas 5:16; Lk 17:3,4; Josh. 7:19; Ps 51
[954] 2Co 2:8–WCF Ch15-vib
[955] Mt 5:23,24

November 21

Good Works

We are going to spend the next ten days on works. Works? But salvation is by grace through faith and not by works, right? That is correct, but as sure as we are saved by grace, our salvation will always be accompanied by good works.

Good works are only such as God hath commanded in his holy Word,[956] *and not such as, without the warrant thereof, are devised by men, out of blind zeal, or upon any pretence of good intention.*[957]

The Bible harmonizes the concepts of faith and works in many areas. In fact, every time an Old or New Testament servant performs the will of God, he is demonstrating his faith by his obedience. We will never hear about a saint believing God, then sitting around waiting for the promise. Noah did not learn that a flood was coming, then plop into a hammock. No, the evidence that he believed God was the fact that he spent many dry years building the ark. He was not thwarted, even in the face of ridicule from everyone around him.

On the other hand, people who perform their works to impress God fail in both faith and good works. God is not impressed with our efforts. In fact, if we are not working out of faith, then our efforts are blasphemous. For efforts without faith are full of pride.

Lord, direct our obedience to be measured only by the faith that you graced us with, not from selfish ambition, but out of love.

---

[956] Mic 6:8; Ro 12:2; Heb 13:21
[957] Mt 15:9; Isa 29:13; 1Pe 1:18; Ro 10:2–WCF Ch16-i

NOVEMBER 22

FRUITS OF FAITH

Some Christians are so tuned to the grace of God that they shun the idea of works out of fear that they might become legalistic in their actions. The problem is, there is no faith without works.

These good works, done in obedience to God's commandments, are the fruits and evidences of a true and lively faith: and by them believers manifest their thankfulness,[958] *strengthen their assurance, edify their brethren.*[959]

When we speak of the biblical view of works, we are not speaking of *works righteousness*. Good works pour naturally out from our faith. It is not a matter of trying to express one's faith, but that faith is expressed through obedience to every command of God. Commands for a holy life, commands for our prayer life, and commands for the application of our spiritual gifts.

From where do these works flow? From a heart of gratitude. Our thankfulness is not a repayment for our faith, but the evidence of it. The Spirit living in us manifests Christ through us, who are the body of Christ, namely the true Church. We are his hands and feet, and Christ is always dynamic.

Lord, take away our misconceptions and fill us with the truth of our good works as the fruits of saving faith. Help us to be glorifying to you in our works, keeping pride obsolete. All good is from above.

---

[958] Jas 2:18,22; Ps 116:12,13; 1Pe 2:9
[959] 1Jn 2:3,5; 2Pe 1:5-10; 2Co 9:2; Mt 5:16–WCF Ch16-iia

NOVEMBER 23

THE WORK OF GOOD WORKS

As the Body of Christ, the Church continues the work that Christ began. Although his work on the cross is finished, believers...

Adorn the profession of the Gospel,[960] stop the mouths of the adversaries, and glorify God, whose workmanship they are, created in Christ Jesus thereunto;[961] that, having their fruit unto holiness, they may have the end eternal life.[962]

Jesus gave the Church one primary mission: to make disciples of all nations. Our good works include every aspect of making disciples. A disciple is a learning believer of Jesus Christ. First, the Gospel is shared with a lost world. Those who come to faith require the teaching of the Word and instruction on repeating the process.

It sounds simple enough. However, the Church has to teach sound doctrine while it fights against false teachers. Where fallible man resides, disruptions are bound to creep in, even between believers. The good work continues in maintaining the unity of believers.

We must remember the good work that Christ began in us. Every aspect of our salvation and sanctification is the direct result of Christ's work in us. Our work should be not only the manifestation of our salvation, but the obedience of the works he has commanded us to continue. Preach, teach, pray, rebuke, and instruct in righteousness.

---

[960] Tit 2:5,9,10,11,12; 1Ti 6:1
[961] 1Pe 2:15; 1Pe 2:12; Php 1:11; Jn 15:8; Eph 2:10
[962] Rom. 6:22–WCF Ch16-iib

NOVEMBER 24

WORKING HIS GOOD PLEASURE

There are countless foundations and opportunities where people can plug in their efforts or financial support. The reasons people participate in these things are just as endless. But to what end? Are good works in God's economy the same as performing a good deed? What is it that believers possess that enables a good work to God?

Their ability to do good works is not at all of themselves, but wholly from the Spirit of Christ.[963] *And that they may be enabled thereunto, beside the graces they have already received, there is required an actual influence of the same Holy Spirit to work in them to will and to do of his good pleasure.*[964]

The depraved, unredeemed man can indeed perform a duty that is beneficial for its own intent. However, without the Holy Spirit, there is no work that pleases God, including works of philanthropy. Good works relate to spiritual matters with godly passion. We must not confuse good intentions with godly purpose.

Good works are those that primarily promote God's riches in grace and in serving the body. The exercise of our spiritual gifts and following the leading of Holy Spirit to do his good pleasure as we are enabled. There is nothing good in ourselves that we can produce a godly work. Believers performing good works do so with a humble heart while acknowledging the Spirit as the source of their ability.

---

[963] Jn 15:4,5,6; Eze 36:26,27
[964] Php 2:13; Php 4:13; 2Co 3:5–WCF CH16-iiia

NOVEMBER 25

STIRRING UP THE GRACE OF GOD

God's good pleasure is the good work that we perform. So what do we do? Wait around for some direction? Not at all.

Yet are they not hereupon to grow negligent, as if they were not bound to perform any duty unless upon a special motion of the Spirit; but they ought to be diligent in stirring up the grace of God that is in them.[965]

The Body of Christ, of which every believer is a part, is to be in motion at all times, fulfilling the instructions he has given. The body is in motion only as its parts are in motion. If the parts stand still, the body stagnates. Therefore, we must individually and corporately press toward the goal.

Because we reside in these limited earthen vessels, we tire easily and are more apt to sit back than we are to step forward. Yet we are to stir up the Spirit and earnestly serve God. This is not to infer that the Spirit is the one who needs energizing. It is through seeking the Spirit in the Word and in prayer that our spirit is prompted.

We are told to *work out our salvation*. This is not working for our salvation, but the exercise of living out the life that salvation brings. This is a life of sanctification and obedience to our Lord. This is a self-challenge to stir up the Spirit within us to activate our sense of urgency to the lost and dying world around us, where we shine his light.

---

[965] Php 2:12; Heb 6:11,12; 2Pe 1:3,5,10,11; Isa 64:7; 2Ti 1:6; Ac 26:6,7; Jude 20,21–WCF Ch16-iiib

NOVEMBER 26

FALLING SHORT IN SELF-EFFORT

When Job was in his deepest anguish, wondering what caused his world to crumble down around him, he still understood one primary thing: God's ways were higher than his own.

They who, in their obedience, attain to the greatest height which is possible in this life, are so far from being able to supererogate, and to do more than God requires, as that they fall short of much which in the duty they are bound to do.[966]

Isaiah tells us that *all of our (self)-righteousness is as filthy rags before Lord*. So pick your very best effort and consider it dung before the Lord. Then why try at all? Again, we must keep in mind that our obedience and good works are the result of grace, not a means to attain God's favor. Works are a duty, but in a manner of it being the natural outpouring of the hope that lives within us. Obedience is love.

If you feel like you are not doing enough to please God, then seek forgiveness. Not for your lack of effort, but for your arrogance. You read that correctly, your arrogance—your pride. Because your efforts are *trying to please*, instead of living a life that is pleasing. In our humanness, we seem to always complicate that which God has already freely given to us. This is just one aspect of walking in the Spirit.

Lord, forgive the days when I live inactive as well as the times when I work with the wrong intentions. Less of me, all for you.

---

[966] Lk 17:10; Ne 13:22; Job 9:2,3; Gal 5:17–TWC Ch16-iv

NOVEMBER 27

NOT SCRATCHING THE SURFACE

When I consider the Apostle Paul, I stand in awe of all that he accomplished to serve God. What is more amazing still is that he understood that he counted it all as loss. Only Christ is of value.

We cannot, by our best works, merit pardon of sin, or eternal life, at the hand of God, by reason of the great disproportion that is between them and the glory to come, and the infinite distance that is between us and God, whom by them, we can neither profit nor satisfy for the debt of our former sins;[967] *but when we have done all we can, we have done but our duty, and are unprofitable servants.*[968]

Paul fulfilled his role as the servant of his king. Was that the norm back then? Is it to be any different for us? These are tough questions. Not difficult to answer, just difficult to swallow. We know the answer is that we are given the same mission as Paul. Not necessarily to travel the globe, but certainly to share the message of hope to the world in which we come in contact. Are you a profitable servant?

There is not one of us who would say we are doing enough. There is always more work to do. The bigger question is, are we doing anything? We can cop out and say that we do not have the gift of evangelism, but the mandate was not to preach to 100 at once. But we do have a mandate. Could you imagine the impact if we all witnessed to just one person a week?

---

[967] Ro 3:20; Ro 4:2,4,6; Eph 2:8,9; Tit 3:5,6,7; Ro 8:18; Ps 16:2; Job. 22:2,3; Job 35: 7,8
[968] Lk 17:10–WCF Ch16-va

November 28

Selfish Works

There can be no self-righteousness in our works. The obedient servant of the Lord performs good works simply as a matter of duty:

And because, as they are good, they proceed from His Spirit;[969] *and as they are wrought by us, they are defiled, and mixed with so much weakness and imperfection, that they cannot endure the severity of God's judgment.*[970]

It is literally impossible to beat the monster of pride, which wants to take even partial credit for the works we perform. This impossibility does not excuse our remaining pride, but should drive us to rely on Christ even more. Failures, in the life of a believer, show us that goodness can only be sourced from the Spirit of God.

I am not saying that any amount of humility is impossible. Humility is the understanding that there is no good in our flesh. The humble person refuses to take credit, but always points to the Spirit. The more we realize that any self-work requires judgment, the more we want to express the goodness of God for enabling us.

Self-recognition of humility is not necessarily an oxymoron. The most humble person in the Old Testament is Moses. The irony is that it is Moses who tells us this. Therefore, we should strive to be humble. We do this by only seeing Christ behind every good work and giving thanks to God for the working in us of his good pleasure.

---

[969] Gal 5:22,23
[970] Isa 64:6; Gal 5:17; Ro 7:15,18; Ps 143:2; Ps 130:3–WCF Ch16-vb

NOVEMBER 29

PLEASING GOD

Up to this point, our focus on good works has been from our point of view. But how does God view the works of his children?

Notwithstanding, the persons of believers being accepted through Christ, their good works also are accepted in him;[971] not as though they were in this life wholly unblamable and unreprovable in God's sight;[972] but that he, looking upon them in his Son, is pleased to accept and reward that which is sincere, although accompanied with many weaknesses and imperfections.[973]

The light at the end of the tunnel is the same light that saved us. Just as we stand blameless in God's sight only because the righteousness of Jesus is accounted to us, our good works are also seen in the light of his Son. The Father is always pleased with the Son. It is the good work of the Son in us that makes our works acceptable.

We can feed and clothe the poor. We can intercede in prayer for the brokenhearted. We can do all things in Christ who strengthens us. It is Christ who called us. It is Christ who works in us. It is in Christ whom the Father is pleased for the entirety of our salvation. We are made perfect in our good works. That is, Christ makes our works in his name perfect and pleasing in the Father's sight. We therefore can and should work unto the Lord, knowing that he is pleased in our sincere efforts. Our sincerity is the humility of working for his glory alone.

---

[971] Eph 1:6; 1Pe 2:5; Ex 28:38; Ge 4:4; Heb 11:4
[972] Job 9:20; Ps 143:2
[973] Heb 13:20,21; 2Co 8:12; Heb 6:10; Mt 25:21,23–WCF Ch16 vi

NOVEMBER 30

MORAL GOOD AND GOD

Can the unsaved man do good? The answer is both yes and no. A person that obeys traffic lights is doing good not to endanger another. Likewise, a person who refrains from stealing my wallet also does good. Especially in areas of philanthropy, our efforts benefit others.

Works done by unregenerate men, although, for the matter of them, they may be things which God commands, and of good use both to themselves and others;[974] *yet, because they proceed not from an heart purified by faith...*[975] *they are therefore sinful, and cannot please God, or make a man meet to receive grace from God.*[976] *And yet, their neglect of them is more sinful and displeasing unto God.*[977]

The world will fight against this doctrine. The unsaved person sees the general benefit of his work and cannot see how this could be an offense to God. How could good be evil? The answer lies in the full extent of that work. If our works proceed from our own doing, then they are not of faith. Without faith, it is impossible to please God.

All work passes through the fire. Just as fire exposes the impurity of gold, so is the source of one's work. A work without the Spirit is shown as corruption, whereas the work manifest by the Spirit through faith is received by God, who is well-pleased with the work of his Son. We must die to ourselves and live in the newness of Christ.

---

[974]   2 Ki 10:30,31; 1Ki 21:27,29; Php 1:15,16,18
[975]   Ge 4:5; Heb 11:4,6; 1Co 13:3; Isa 1:12; Mt 6:2,5,16
[976]   Hag 2:14; Tit 1:15; Am 5:21,22; Hos 1:4; Ro 9:16; Tit 3:15
[977]   Ps 14:4; Ps 36:3; Job 21:14,15; Mt 25:41,42,43,45; Mt 23:3

DECEMBER 1

PERSEVERANCE OF THE SAINTS

Today, we begin with the most comforting doctrine attached to salvation. The perseverance of the saints is the promise that for that every person whom God justifies, he will definitely bring to glory.

They, whom God hath accepted in his Beloved, effectually called and sanctified by his Spirit, can neither totally nor finally fall away from the state of grace; but shall certainly persevere therein to the end, and be eternally saved.[978]

What could be better than knowing your salvation cannot fail? If there is anything a Christian wrestles with, it is the thought of losing so great a salvation. The more we understand our unworthiness, the less it makes sense that God could love us in spite of ourselves and our continued failings. The fact is, if it were left up to us, we would lose our salvation. But grace is not based on our performance, but on Christ's.

The Scriptures so clearly paint a picture of God completing the work he begins. He will never lose any of those he saves. This doesn't mean we will not die. For every saint, there is the promise of resurrection. This doctrine might be better called the perseverance of faith. For it is our God-given faith that perseveres, not by our own will.

As we dig into this doctrine over the next few days, be sure to see whose power is at work in the supporting scriptures. Be on the ready to repent of your pride when you think this is about you.

---

[978] Php 1:6; 2Pe 1:10; Jn 10:28,29; 1Jn 3:9; 1Pe 1:5,9–WCF Ch17-i

DECEMBER 2

GOD'S UNCHANGEABLE LOVE

Children do many things to try our patience. There is nothing they can do to change our deep-seated love for them.

This perseverance of the saints depends not upon their own free will, but upon the immutability of the decree of election, flowing from the free and unchangeable love of God the Father;[979] *upon the efficacy of the merit and intercession of Jesus Christ.*[980]

The love of God extends infinitely deeper than our own capacity. Although our love might have its limits, God's love can never be exhausted. So although I continue to fall short of being a *good* child of God, my saved position never changes. This is because, for those whom God sets his love, it remains by grace alone and nothing in us.

The children of God receive the promise of eternal inheritance. We have the seal of the Holy Spirit as our guarantee. If the work of salvation is fully of Christ, then what part of maintaining salvation is based one's own effort? None. Does this mean we throw caution to the wind and sit back and let God pick up our trail of transgressions? Never. The question, although answered, is truly an empty question for those who recognized the price paid for their salvation.

The promise of God is that nothing shall separate us from his love. Believers understanding this will not go on sinning, but will separate themselves by the sanctifying power of the Holy Spirit.

---

[979] 2 Ti 2:18,19; Jer 31:3–WCF Ch17-iia
[980] Heb 10:10,14; Heb 13:20,21; Heb 9:12-15; Ro 8:33-39; Jn 17:11,24; Lk 22:32; Heb 7:25

DECEMBER 3

THE LOVE WITHIN

Believers will persevere in saving faith, not out of human effort, but through the intercession of Jesus Christ and...

The abiding of the Spirit, and of the seed of God within them;[981] and the nature of the covenant of grace:[982] from all which arises also the certainty and infallibility thereof.[983]

If the continuation of our salvation, for one minute, depends in any portion on ourselves, we are doomed. God's holy standard does not change after regeneration. If perfection is the only performances that pleased God to be saved, i.e., the work of his Son, how much more so in the continuation of our acceptance?

Believers have God at work in them. His Spirit dwells within every believer, where he continues the work he began until their final breath. His Spirit guides, teaches, and sustains our righteousness in Christ. This is an everlasting covenant of God. It is a one-sided, guaranteed promise that his people will not depart from him.

Salvation is eternal life. If you are saved, you possess eternal life. If you could lose it, there is nothing eternal about it. For those who do walk finally away from Christ, the Scriptures tell us that they were never truly saved to begin with. God loses no one. Again, it is not because we have unwavering faith, but because the Lord is faithful.

---

[981] Jn 14:16,17; 1Jn 2:27; 1Jn 3:9
[982] Jer 32:40
[983] Jn 10:28; 2Th 3:3; 1Jn 2:19–WCF Ch17iib

DECEMBER 4

CONTINUED SIN

Only God can see into the heart of man. It is not possible for us to certify the salvation of another. How do we handle those who appear to have their lives changed by God, but for a season, fall back to their old sinful life? If they truly belong to God, the promise is they are saved eternally.

Nevertheless, they may, through the temptations of Satan and of the world, the prevalency of corruption remaining in them, and the neglect of the means of their preservation, fall into grievous sins;[984] and, for a time, continue therein:[985] whereby they incur God's displeasure.[986]

We all sin after salvation; the only difference is the degree and the duration. Some sin is hidden from public, some sin is very visible. Is sin worse in the open? No, because our sin is against God and nothing is hidden from him. There is no excusable transgression.

The security of our salvation is not a license to sin. Why some fall harder and deeper back into their old sinful habits is beyond our comprehension. We know that sin is a result of yielding to temptations. We are tempted by Satan, by the lust of this world, by the lust of our eyes, and by our flesh. Some may fight through addictions that made them feel powerless. Some remain in their sin, and they reap its consequences, plus a displeased Lord.

---

[984] Mt 26:70,72,74
[985] Ps 51:(title), 14
[986] Isa 64:5,7,9; 2Sa 11:27–WCF Ch17-iiia

DECEMBER 5

TEMPORARY JUDGMENT

We ended yesterday with God's displeasure with our remaining sin. Salvation does not mean that sin is less offensive. God is unchanging, and he forever hates sin. Therefore, we can displease God;

And grieve his Holy Spirit, come to be deprived of some measure of their graces and comforts;[987] have their hearts hardened, and their consciences wounded;[988] hurt and scandalize others, and bring temporal judgments upon themselves.[989]

Do not confuse grieving the Holy Spirit with disappointing God. God cannot be disappointed. For one to be disappointed, it means that they were expecting a different result. God, in his omniscience, is never surprised. So while God grieves over our sin, he accounted that sin to his Son at the cross and the believer remains sealed forever.

While sin cannot separate us again from the love of God, it can create misery. A drunk driver can kill a person and end up in jail. The guilt and consequence of this sin will have a dramatic effect on their remaining time in this life. Name the sin; it will affect your walk.

We may be tempted to ask the Lord why he allows us to fail. We know that *God works all things together for our good*, but what possible good could come from our continued disobedience. Rest assured, God has eternal purposes even through our failures.

---

[987] Eph 4:30; Ps 51:8,10.12; Rev 2:4; SS 5:2,3,4,6
[988] Isa 63:17; Mk 6:52; Mk 16:14; Ps 32:3,4; Ps 51:8
[989] 2Sa 12:14; Ps 89:31,32; 1Co 11:32–WCF Ch17-iiib

December 6

False Security

Sharing the gospel, especially in our post-modern culture, is difficult. Telling people that Jesus *came to seek and save that which was lost* falls on many deaf ears. People just do not realize their need for a Savior because they do not think they are lost.

Hypocrites and other unregenerate men may vainly deceive themselves with false hopes and carnal presumptions of being in the favor of God, and estate of salvation;[990] *which hope of theirs shall perish.*[991]

The first failing with fallen man's false security is his own comparison with the world around him. We can always find plenty of people who are worse than ourselves. The second is their idea that their good deeds outweigh their sin. Another is the false concept that everyone has their own way and there are many paths to God.

I think most of us can sympathize with these arguments. The problem is God does not grade on a curve. The only person that we should compare ourselves to is Jesus—the standard of perfection. The other lesson is that just one sin is ultimate failure. I agree that many paths lead to God. Now, there is only one way of salvation: that is through the Lord Jesus Christ. But all other paths lead to God and his Judgment, where their false hope shall perish. There will be no one else to blame as they face God on that day.

---

[990] Job 8:13,14; Mic 3:11; Dt 29:19; Jn 8:41
[991] Mt 7:22,23–WCF Ch18-ia

DECEMBER 7

CERTAINLY SECURE

For those who rely on any means, other than Jesus, they will find only condemnation for their false belief.

Yet such as truly believe in the Lord Jesus and love him in sincerity, endeavoring to walk in all good conscience before him, may, in this life, be certainly assured that they are in the state of grace,[992] *and may rejoice in the hope of the glory of God; which hope shall never make them ashamed.*[993]

Although believers may not have the feeling of assurance, they have been given the right to be assured by the promises provided in the Scriptures. We are further assured by the testimony of the Holy Spirit that lives within us, which is evidenced by our desire is to keep his commandments. If we have trouble believing our own hearts, we know that we can believe God. Align your heart with his Spirit.

Contrast the available assurance of the believer with the presumed assurance of the hypocrite. The reprobate has no real assurance, yet might feel completely secure. The redeemed person may not feel assured, but they are indeed secured and have the rights to this comfort.

God, may you remove the blinders of false assurance from those who need the True Savior. Grant your peace to those who believe, yet struggle with the assurance you offer.

---

[992] 1 Jn 2:3; 1Jn 3:14,18,19,21,24; 1Jn 5:13
[993] Ro 5:2,5–WCF Ch17-ib

DECEMBER 8

INFALLIBLE ASSURANCE

Some have a false hope that their merits will earn them a heavenly reward. The Christian however, does not have to feel insecure about his salvation. It is a hope with biblical evidence.

This certainty is not a bare conjectural and probable persuasion, grounded upon a fallible hope;[994] but an infallible assurance of faith, founded upon the divine truth of the promises of salvation.[995]

The world knows nothing of biblical faith. They say faith is empty belief without foundation. The problem is there are some Christians who believe without being able to give a sound reason to that which they believe. This need not be the case.

The believer has the entirety of Scripture to set their trust in. Every fulfilled promise of God gives testimony to future promises. We can be just as sure in our future as we are in knowing the past. He is the God over all eternity and his plans fail not.

The Christian's hope is biblical faith exercised on the promises yet to come. It is no less certain that we will see final glory than it is that we have been saved at all. As believers, we do well to focus on the promises of God. For if we stand on this solid ground, we do not have to walk on the shakiness of our unnecessary doubts. It is impossible for God to lie and we lay hold of the hope set before us.

---

[994] Heb 6:11,19
[995] Heb 6:17,18–WCF Ch17-iia

DECEMBER 9

THE SPIRIT OF ADOPTION

Have you forgotten to whom you belong? We are the children of God, born again by the Spirit, who also guarantees our adoption.

The inward evidence of those graces unto which these promises are made,[996] *the testimony of the Spirit of adoption witnessing with our spirits that we are the children of God:*[997] *which Spirit is the earnest of our inheritance, whereby we are sealed to the day of redemption.*[998]

With ever-securing evidence, God has shown us that our salvation cannot fail. He bestows his grace upon those he loves. By his death and righteousness, we are redeemed, and we are given his Spirit, who seals us with his promise. What could be more sure?

Our assurance lies not in ourselves, yet is realized by faith in the One who redeems. We further have the testimony of God's Spirit within us. His Spirit does not make us fear being cast out, but shows us that we are indeed his children. If we find comfort in the arms of our earthly fathers, how much more so in our heavenly Father's arms?

Take hold of the assurance of your salvation. Trust, do not doubt, in the One who has the power to complete that which he has begun in you. God cannot fail, and therefore, our redemption will certainly finish just as powerfully as it began.

---

[996] 2Pe 1:4,5,10,11; 1Jn 2:3; 1Jn 3:14; 2Co 1:12
[997] Ro 8:15,16
[998] Eph 1:13,14; Eph 4:30; 2Co 1:21,22–WCF Ch17-iib

DECEMBER 10

ALL IN DUE TIME

For many of us, assurance takes some time. Although, as God's children, we have the reality of eternal salvation, assurance of this security does not instantaneously accompany it.

This infallible assurance doth not so belong to the essence of faith, but that a true believer may wait long, and conflict with many difficulties, before he be partaker of it:[999] *yet, being enabled by the Spirit to know the things which are freely given him of God, he may, without extraordinary revelation, in the right use of ordinary means, attain thereunto.*[1000]

Those who wish to attain assurance of their salvation shall find its means in the Word of God. The reading of the Bible and its promises is the key to knowing what we know is so. Our meditation on these promises increases our assurance. Those who do not study his Word will have little in which to place their trust. How can we trust what we do not know? Where is the comfort of hoping in ambiguity?

We can know his Word because his Spirit leads us in all truth. The Spirit enlightens the Scriptures to us, showing the depth of his love. Our trust is not simply a gut-shot anticipation, but the spirit of our inner man agrees with the testimony of the Holy Spirit. We grow through the increased knowledge of his revealed promises to us. Without the Word, the Spirit will have nothing to testify to.

---

[999] 1 Jn 5:13; Isa 1:10; Mk 9:24; Ps 88; Ps 77:1-12
[1000] 1 Co 2:12; 1Jn 4:13; Heb 7:11,12; Eph 3:17,18,19–WCF Ch17-iiia

DECEMBER 11

MAKE YOUR ELECTION SURE

The title is not to infer that we guarantee our own calling and election. Our duty is to search out the assuring promises of God.

And therefore it is the duty of everyone to give all diligence to make his calling and election sure;[1001] that thereby his heart may be enlarged in peace and joy in the Holy Ghost, in love and thankfulness to God, and in strength and cheerfulness in the duties of obedience,[1002] the proper fruits of this assurance: so far is it from inclining men to looseness.[1003]

There are some that falsely teach that assurance of one's salvation leads to a reckless life. Their idea is that if a person understands they cannot lose their salvation, they will abuse grace and sin all the more. However, this is a false presumption and could just as falsely be presumed upon someone who might fulfill their lust, knowing that they could just repent of it later.

What true faith demonstrates is a disdain for sin and an all-out effort for a sanctified life. While there is a sense where all men take advantage of God's forgiveness, the thankful heart strives for obedience. Not that his duty is burdensome, but that out of a joyful knowledge of one's salvation, obedience is a cheerful and natural response. Throughout spiritual maturity, God continues to enlarge our hearts in love. Our sin decreases and desire for God increases.

[1001] 2 Pe 1:10

[1002] Ro 5:1,2,5; Ro 14:17; Ro 15:13; Eph 1:3,4; Ps 4:6,7; Ps 119:32- TWC Ch17-iiib

[1003] 1 Jn 2:1,2; Ro 6:1; Tit 2:11,12,14; 2Co 7:1; Ro 8:1,12; 1Jn 3:2,3; Ps 130:4; 1Jn 1:6,7

December 12

Assurance Diminished

Some people are not diligent to pursue making their calling and election sure. Although a believer's salvation will never be lost, the assurance of that salvation may weakened.

True believers may have the assurance of their salvation divers ways shaken, diminished, and intermitted; as, by negligence in preserving of it; by falling into some special sin, which wounds the conscience and grieves the Spirit; by some sudden or vehement temptation; by God's withdrawing the light of his countenance, and suffering even such as fear him to walk in darkness, and to have no light.[1004]

Post-salvation sin can still drive a stake of separation between a man and his God. It is not that God has turned his back on his elect, but that the sin takes man's focus off of God. One cannot both enjoy God and fulfill his lusts. It is the same as a man trying to serve two masters. Sin and its continuation may cause God to withdraw the comfort of his Spirit from man. Not salvation, but its joy therein could be lost.

Outside of sin, if one is not deepening themselves in the study of the Word, they also may lose assurance. God communicates by his living Word. As in any relationship, it suffers when communication is lacking. Where is the comfort if we do not know his promises? It is the believer's duty to be diligent to rightly divide the Word of Truth.

[1004] SS 5:2,3,6; Ps 51:8,12,14; Eph 4:30,31; Ps 77:1-10; Mt 26:69-72; Ps 31:22; Ps 88; Isa 1:10–WCF CH 17-iva

DECEMBER 13

ASSURANCE REVIVED

The Lord is not slack concerning his promise. No one misses the finality of their redemption. A believer might lack assurance;

Yet are they never utterly destitute of that seed of God, and life of faith, that love of Christ and the brethren, that sincerity of heart and conscience of duty, out of which, by the operation of the Spirit, this assurance may, in due time, be revived;[1005] *and by the which, in the mean time, they are supported from utter despair.*[1006]

Believers can lose their trust in the assurance of their salvation, but God does not fail in sustaining the work he began. In review, we know that salvation is by grace alone, a regeneration work performed by the Holy Spirit. We further know that we bring nothing that adds to the work of God. Therefore, as emotionally far away from God one might feel, his Spirit remains. The Spirit cannot testify against himself.

Understanding the promise that God will not forsake his children should revive all believers to an increased assurance. As the body of Christ, the Church should also be prominent in comforting the brethren in their times of despair. Through personal testimony and reminded promises, a person can be revived from their despair.

None of us lives perpetually on the mountain. We have been promised tribulation in this life. Praise God that Jesus has overcome! Hold on to this promise when you feel overtaken by the world.

[1005] 1 Jn 3:9; Lk 22:32; Job 13:15; Ps 73:15; Ps 51:8,12; Isa 1:10
[1006] Mic 7:7,8,9; Jer 32:40; Isa 54:7-10; Ps 22:1; Ps 88–WCF Ch17-ivb

DECEMBER 14

CHRISTIAN LIBERTY

If the Son makes you free, you shall be free indeed.

John 8:36

The liberty which Christ hath purchased for believers under the Gospel, con-
sists in their freedom from the guilt of sin, the condemning wrath of God, the
curse of the moral law;[1007] *and, in their being delivered from this present evil*
world, bondage to Satan and dominion of sin;[1008] *from the evil of afflictions,*
the sting of death, the victory of the grave, and everlasting damnation.[1009]

In short, Christian liberty is the restoration of everything that was
lost at the Fall of man. The only thing that remains under sin is our flesh.
The death of Christ redeemed God's elect souls, yet the final redemption of our flesh will be manifest at the Resurrection.

Our liberty in Christ does not give us freedom to sin, but from sin.
Liberation does not take advantage of the forgiveness of sins, yet it does
bring freedom from the guilt of sin and the wrath to come. People who
dare see their liberty as opportunity to fulfill their flesh do not understand liberty in godly terms.

What does liberty look like? Picture yourself chained in a holding
cell, awaiting the just execution for your sins. Upon faith in Christ, the
chains drop off and the cell door opens. You are free, free from the consequence of sin and your bondage to Satan. Free indeed.

[1007] Tit 2:14; 1Th 1:10; Gal 3:13
[1008] Gal 1:4; Col 1:13; Ac 26:18; Ro 6:14
[1009] Ro 8:28; Ps 119:71; 1Co 15:54-57; Ro 8:1–WCF Ch20-ia

DECEMBER 15

THE FREED SLAVE

Before the death of Christ, only the high priest had access in to the Holy of Holies, where God dwelt among his people. However, when Christ died, the veil that separated this tabernacle was torn in two. This literal and symbolic event provided direct access for all believers.

As also, in their free access to God,[1010] *and their yielding obedience unto him, not out of slavish fear, but a child-like love and willing mind.*[1011] *All which were common also to believers under the law.*[1012]

All men are restrained by the moral law. That is, they keep the law as a means to avoid punishment. However, for those liberated by Christ, we now exercise obedience out of love. Although we do not do so perfectly, our will is aligned with the mind of Christ, and now, we hate the sin that remains. We are no longer slaves of sin.

We can observe the will of unredeemed man in the life of a child. Never has a child needed instruction on being bad. We begin to discipline as a child can comprehend to restrain their selfish and sinful wills ruling within. Self-will seeks only self-gratification.

The liberated child of God, out of love, seeks to please God. While we still fight against the lust of our flesh, our spirit likens us to a child who seeks for parental approval. God frees our spirit to obey.

[1010] Ro 5:1,2
[1011] Ro 8:14,15; 1Jn 5:18
[1012] Gal 3:9,14–WCF Ch20-ib

DECEMBER 16

THE FINISHED WORK

The never-ending atoning sacrifices of the Old Covenant were a brutal reminder of the wages of sin. The blood of these sacrifices ran continuously from the altar as a remission of sins. One important truth to remember is that these sacrifices never forgave a single sin, but only placated God's wrath for a season.

But under the New Testament, the liberty of Christians is further enlarged in their freedom from the yoke of the ceremonial law, to which the Jewish Church was subjected,[1013] *and in greater boldness of access to the throne of grace,*[1014] *and in fuller communications of the free Spirit of God, than believers under the law did ordinarily partake of.*[1015]

The work of priestly intercession never ended that is, until our high priest, Jesus Christ, shed his blood as the final sacrifice. The righteous act of one man, the Son of God, did effectively and finally atone and forgive the sins of all generations. The temple work ended when Jesus declared, "It is finished." The debt had been satisfied in full.

In liberty, we now have access to the throne of grace. Not in boldness by our own right, but by the open door through which Jesus calls us. We are no longer in bondage to be hidden from God's glory, but now we are being ever changed more into the image of Christ, by his Spirit who gives us communion with the Father.

[1013] Gal 4:1,2,3,6,7; Gal 5:1; Ac 15:10,11
[1014] Heb 4:14,16; Heb 10:19-22
[1015] Jn 7:38,39; 2Co 3:13,17,18–WCF Ch20-ic

DECEMBER 17

THE LIBERTY OF CONSCIENCE

Faith comes by hearing, and hearing by the Word of God. So everyone who hears, believes? No. Only those of whom the Lord opens their understanding are *they* able to believe.

God alone is Lord of the conscience,[1016] *and hath left it free from the doctrines and commandments of men, which are, in anything, contrary to his Word, or beside it, in matters of faith or worship.*[1017] *So that to believe such doctrines, or to obey such commands out of conscience, is to betray true liberty of conscience:*[1018] *and the requiring of an implicit faith, and an absolute and blind obedience, is to destroy liberty of conscience, and reason also.*[1019]

God liberates our conscience. This is not saying that he forces Christianity down our throats. He removes the spiritual blindness that we may fully see the truth. By the knowledge of truth, we can distinguish false doctrines. Furthermore, to try and hold on to a false teaching is to betray the work God has done in us.

Believers, of good intention, might express to others, "You just have to exercise faith," as if the will of faith has any power in itself. Blind faith and biblical faith are opposites. True faith is exercised by one's conscience. They set their beliefs upon reasonable logic that is based on the nature of this knowledge: God is truth.

[1016] Jas 4:12; Ro 14:4
[1017] Ac 4:19; Ac 5:29; 1Co 7:23; Mt 23:8,9,10; 2Co 1:24; Mt 15:9
[1018] Col 2:20,22,23; Gal 1:10; Gal 2:4,5; Gal 5:1–WCF Ch20-ii
[1019] Ro 10:17; Ro 14:23; Isa 8:20; Ac 17:11; Jn 4:22; Hos 5:11; Rev 13:12,16,17; Jer 8:9

DECEMBER 18

DESTROYING LIBERTY

One of my most troubling experiences comes when nonreformed believers state that the knowledge of liberty in Christ leads to a loose life: *We are free, therefore we are free to sin.* How awful!

They who, upon pretence of Christian liberty, do practice any sin, or cherish any lust, do thereby destroy the end of Christian liberty; which is, that, being delivered out of the hands of our enemies, we might serve the Lord without fear, in holiness and righteousness before him, all the days of our life.[1020]

A believer, being freed from sin, cannot in good conscience remain in sin. The practice of sin puts an end to Christian liberty. Our liberty in Christ is to be free from sin through the knowledge that sin brings the chains bondage. Our flesh might still long for satisfaction, yet our spirit desires the righteousness of God by which we are free.

The proper look at our liberty is understanding what we have been liberated from. We are no longer slaves to sin. We can now function freely in our faith as disciples of Christ, where we can serve one another in his love. Since Christ has liberated us, we are free to serve God without fear of judgment. His love casts out all fear.

It is critical that we maintain a biblical view of our liberty in Christ. Our freedom is never self-serving. Let us not abuse our liberty. We have the God-given right to worship him in spirit and in truth.

[1020] Gal 5:13; 1Pe 2:16; 2Pe 2:19; Jn 8:34; Lk 1:74,75–WCF Ch20-iii

DECEMBER 19

THE RIGHT TO LIVE JUSTLY

Does our freedom from the Old Testament ordinances and ritual excuse us from observing civil law as well? Of course not.

And because the powers which God hath ordained, and the liberty which Christ hath purchased, are not intended by God to destroy, but mutually to uphold and preserve one another; they who, upon pretence of Christian liberty, shall oppose any lawful power, or the lawful exercise of it, whether it be civil or ecclesiastical, resist the ordinance of God.[1021]

The idea is that we are not to use our liberty in Christ to be trouble-makers. The law that government upholds in our daily lives is designed for our protection and the protection of others. In areas where these powers over us do not conflict with the moral law of God, we are to be obedient. To go against the rule of those over us is seen in God's eyes as though we are offending him directly.

God reigns over all authorities. God ordains government for our good. Now, this remains true as long as those over us do not go against the moral law. For example, some governments demand abortion for population control. Abortion is murder; therefore, you not only can disobey, but you must disobey such laws.

There are many facets to this discussion. However, our goal is to live to God's glory in every way. Are you in pursuit of holiness?

[1021] Mt 12:25; 1Pe 2:13,14,16; Ro 13:1-8; Heb 13:17–WCF Ch20-iva

DECEMBER 20

FALSE LIBERTY REBUKED

The doctrine of our liberty in Christ is for our freedom from sin and to the glory of God. The abuse of liberty is not to be tolerated.

And, for their publishing of such opinions, or maintaining of such practices, as are contrary to the light of nature, or are destructive to the external peace and order which Christ hath established in the Church, they may lawfully be called to account.[1022]

The Body of Christ, being set free from the condemnation of the Law, is now able to freely worship because we have the mind of Christ. Those who would live purposefully contrary to true liberty are to be rebuked, corrected, and trained to live rightly if they wish to remain part of the assembly.

The Scriptures confirms that a person who practices outside of a wholesome life does not understand true liberty. They will dispute against wisdom, and therefore, we are not to remain in their company. Some may be acting this way ignorantly and would be open to receive rebuke to be returned to a sound doctrine of faith.

What about repeat offenders? We are to forgive, but we cannot allow sin to continue. Those who are earnest in their repentance will trend toward a decreased degree and frequency of their offenses. A person who is lead by the Spirit should receive correction with a heart that desires to honor God in every aspect of their lives.

[1022] Ro 1:32; 1Co 5:1,5,11,13; 2 Jn 10,11; 2Th 3:14; 1Ti 6:3,4,5; Tit 1:10,11,13; Tit 3:10; Mt 18:15,16,17; 1Ti 1:19,20; Rev 2:2,14,15,20; Rev 3:9—WCF Ch20-ivb

DECEMBER 21

HELD ACCOUNTABLE

Believers are to be seeking after God and his righteousness. Pursuit of liberty outside of holiness is sinful and self-serving. Unrighteous lifestyles are to be confronted by the body of believers.

And proceeded against by the censures of the Church.[1023]

There is no room for unrighteousness when this is exactly what Christ died for. The price he paid for redemption is not to be used as an unlimited credit card for the continuation of our trespass. To misinterpret liberty in Christ is to ignore the Word of God. If liberty, by chance, did mean a license to sin, there would be no reason for the continuous admonishing instructions to the church.

The fact is a righteous lifestyle of humility is expected and is to be enforced. Those who ignore their sin are to be reprimanded by those upholding the righteousness of Christ. The degree of rebuke is to be proportional to the offender's resistance to being corrected. If they see the error of their ways with a penitent heart, no further action is necessary. However, if rebuke is resisted, further disciplinary action is to be used, up and to the point of excommunication.

The Church's primary goals are to restore believers to the church and also to keep apostates from influencing the brethren. The liberty we have in Christ is the freedom from being subjects of Satan and the right to live a holy life in service unto our King of kings.

[1023] Dt 13:6-12; Ro 13:3,4; 2 Jn 10,11; Ezr 7:23,25-28; Rev 17:12,16,17; Ne 13:15-30; 2Ki 23:5,6,9,20,21; 2Ch 15:12,13,16; Da 3:29; 1Ti 2:2; Isa 49:23; Zec 13:2,3–WCF Ch 20-ivc

DECEMBER 22

DEATH IS NOT THE END

There are many philosophies of what happens to a person who dies. Some say that death is the end of consciousness; you die and your body rots to feed the plants. Others claim reincarnation; coming back to this world in another form, a person or otherwise. The Bible provides the only clear description of the truth of this matter.

The bodies of men, after death, return to dust and see corruption,[1024] but their souls, which neither die nor sleep, have an immortal subsistence.[1025]

Mankind is body and soul. While the body, after death, continues its process of decay, the soul is eternal. The physical body degrades, yet the spirit endures. The question that follows is what happens to the soul once separated from its earthly dwelling? This question is asked by everyone, yet every reply outside of the Scripture is speculative at best and entirely wrong at worst.

As in all things pertaining to God, our only source for truth is his Holy Word. His truth is relevant in this life and in eternity. The Bible only describes two possibilities of a person's soul in eternity. Heaven and hell. There is nothing outside of these two. They are exact opposites in every respect. The only way in which they are the same is that they are eternal dwelling places for every man and angel ever created. One place is void of judgment, the other is void of mercy.

[1024] Ge 3:19; Ac 13:36
[1025] Lk 23:43; Ecc 12:7- WCF Ch32-ia

DECEMBER 23

SOULS OF THE RIGHTEOUS

The souls of the righteous are those whom the Lord has redeemed and declared righteous. No one is righteous of themselves.

But their souls immediately return to God who gave them: the souls of the righteous, being then made perfect of holiness, are received into the highest heavens, where they behold the face of God, in light and glory, waiting for the full redemption of their bodies.[1026]

What an amazing truth to grasp! Here we are, sinners who have been purchased by the blood of Christ, and we shall one day be forever in the presence of our Creator, our Father, who has bestowed his love upon us. We are left to wait for that day with joyful anticipation.

Upon death, we are immediately ushered to be with Christ. The sin that remained in this life will meet its final release. Can you imagine, not another temptation, not another failing, no mood swings, no harsh words, no disappointments, no anxiety, no tears.

Thoughts such as these make us want to leave right now. Yet we are here for a purpose: to glorify God and to make disciples. We have the peace of God now. We have his promises now. Therefore, knowing we are secure by the assurance of the Holy Spirit, we can live out this life, striving for the goals he has set before us.

[1026] Heb 12:23; 2Co 5:1,6,8; Php 1:23 with Ac 3:21; Eph 4:10–WCF Ch32-ib

December 24

Souls of the Wicked

Who are the wicked? These are those who hate God. They hate God by their unbelief. These are people who could be the nicest person you have ever met. This is not about personality, it is only about our sinfulness and the One who takes away sin.

And the souls of the wicked are cast into hell, where they remain in torments and utter darkness, reserved to the judgment of the great day.[1027] Beside these two places, for souls separated from their bodies, the Scripture acknowledges none.

Choose your sin: adultery, theft, hatefulness, envy, drugs, lying, homosexuality, disobedience to parents—it matters not. Whoever would practice or call any sin "good" hates God for his holiness. The wicked are those who dare call God a liar by not acknowledging what he calls sin. A righteous person repents and seeks forgiveness.

It is not that people do not recognize their sin, it is just that they would rather fulfill it than repent of it. But some will argue they were *born that way.* I might grant you this point, in that the Bible says we are conceived in sin. However, unless you can excuse every action of wickedness with this same excuse, you have no right to pick and choose. God sets the standard, end of story. You believe or you deny.

You see, all people recognize God and his moral law; however, the wicked person cannot deny the very God they shall face.

[1027] Lk 16:23,24; Ac 1:25; Jude 6,7; 1Pe 3:19–WCF Ch32-ic

DECEMBER 25

OUR RESURRECTION

The topic of the Christ's return is a favorite among believers. It is the hope for which we wait, his glorious appearing for all saints.

At the last day, such as are found alive shall not die, but be changed:[1028] and all the dead shall be raised up, with the self-same bodies, and none other (although with different qualities), which shall be united again to their souls forever.[1029]

The resurrection is not just a New Testament revelation. Job knew that one day, in his flesh, he would be face-to-face with his Creator. Although there are many thoughts about the exact timing of the resurrection of the saints, one thing is certain: all who take the Scriptures seriously do not doubt that one will occur.

Not everyone will be dead at the resurrection, so the question is, *What becomes of believers who are alive at this time?* The Scriptures tell us that just after the resurrection of those who have previously died, those who are alive will be instantaneously transformed into their new heavenly bodies. These will escape physical death. I think it is something most of us secretly hope for, straight away to be with God.

Can you imagine that day? Millions of Christians, going about a myriad of activities, will one day vanish off this planet at the command of Christ's call. Are you secure in Christ, knowing that when his call comes, you will hear his voice? If you love God, you can be sure.

[1028] 1 Th 4:17; 1Co 15:51,52
[1029] Job 19:26,27; 1Co 15:42-44–WCF Ch32-ii

DECEMBER 26

THE JUST AND THE UNJUST

An exciting resurrection is coming for God's people. However, a very troubling resurrection will be attached to the nonbelievers.

The bodies of the unjust shall, by the power of Christ, be raised to dishonor: the bodies of the just, by His Spirit, unto honor; and be made conformable to His own glorious body.[1030]

All resurrected bodies will be both physical and eternal. The new bodies will be such that they will not grow old or degrade. For those of us in Christ, we will experience the pleasure of touch and eating. For the wicked, their new bodies will feel the wrath of God's judgment. They will find no comfort and never experience relief.

We have a hard time understanding God's eternal punishment for the damned. However, we know that God's judgments are perfectly just. We should place our focus on the understanding that by our own sin and rebellion, we deserve God's judgment. Yet God, being full of mercy, has set his grace upon us and saved us from his wrath.

Even if we live to be a hundred, it is a blink compared to eternity. The rebellious know God, but they refuse to glorify him. They let their foolish hearts fulfill their hidden lusts. In the final picture, they, even though they understand their pending judgment, not only do these things, but they call wickedness good. No remorse. They choose to live in the darkness of now with no fear of the eternal darkness to come.

[1030] Ac 24:15; Jn 5:28,29; 1Co 15:43; Php 3:21–WCF Ch32-iii

DECEMBER 27

GOD AS JUDGE

If the thought of God's judgment does not make you swallow hard, then nothing will. Every person will one day face their Creator.

God hath appointed a day, wherein he will judge the world in righteousness by Jesus Christ,[1031] *to whom all power and judgment is given of the Father.*[1032]

I am completely sure that Christ has saved me, yet I also understand that if his mercy was withheld from me at Judgment I would be deserving of his full wrath. There is no pride on Judgment Day. There will be only thanksgiving for his grace and forgiveness.

We should tremble at the expression of being *judged in righteousness.* If the standard is perfection, then every nuance of our imperfect selves is under scrutiny. Our only comfort is that we shall face judgment from the very One who saved us. Because Jesus has promised our redemption in him, we have already been judged at the cross with Christ. Only the unrighteous will see their sins that day.

God the Father entrusts the Son to represent the elect and to place condemning judgment on the wicked. The unrighteous will give an account for every careless thought. We shall all see the same Judge on that great day, yet we shall not all look the same to him. The Bible describes two groupings: sheep and goats. The goats depart into everlasting fire. The sheep enter into comfort. God is righteous.

[1031] Ac 17:31
[1032] Jn 5:22,27–WCF Ch33-ia

DECEMBER 28

JUDGMENT OF MEN AND ANGELS

The Last Judgment is for men and angels. Angels will be judged as righteous or condemned on God's same, holy, and perfect standard.

In which day, not only the apostate angels shall be judged,[1033] *but likewise all persons that have lived upon earth shall appear before the tribunal of Christ, to give an account of their thoughts, words, and deeds; and to receive according to what they have done in the body, whether good or evil.*[1034]

How is it that some angels fell from righteousness? The Bible tells us that Lucifer fell because of his pride; he wanted to be like God. When God kicked Satan out of heaven, a third of the angels joined him in his rebellion. Having understood the holiness of God and their perfect first estate, fallen angels may face even a greater judgment.

The Bible speaks in greater detail about the judgment of man. The deeds of man will be judged, and even more terrifying, so will his thoughts. Imagine for one moment, your impure thoughts being flashed on a screen, for all to see. We know the depths of our wicked thoughts. Those without Christ will have to account for theirs.

If any soul dare think they have done a decent job, keeping God's command, think again. Jesus told us that if we even thought about it, then we are guilty of it. In God's eyes, lust equals adultery and hate equals murder. We are all guilty of breaking every command.

[1033] 1 Co 6:3; Jude 6; 2Pe 2:4
[1034] 2 Co 5:10; Ecc 12:14; Ro 2:16; Ro 14:10,12; Mt 12:36,37–WCF Ch33-ib

DECEMBER 29

SALVATION AND DAMNATION

A few days ago, we mentioned the separation of the sheep and goats at the Judgment of Christ. These are righteous and wicked people throughout history. There is no one who crosses the aisle after death. The distinction? The sheep are those for whom the Lord lay down his life. He is the Good Shepherd.

The end of God's appointing this day is for the manifestation of the glory of his mercy, in the eternal salvation of the elect; and of his justice, in the damnation of the reprobate, who are wicked and disobedient.[1035]

The difficultly with understanding the sheep and the goats is to not attribute a scale of personal merit to either grouping. The parable certainly points toward the level charity each group showed unto Jesus' brethren. However, the message emphasizes that true believers will manifest their love to brothers and sisters in Christ.

Because salvation is by grace alone, we must conclude that the sheep are those to whom God has shown mercy, and their righteous works are only a result of the work the Holy Spirit has done in them. The wicked hate the brethren (elect) because they first hate God.

The Last Judgment is to the glory of God. It is the display of his perfect righteousness in those whom are damned and of his mercy in those whom he saves. Oh! The riches of his love and tender mercies!

[1035] Mt 25:31 to the end–WCF Ch33-iia

DECEMBER 30

REWARD OR PUNISHMENT

Believe it or not, every person will face God and his righteous judgments. Your guilt or innocence is ruled by Christ the Righteous. His judgment is final and eternal.

For then shall the righteous go into everlasting life, and receive that fullness of joy and refreshing, which shall come from the presence of the Lord; but the wicked who know not God, and obey not the Gospel of Jesus Christ, shall be cast into eternal torments, and be punished with everlasting destruction from the presence of the Lord, and from the glory of his power.[1036]

Our objective in this world is the same as it has been for God's people for all time—a message of repentance. To share the gospel with the world, allowing God to redeem the lost. Those whose eyes are opened will see their sin and its penalty, repent, and believe.

Those who remain unrepentant will perish in their sins. They hate God, his Law, and his only begotten Son. For the love of their sin and their short prideful life, they will reject the eternal on behalf of the temporary. Their regrets will be too late and will last for eternity.

We cannot scare people into believing. However, our words of biblical truth may cause them to contemplate their own mortality, their sin, its punishment, and the Holy God who will judge us all. By his grace, may their hearts be made new, that they will repent and believe.

[1036] Ro 2:5,6; Ro 9:22,23; Mt 25:21; Ac 3:19; 2Th 1:7-10—WCF Ch33-iib

DECEMBER 31

OUR GLORIOUS HOPE

The Judgment of man's sin is proclaimed that all will understand and be persuaded of God's holiness. The return of Christ is feared of the wicked and awaited in joyous anticipation for believers.

As Christ would have us to be certainly persuaded that there shall be a day of judgment, both to deter all men from sin; and for the greater consolation of the godly in their adversity:[1037] *so will he have that day unknown to men, that they may shake off all carnal security, and be prepared to say, Come, Lord Jesus, come quickly, Amen.*[1038]

The closer we grow to Christ, the more we resent sin. Growing in Christ is equivalent to having more of his Word written on our hearts. Jesus' prayer for us is that the Father would sanctify us in his truth. God's Word is truth. Jesus is the Word manifest unto us.

Do you want more of Jesus? Study and meditate on his Word. This devotional book is written as an encouragement to know him more and more each day. The more truth we know, the less we have to rely on false hope. The hope of our salvation is sure in Christ.

It is my prayer that I have given an adequate reason for that hope in which I believe. I know that God's Word does not return void. Do not seek the things of this world, for they are fading away. Seek his truth and look up, for our redemption draws near! To God be the glory!

[1037] 2 Pe 3:11,14; 2Co 5:10,11; 2Th 1:5-7; Lk 21:7,28; Ro 8:23-25
[1038] Mt 24:36,42,43,44; Mk 13:35-37; Lk 12:35,36; Rev 22:20–WCF Ch33-iii